AF676545

Online, On Time, On Target

Lessons from Churchill's Information Portal

Online, On Time, On Target

Lessons from Churchill's Information Portal

Mark Kozak-Holland

MC PRESS

IBM Press™

Online, On Time, On Target: Lessons from Churchill's Information Portal
Mark Kozak-Holland

Published under IBM Press by MC Press Online, LP
IBM Associate Publisher: Tara B. Woodman, IBM Corporation
IBM Press Alliance Publisher: David M. Uptmor, MC Press

For information on translations and book distribution outside the United States or to arrange bulk-purchase discounts for sales promotions or premiums please contact:

MC Press Online, LP
Corporate Offices:
125 N. Woodland Trail
Lewisville, TX 75077

Sales and Customer Service:
P.O. Box 4300
Big Sandy, TX 75755-4300

First edition
First Printing: March 2004
ISBN: 1-931182-15-9

Printed in Canada. All rights reserved. No part of this publication may be reproduced in any form without prior permission in writing of the copyright owner.

© 2004 by International Business Machines Corporation
Portions © 2004 by MC Press Online, LP

Every attempt has been made to provide correct information in this book. However, the publisher, the editors, nor the authors guarantee the accuracy of the book and do not assume responsibility for information included in or omitted from it.

The following terms are trademarks or registered trademarks of International Business Machines Corporation in the United States, other countries, or both: DB2, Lotus, Tivoli, WebSphere, IBM, the IBM logo, IBM Press, and the e-business logo.

Rational, Rational Developer Network, and ClearCase are registered trademarks of Rational Software Corporation and/or IBM Corporation in the United States, other countries, or both.

Microsoft, Windows, Windows NT, and the Windows logo are trademarks of Microsoft Corporation in the United States, other countries, or both.

Java and all Java-based trademarks are trademarks of Sun Microsystems, Inc. in the United States, other countries, or both.

Intel, Intel Inside (logos), MMX, and Pentium are trademarks of Intel Corporation in the United States, other countries, or both.

UNIX is a registered trademark of The Open Group in the United States and other countries, licensed exclusively through The Open Group.

Other company, product, and service names may be trademarks or service marks of others.

To my wife Sharon and children Nicholas, Jamie, and Evie

Contents

Preface

Business organizations are continually looking to be responsive enough to anticipate market conditions and customer needs. To do this, they need to understand the impact of business events in real-time, compare these against various scenarios, make sound decisions, and take actions to counter competitive threats. This book is about reacting to these events proactively, so your organization can stay ahead of its competition and thrive. It is about leveraging today's emerging technologies and creating an on demand business by using information, resources, and people to provide faster and better decision-making.

A business organization can start to achieve this on demand status by getting the right information to the right person in the right timeframe, through an on demand solution like a portal. Essentially, this is an information-management tool that links people across organizations, customers, or partners with relevant information, services, and other people, through a single access point, like a broker.

To further illustrate the concept of how portals can help you create an on demand solution, the book reaches back into history to show the fascinating story of how an organization under tremendous pressure built the equivalent of a modern-day portal solution using the emerging technologies of the day. The book uses Churchill's story for several reasons:

- Churchill faced the challenges many business organizations face today. In June 1940, he was facing a dire situation. Not only did he have to stave off an imminent threat, but he had to quickly turn a disjointed peacetime economy around, unify it, put it on a war footing so that it could sustain total economic warfare, and direct its output into immediate military use.

- Churchill responded with an on demand solution, pushing 1940s emerging technology to its limits. He created, in concept, a modern federated portal, an information-management tool that has been around as long as we have been managing information on paper or electronically.
- The portal solution allowed Churchill to harness disparate organizations from all walks of life and command, and control the meager resources of a nation. It provided a sophisticated military response system integrated to a supply chain. As a result, Churchill was also able to turn the battle around. He put the UK back into the war, which he then conducted with this solution. Eventually, it helped him defeat a more powerful enemy.

The portal was a breakthrough in the use information-management concepts and led to the birth of the electronic computing age. Of course, on demand is more than just a portal, but what Churchill achieved was central to on-demand. With it, Churchill's government was

- Responsive enough to anticipate changing conditions and threats, and react to events
- Flexible enough to manage multiple projects, resources, and costs
- Focused enough to manage the core business, specifically the military supply chain, and leverage partners for the rest
- Resilient enough to keep the core business accessible, yet safe and secure

THE BOOK'S ORGANIZATION

The book is organized into eight chapters, following a standard project method, from defining the problem to deploying the solution. A historical narrative is woven into the book's structure, highlighting how to evaluate business situations and determine the right solution for your organization. At the end of each chapter, best practices are presented.

THE READER

This book is for the business executive responsible for Information Technology (IT) spending and approving new IT projects. Its goal is to help ensure your organization has the wherewithal to be competitive. It is also for the IT professional who needs to know how to align and deliver a portal solution that meets the needs of the organization and is widely accepted by it.

The Reader's Work Environment

In the past, when industry events like product launches, marketing initiatives, or changes in legislation occurred, their impact was not apparent for weeks, months, or possibly years. Typically, in the past, such events affected everyone equally, so organizations had time to counter the events. However, emerging technologies and the Internet have altered the reaction time. Organizations have to understand these events in real-time and react accordingly with countermeasures. Many organizations know the information to do this is there in the enterprise, but are challenged in putting it in front of the right people, in the right timeframe to leverage it.

The Reader's Choice of the Book

There are several reasons why you might have chosen this book, for example:

- You are looking for better insight into portal technology and the intricacies of this complex subject.
- You are considering creating an on demand solution with emerging portal technologies, or you have had some experience, but with mixed results.
- You want to take part in a project, and knowing the rationale for and timing of deliverables enables you to be a full participant in the process.
- You know from experience that considerable project effort is outside of the technology, in setting up the organization into communities and integrating processes.
- You want to mitigate the risk through strategies and avoid the pitfalls of these projects.
- You want to visualize the outcome of this project and the output of a portal solution.
- You are familiar with and interested in the historical analogy.

Problems Addressed by the Book

This book will help you start to solve these four problems:

1. Organizations lack the ability to successfully sense and respond to events, discern "signal from noise," and make use of all the potential

information, knowledge, and intelligence stored around them. They create, collect, and handle huge volumes of data in large warehouses, but are challenged in making use of the most critical information and in discerning useful intelligence from the glut of information. They are challenged in extracting, aggregating, and presenting the information to the right decision-maker(s) in a relevant timeframe, so it can be actively used as a potent weapon.

2. There is a huge disparity in the way organizations implement and leverage emerging technologies across the enterprise. For example, some business units fail to buy into an enterprise project. They proceed with their own project with similar technologies and fail to integrate at an enterprise level. As a result, the enterprise project never achieves the envisioned benefits, the organization presents mixed messages to customers, and the output just further propagates the confusion.
3. Organizations view emerging technology projects as "technology-only" projects, where the focus is on the implementation of the technology. These projects are not about technology, but about business and communities. Organizations fail to exploit the new technology available and end up not achieving the desired return on investment because they don't focus on payback or work within a business-case framework.
4. Organizations struggle to realign business processes and the organizational structure for the emerging technology project. They fall short in matching the same investment and effort that is usually apportioned to the technology. For example, they fail to establish the communities that can collaborate and create knowledge for their organizations.

Author Profile

Mark Kozak-Holland is a Senior Management Consultant with IBM Global Services. Mark has many years of international experience working with organizations in formulating projects and initiatives for developing and integrating solutions that leverage emerging technologies. He has been working with mission-critical solutions since 1985. He conceived the idea for this book when he was visiting Storey's Gate (the Cabinet war rooms) in London, England. At the time, he was working with several financial institutions in defining business intelligence solutions. The visit to Storey's Gate was instrumental; he was struck by the way the operations center was organized to manage information for decision-making and control all the available resources, from the supply chain to the response systems. It struck Mark that this was, in essence, a precursor to today's portal technology.

Acknowledgments

I am indebted to the many colleagues, friends, and associates who helped put shape to this book and its prequel, *On-line, On-time, and On-Budget*. I would like to recognize architects Andrew Makowski, Ron Laudadio, Alister McGuinness, and Richard Budel for reviewing the early drafts. I would like to thank Tim Lalonde, not only for his review, but also for his guidance on the historical accuracy of the case study. Finally, I would like to thank Tara Woodman and Merrikay Lee for their guidance in finalizing the "on demand" threads.

Introduction

This book will help you plan and establish your on demand presence through a portal and other emerging technologies. In the progression, it shows the technology, processes, and management issues that affect the move.

As you go through this book, you will learn that the biggest task isn't buying the technology, but doing the planning. This includes identifying the key problems facing the organization, the users, and the communities. It also includes managing and synthesizing intelligence from the profusion of information available, so users can make decisions in a timely manner, in the right context and place.

What Is On Demand?

On demand is when companies go beyond integration of processes, to sense and respond to fluctuating market conditions and provide products and services to customers. An on demand business is responsive enough to anticipate changing customer, employee, and partner needs and react to business events; flexible enough to manage multiple projects, resources, and costs; focused enough to manage the core business and leverage partners for the rest; and resilient enough to keep the core business accessible, yet safe and secure.

A portal helps an organization achieve on demand through proactive decision-making, which requires the ability to proactively recognize changes and business events through an early-warning system. This book will help you plan your on demand presence, make it operational, and most important, continually assess and improve it. To help your organization deliver on demand, you need to answer the following questions:

- What events do I need to be aware of that affect my business?
- What actions do I need to take to react to these events? What are my options?
- What is the impact of (not) doing so?
- What is my return on investment for this?

What Is a Portal?

In brief, portals are mechanisms that enable a decision-making environment. They provide the ability to recognize events and set alerts, they broker information requests against needs, and they focus supply based on a changing demand.

Some Definitions of Portals

The term *portal* has many definitions, from a simple Web site to a complex site with interconnected business applications and information. In many organizations, each employee acts as a portal—getting and collecting information, analyzing it, and then making decisions. Much time is wasted in these processes that could be better spent on making decisions.

The portal automates many functions that enhance decision-making by removing menial and repetitive tasks related to information aggregation and dissemination. A portal is a major broker for these and other business initiatives. Figure I.1 illustrates a portal, an electronic broker that is targeted to specific audiences and communities, bringing together information and services relevant to them. Most communities have very different requirements, expectations, and functions.

The Composition of Portals

Portals today are suites of loosely integrated tools and connectors. They consist of enterprise software that delivers value by brokering data streams. They aggregate multiple information sources, applications, and business processes from an endless source of services inside and outside the organization. They provide a single source of seamless and personalized access for their users. They also provide the ability to manage this access and support multiple devices, and have some level of shallow integration, such as mail and a calendar in the same place.

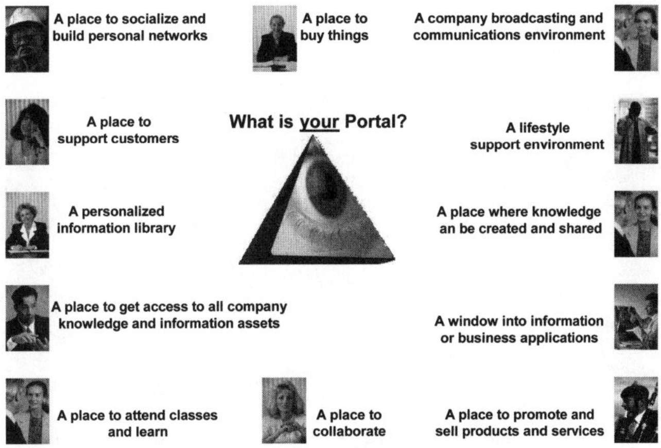

Figure I.1: There is no single answer to what a portal is. It means different things to different people and can be many different things.

The Importance of Portals

The portal is at the heart of process-centric integration, which manages all events in real-time, giving access to data, applications, and people. It brokers between different types of servers or applications, routes messages, configures applications and business processes, and connects these in real-time based on user interactions. It supports complex analysis through business intelligence technologies and agents. It is the common framework for sharing data and metadata by applications and people across multiple Web sites running adaptive applications.

Different Faces of a Portal

When an organization evaluates a portal, it needs to consider its target audiences, including customers, employees (senior executives, line managers, customer-facing employees), partners, and suppliers. Figure I.2 illustrates the different ways these target audiences can interact with a portal through interfaces. Typically, the portal is used to deliver services to customers, collaboration for employees and agents, and procurement for suppliers. The governors are accountable for the portal.

Types of Portals

Portals can be differentiated by their target audiences, scope of content, and the services they offer. Vertical portals are niche, like a sub-portal or industry portal. They focus on a specific community and provide specific business functions. Horizontal portals focus on an entire community and offer less business functionality, as shown in Table I.1.

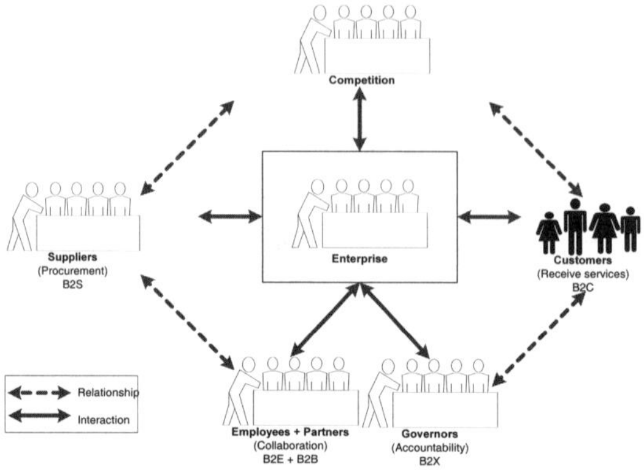

Figure I.2: Target audiences can interact with a portal in many different ways. Typically, this is reflected through several portals.

Table I.1: Different Types of Portals and Support

Type of Portal	Content	Function	Community
Knowledge Portal (B2E or E2E)	Content is focused on creating knowledge.	Function supports knowledge creation, sharing, collaboration, and learning.	Provides some support depending on whether process working or collaborative knowledge sharing.
Role-based Portal (Vertical, B2B, or B2E)	Content is focused on process information or creating knowledge, mainly sourced from internal systems.	Function supports roles, specialized toolkits, and process integration function.	Provides some support, depending on role.
General-purpose Portal (Horizontal or B2C)	Massive amounts of content come from a wide variety of sources.	General-purpose function is limited to search, classify, and locate.	Provides little community support.

Within an organization, you can expect three types of portals:

- Employee portals (B2E) provide access to corporate information and applications, build better employee–corporate relationships, and improve business decision-making and operational execution.
- Supplier portals (B2S) are buy-oriented. They are designed to include everything from setting up a global supply-chain extranet to a dealer or

distributor information system. Often, these portals involve networks of trading partners.

- Customer portals (B2C or B2B) are sell-oriented. They are designed to attract and keep the attention of customers/businesses, collect information about them, and drive future sales.

No single portal meets all the needs of all target audiences. Different target communities impose different business and functional requirements on a portal. You need to find the right mix of functionality for each target audience.

A federated portal or *federation of portals* is a collection of associated or related portals that coexist and interact in either a loosely or tightly coupled arrangement.

Difference between Portals and Web Sites

Web sites fail to enrich interactions by not providing targeted information or integration to businesses processes. Portals offer targeted information and services, as well as integration across different channels. Hence, they keep the promise of improving richness and reach at equal costs. This improves the transaction value for both producers and consumers. Without a portal, users create their own channels for moving information. With a portal, the information flow is greatly simplified and is based on a need and level.

Why Portals Are Beneficial to an On Demand Business

The following pages look at the fundamental benefits of a portal, its costs, why portals are so popular, and what different industries are doing about on-demand and portals. On demand goes beyond a portal, but at the heart of every on demand environment is a portal.

Fundamental Benefits of a Portal

Portals reduce interaction complexity and costs by eliminating multiple links or peer-to-peer connections and mediating more effective interaction between partners. The portal matches these interacting partners and their required content, taking care of the data conversion and distribution.

The value of portals can be summarized as follows:

- Connecting all your communities, anytime, anyplace, using multiple devices that extend the reach and range of the enterprise
- Creating and leveraging shared knowledge pools among all an organization's constituencies

- Personalizing company content and services to all your constituencies, so that "the" company becomes "my" company
- Dynamically responding to business situations by ensuring that the right knowledge is available to the right people at the right time in order to take appropriate action

Fundamental Costs of a Portal

The costs of a portal go way beyond the infrastructure and operation. Effective portals require significant organizational and cultural change, and this can consumes much of the implementation effort. For example, employee portals involve the redesign of business processes, the elimination of stovepipes, and the establishment of a knowledge-sharing culture. This also requires getting over different levels of organizational resistance.

Why Are Portals So Popular?

The benefits of a portal, by community (customer, supplier, and employee), are as follows:

- Improves customer service, streamlines processes, and simplifies transactions
- Improves response times to changing content/services, improves agility, and reduces overhead
- Saves money in replacing functions such as an in-house travel resource center or a printing center
- Increases collaboration, which generates knowledge, improves products and services, and in turn drives revenue
- Increases individual productivity
- Improves decision-making and provides the ability to react to events more proactively
- Increases business velocity
- Retains valued customers/employees by reducing bureaucracy and increasing trust
- Reduces time spent in non-value-producing tasks like searching for information

Commercial Application of Portals

Organizations use portals to meet the changing expectations and experiences that customers are looking for. This is driven by a constantly changing environment of pricing pressure, time sensitivity, security threats, and demand for faster innovation. For example, consumers today expect more information and value when they access electronic services such as banking, telephone, retail, travel, or healthcare.

Consumers want to be able to react to events, make informed decisions with accurate and timely information, and get improved intelligence. These needs are increased by the reduction in face-to-face interaction and the growth in nonhuman delivery channels like automated tellers, kiosks, and wireless devices. As a result, organizations need to constantly improve their designs and processes and unlock hidden value by making processes and data accessible in new ways.

What Are the Different Industries Doing about On Demand and Portals?

The following bulleted items provide a clearer definition of what portals are within various industries and sectors and how they are being used. Reading these items—and seeing your company in the descriptions—will help you get a feel for the possibilities that this technology can bring you:

- *Financial institution*—Portals recognize customers and provide personalized content, relationship pricing, and consistent delivery. Customers set automatic alerts to maintain their account balances. They define how they receive online statements showing all accounts, investments, and recent transactions, consolidated in one currency every 24 hours. They set preferences, download information to spreadsheet programs, and access online history. Through portals, financial institutions present customers their complete financial picture and the necessary intelligence for making decisions.
- *Insurance*—Portals provide motorists fairer insurance rates, based on actual automobile use. The portals monitor automobile usage through real-time tracking, using telematics. Captured information is analyzed, and more accurate rates are calculated. The portals are also able to track stolen cars.
- *Telecommunications*—Portals simplify for customers and employees what has become a very complex combination of services and products. An explosion of offerings has become available as wireless and digital technologies have merged. A portal provides improved decision-making and better targets consumer choices for plans.
- *Retail*—Portals are valuable to consumers because they make life simpler (structuring and netting out information, providing one-stop shopping), offer personalization, provide lifestyle-oriented services, and foster communities (through bulletin boards and chats). The commercial value of portals is evolving from advertising (pay-per-click) to e-commerce and

business intelligence, and retailers are harvesting the information from portals to better understand consumer behavior and habits.

- *Distribution*—Portals provide business-to-business trading exchange and bring shippers and carriers together. For example, consider carriers who have the spare capacity to carry cargo. Through a reverse auction, shippers bid for this space in partially empty trucks. This improves the economics for both carriers and shippers, and benefits other road users and the environment.

- *Manufacturing*—Hard portals offer intriguing opportunities. A manufacturer of car parts, by adding sensors to the parts and working with a networked car portal, might learn how different drivers with different behaviors experience different failures. In addition to market research data, hard portals provide real-time supply information for just-in-time manufacturing. They allow employees to collaborate with staff and partners inside and outside the plant.

- *Healthcare*—Portals are used by physicians, healthcare providers, and patients. Physician portals access online journals, clinical guidelines, drug databases, and upcoming conferences, and provide opportunities for collaboration. Patient portals allow users to request medications, schedule physician appointments, and view their charts. Healthcare portals integrate applications into their workflow. Applications written for personal digital assistants (PDA) provide physicians, nurses, and caregivers connectivity anytime, anywhere, anyplace for lab results and nursing unit communications.

- *Government*—Portals are a priority for governments as populations move increasingly online. Portals are at the center of e-Government transformation because they provide online transaction services for citizens and businesses, economic development boosters, digital democracy capabilities, communities of interest, improved internal operations, tourism, and even weather information. These are citizen-centric, built around life events.

- *Transportation*—Portals provide a single interface and integrate complex processes, allowing air, road, and rail transporters to offer online, integrated booking that responds to inquiries with the best routes and fares. For example, trucking companies have the ability to schedule rendezvous points to provide on-time delivery of goods to just-in-time manufacturers.

- *Airlines*—Portals open up scheduling, booking, and reservation systems to customers, enabling them to download flight research, perform planning, and purchase tickets. Customers determine the best deals and purchase e-tickets when discount pricing can be adjusted automatically to match customer profiles and maximize capacity. Clever integration provides bundling of services to include travel, leisure, hospitality, and entertainment, enabling everything from hotel and car rentals, to tickets for sports events and concerts.

In addition to the industry portals listed above, nonindustry portals like AOL and Yahoo! have been phenomenally successful. These have relied on building up a critical mass of users through family and friend associations and creating online communities.

BUILDING A PORTAL USING A LIFECYCLE

The framework for the chapters in this book is based on a project lifecycle model, which highlights all the stages required. Each chapter is intertwined with two threads: Churchill's portal, and how to build a federated portal through the stages of a project.

Chapter Framework

The chapters are laid out so you can appreciate the evolution of a project from conception to implementation, and anticipate some of the more complex issues you will encounter. This framework also allows for a rapid audit of your organization's ability to create a solution. Each chapter is written so a business manager has a better appreciation of the kind of questions that need to be asked at each stage in the project lifecycle, which is shown in Figure I.3.

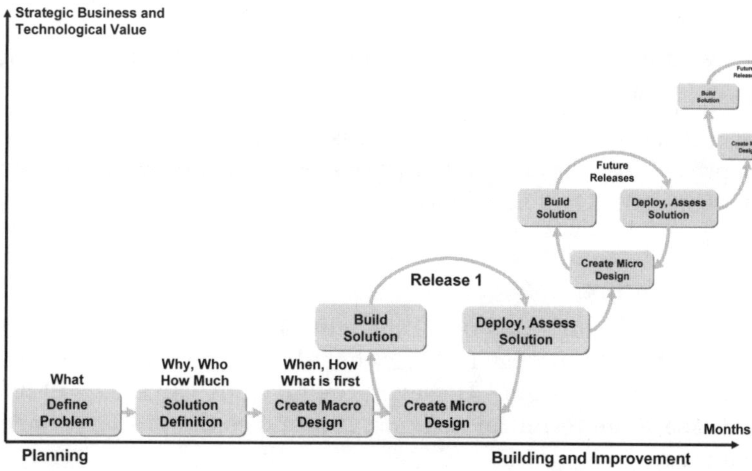

Figure I.3: This project lifecycle is used throughout the book.

An evolutionary approach to the portal involves a single pass through the outline solution and macro design phases, and then repeated iterations through the micro design, build, and deploy and assess phases. This approach divides the development effort into release cycles, which incrementally add capability to the portal. Micro design drills down on a specific release and refines many of the same deliverables as macro design.

The lifecycle is governed by a philosophy to build in small releases and scale quickly. The book tracks the first release of a project from chapters 1 to 6. Chapter 7 addresses how to start the next of many releases.

Benefits of the Lifecycle

The approach used in this book starts small, but scales fast. In each evolution, the model increases in functionality and availability. This approach allows the immediate testing of the working model early on. A feedback loop improves each evolution, allowing lots of minor adjustments to be made quickly, which helps measure the overall progress and gauge the likelihood of success. This approach is the most effective for portal projects for the following reasons:

- It provides incremental proof points to demonstrate value and maintain buy-in.
- It transitions quickly into the mainstream of operations.
- It catches major flaws very early, and so is cost-effective.
- It creates something quickly, so adjustments to scope can be readily made.
- It gets executive buy-in and organizational support by showing early success.

As a result, it provides the business flexibility and the ability to constantly improve business design and processes. It also reduces risk considerably and increases the chances of success.

Technicality Index

As you go through this book, you will find some sections more technical than others. This cannot be avoided when dealing with a complex subject about emerging technologies. However, the index in Table I.2 will help you better anticipate the technical sections. It assumes the primary reader is a business manager.

Table I.2: Chapter Technicality Index

Chapters	Technicality	Description
1	Little	A breeze.
2	Low	Some complexity.
3	High	Might be heavy going, with conceptual and technical architectural models.
4	Medium	A little lighter. Refines the architectural models.
5	Medium	Still technical. Covers building and testing.
6	Low	Much lighter. Covers deployment, final testing, and assessment.
7	Little	A breeze.
8	Little	A breeze.

Churchill and His On Demand Solution

As you go through the chapters, you will be introduced to the Churchill analogy. You will see how each of the federated portals, part of the overall on demand solution, emerged. You will also see how they provided Churchill's government and organizations with different on demand characteristics, for example:

- *Bletchley Park* was responsive enough to anticipate changing conditions and to accurately predict when and where an incoming raid would fall. It did this by intercepting and decoding enemy communications and harvesting critical enemy intelligence into a knowledge repository.
- *Bentley Prior* was responsive enough to respond to real-time threats like incoming raids, based on Bletchley Park intelligence. It was able to take appropriate actions and repel these within a time-critical window.
- *Storey's Gate* was flexible enough to map out various scenarios, define strategies, and manage multiple projects, resources, risks, and costs. It was the focal point for decision-making and employed variable cost structures for the projects to outpace the enemy with new capabilities.
- *Whitehall* was focused enough to manage the core business, specifically the military supply chain, and leverage partners for the rest. It

optimized the critical fighter production through a variable cost structure encompassing everything from factories to garages to repair shops. It reallocated nonessential parts of the supply chain to partners and synchronized fighter production to Bentley Prior's demand.

- The whole federated portal was resilient enough, through redundancy, to keep the core business accessible, yet safe and secure. This was specifically exemplified by Bletchley Park, where security was an obsession.

Emerging technologies were leveraged where they could be. Otherwise, human operators completed the operation, to make the whole system work. And it did work. From the moment the first communication of an incoming raid was detected and decoded, a response was triggered, and a ripple went through every portal in the federation. As the threat was responded to and dealt with, the supply chain kicked in to meet the new demand. This included everything from logistics, to manufacturing, to distribution. Also, the operational headquarters reviewed and adjusted its strategies and tactical projects for retaliatory action. This was a truly remarkable on demand solution.

CHAPTER 1

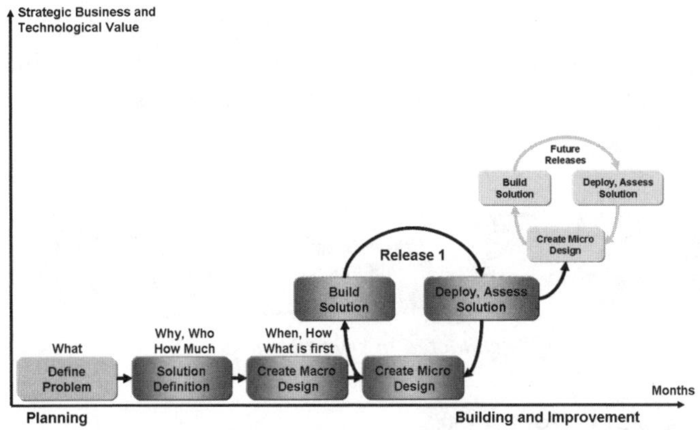

Define the Problem

I would say to the House, as I said to those who have joined this Government: I have nothing to offer but blood, toil, tears, and sweat.

Winston Churchill, Prime Minister
May 13, 1940

Chapter Objectives

In this chapter, you learn how to articulate the business problem and specify alternative solutions. You also evaluate the governance framework. With this information, you will be ready to move on to chapter 2, in which you start to define the solution in detail.

What Steps Do I Need to Follow?

The four steps shown in Figure 1.1 help to define your organization's problems:

1. Initiate problem definition.
2. Articulate the business problem.
3. Define alternative solutions to the problem.
4. Evaluate governance framework.

To get you warmed up to the subject, we'll walk through these four steps, using Churchill's portal as a backdrop in helping you to define your own business requirements.

Initiate Problem Definition

The first phase, shown in Figure 1.1, defines the business problem by carefully articulating it, and then identifies alternative solutions to it. This phase also reviews whether a governance framework exists, or what must be done to enable one.

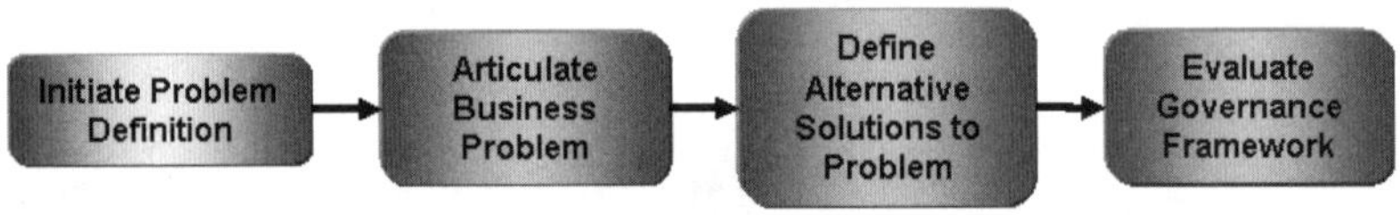

Figure 1.1: Problem-definition is conducted in several weeks.

Articulate the Business Problem

The phase of articulating the business problem explores and clarifies the changes affecting your organization. It also determines the gap between your current and desired capabilities.

The following pages look at the key events prior to and at the start of the Second World War, to determine how a solution for winning the war was conceived and the extent of this initiative. As you go through the next several chapters, you will see the technology emerge and grow, driven by the business problem. Most important, the portal is not a goal in itself.

Changes Affecting Your Organization

External change acts as a catalyst for the organization to do something and initiate some sort of idea or project. For example, the competition introduces a new service, or a new emerging technology opens up a new opportunity to solve a pervasive business problem.

In 1939, Germany was prepared for a lightning war, or *Blitzkrieg*. Heavy military spending sustained over six years had re-armed the military with modern equipment. A new military doctrine envisioned rapidly overcoming the enemy through hard-hitting attacks led by air strikes and panzer divisions. This was a massive change in strategy to the Great War of 1914, a static war of stalemate and attrition. Even as late as August of 1939, the British government was still holding out for a status quo in hopes of averting war. The United Kingdom was largely unprepared for war. Its military spending had shrunk since 1918, and the military doctrine was still steeped in that era.

You need to recognize these changes and determine their potential impact on the organization and the situation facing you. You need to take stock of the current thinking among leading figures in your organization so you can start to determine a course of actions.

In May 1940, France had just fallen—to the shock of the British public, who had been kept in the dark about the gravity of the situation in Europe. On May 10th, Neville Chamberlain resigned, and Winston Churchill was swept into power. The hopelessness of the situation had convinced leading figures in Britain to sue for peace. Churchill, however, had been pushing for stepping up armaments since 1935. Upon becoming prime minister, he had to make a stand and bolster confidence. He outlined his mission to the British Parliament:

> *"You ask what is our aim? I can answer with one word: Victory—victory at all costs, victory in spite of all terror, victory however long and hard the road may be; for without victory there is no survival."*

Current Capabilities

In taking a course of action to address the changes in your organization, you need to determine current capabilities, as well as the gap between these capabilities and the desired ones.

Churchill faced a dismal situation. Britain had evacuated Allied forces at Dunkirk, leaving most of its heavy fighting equipment behind. They kept scarcely enough to equip two divisions. The RAF was about 50 percent below target strength and was woefully behind in its ability to fend off the Luftwaffe, having lost 509 fighters in April and May. Aircraft production needed to be stepped up, but more important, the number of pilots needed to increase. The Allied land forces were hopelessly outclassed by much greater Axis forces with hardened battle experience. In summary, Churchill's capabilities were very limited.

Likewise, in today's world, events can rapidly overwhelm your organization if you are not prepared with contingencies. You have undoubtedly seen organizations rise from nowhere, enter an industry, and become a major force. These organizations prevail through the application of new thinking to an industry, or through superior capabilities based on emerging technology, or through migrating best practices across industries. An inadequate IT infrastructure or inflexible organization limits your capabilities and therefore your ability to fend off the competition.

Churchill's problem was to prevent an imminent invasion by a much more powerful military opponent. He had to restore the nation's confidence in its government and himself. Once he overcame this “small” problem, he had the inevitable task of waging war for many years against a much stronger and experienced enemy.

Desired Capabilities

To match or overtake your competition, you need to define a desired set of capabilities to put you ahead. Innovation, new thinking, new approaches, or new technologies might be required.

Churchill had several aces up his sleeve as opportunities presented themselves. The first one was presented by the Poles in 1939. This opportunity laid the groundwork to cracking the German secret intelligence codes used by Enigma. By early 1940, the British code-breaking system Ultra had started to become operational at Bletchley Park. However, it was desperately short of resources, and results were sparse.

The second opportunity involved leverging emerging technologies. For example, radar could provide an early warning of enemy activities.

The third opportunity was the newly completed cabinet war rooms, which could now be made operational. All these options could give Churchill a desired set of capabilities and significantly maximize the effectiveness of his much smaller forces.

Your desired capabilities can be through new, emerging technologies that can help improve the integration of disparate information, and the use of indicators and an executive dashboard. The capabilities such technologies provide include better and earlier warnings of key business events, enabling you to sense and then respond to these through improved decision-making. Overall, this helps your organization react better to threats and stave off the competition. Small, nimble companies are able to take on the giants very much like Churchill did.

The changes related to Churchill’s situation included the real pressures of an imminent invasion threat; a small, ill-equipped ground fighting force with aging technology and in disarray from Dunkirk; a powerful navy; and a small but effective air force. He also had the option of piecing together new, emerging technologies into a new and sophisticated decision-making infrastructure. This capability had to effectively combat the Axis powers to delay the invasion until sufficient resources could be garnered, which would take years.

Define Alternative Solutions to the Problem

The first step in defining one or more solutions is to examine all the alternatives determined in the previous phase. After you select the best one, you must set out the short- and long-term objectives for addressing the business problem. Again, let's start by looking at Churchill.

Churchill's problem was setting up an adequate defense. As the first solution, he had the choice of stepping up military production and increasing ground fighting forces. However, time and the availability of resources nullified this option. Even with better equipment, the remnants of his smaller forces would be overwhelmed by the quantity and the superiority of troops. He could only muster about two armored divisions (600 tanks), which would be pitted against several thousand tanks.

Likewise, in today's competitive world, you can increase your ground troops and "copy" successful business strategies through newer technologies. This gains better service and an increase in revenue, or more functionality with lower operational costs. However, it also requires large investments and resources, and has a payback over a relatively long period.

A second choice for Churchill—and his best hope—was to defeat the enemy in the air. If he could hold the air space, the Royal Navy could be protected and hence could fight off the invasion fleet. Resources would have to be poured into aircraft production, but there was still the limiting factor of the number of available pilots.

Likewise, in today's world, you can invest in your high flyers—a highly skilled and elite work force. However, this is time-consuming in terms of education, training, and motivation, and has to be deployed effectively.

A third choice for Churchill was to leverage new technologies and pour resources into radar and particularly "Ultra." These would allow him to better orchestrate the limited fighting forces by sensing imminent threats. Churchill would need a command framework consisting of a command-center hierarchy to do this. Fortunately, the cabinet war rooms were physically available by August 27, 1939, a week before Britain's declaration of war. These gave Churchill a centralized location from which to run the war, although he was now facing an enemy no more than 21 miles across the English Channel.

Likewise, in today's world, you can invest in emerging technologies that provide a framework for information. This gives you a competitive advantage through superior decision-making.

A fourth choice for Churchill was to turn the UK's economy around. This meant unifying a disparate peace-time economy and putting it onto a war footing so that it could sustain total economic warfare for many years. This would require running the economy like a supply chain, where everything from raw materials, to production, to distribution would be carefully managed. This would require masses of information, organized through a portal nerve center like the cabinet war rooms. His bigger vision was expanding the war and creating an alliance with the United States. But in the meantime, the UK had to hold its own.

Likewise, in today's world, you can make longer-term changes to enable a bigger vision. However, these changes require a sustained effort, planning, and commitment.

So what solution did Churchill select? To solve the problem of setting up an adequate defense, he had to increase RAF capability and invest in emerging technologies in the short term. In the long term, he had to implement a war economy. The UK was the most industrialized country in the world, but it was also over-populated. Almost all raw materials except for coal were imported—including wood, oil, and two-thirds of the food.

The selected solution was a combination of options two, three, and four. On May 22, Parliament granted Churchill government-wide emergency powers and the opportunity to implement these solutions. On May 28, he met twenty-five members of his new government and said, quite casually, "Of course, whatever happens at Dunkirk, we shall fight on." This, at a time when many senior people were ready to throw in the towel.

Likewise, in today's world, you may choose a new business strategy based on the integration of several new, emerging technologies. In selecting a solution, you might well have to change your business model, processes, and organization, as well.

The core of Churchill's solution was a federation of portals. Primarily, this meant a secure access point from which Churchill and his staff could access military and civilian intelligence, such as the Enigma signals cracked by Ultra and the order of battle in battlefronts. As a result, decisions could be made that affected strategic planners planning military initiatives and field commanders running tactical operations. Of course, Churchill didn't call this a "federated portal," but as you go through the book, you will determine that this is actually what it was.

The solution integrated several portals that could have been built in isolation. It integrated the complex business processes and workflows into a single entity that provided benefits like security, personalization, and single entry. Everything depended on who you were in the organization. For example, the highest-grade intelligence was delivered only to specific personnel identified by function with the topmost security clearance.

Evaluate the Governance Framework

A governance framework is a collection of people and resources that have the legitimacy and authority to create a portal. A critical part of creating a portal is determining how to manage it to meet overall organization objectives. Organizations generally must address two questions:

- What actions do you need to take to ensure that you move forward swiftly and effectively in creating a portal?
- How do you organize or manage the portal efforts?

Churchill took actions to provide some important breathing space, create momentum for his solution, and organize the creation efforts. He delivered to the House of Commons his famous "we will never surrender" speech. Hitler hesitated in invading the UK, in the hope of negotiating a peaceful settlement, and Churchill's aggressive stance forced further delays.

Today, it is important to take stock first and make sure these questions are addressed, as they are driving organizations towards formal governance frameworks. Individual portal approaches are unique, and the type of governance framework that is required depends on the existing structure and culture. Typically, a governance framework should already be in place, but if it is not, you need to create it. This area is very important, and yet often overlooked. Hence, it needs to be evaluated very early in the project.

These same challenges faced Churchill, but in a more acute and pressing way. His federated portal was not built overnight, but through a sustained development effort over many months. This was possible because Churchill had a very clear vision of what was needed, and he had complete control of what had to done. He also had the pieces of a governance framework around him in the fabric of the UK government.

There are three types of governance:

- *Centralized*, in which all functions, investments, and activities are centrally controlled, including content creation
- *Decentralized*, in which all functions and activities are delegated to business units and functions, so that business units and brands are more important than the overall company brand
- *Hybrid*, a mixture of the other two, in which, for example, ownership of some activities, such as content creation and strategy execution, is passed to the business units

Churchill's organizations consisted of government, military, and commercial groups. These were well-organized, highly institutionalized, and hierarchical.

However, a certain amount of autonomy was required, so the final model was a hybrid of centralized and decentralized control.

A best practice is to structure the governance framework after the structure of the organization. If an organization is run in a centralized manner, a centralized governance structure is the most likely to be effective. The potential problems of working against culture and structure include the lack of business-unit support or employee acceptance, the lack of control and consistency, missed opportunities due to over-control, misallocation of funds, unclear initiative prioritization, overlapping responsibilities, and political conflicts. Governance also covers adoption and includes the plans needed to overcome barriers to a successful launch.

Without doubt, Churchill's organizations had unique cultures and structures, used to working in their own ways. These had to be carefully drawn together to work harmoniously without upsetting their balance, so they could continue to be effective.

Typically, most of today's organizations are run in a hybrid mode and adopt a similar governance structure, taking direction from a "head office," but maintaining some autonomy on how to implement that direction.

Superficially, Churchill's governance framework might appear centralized and hierarchical. In reality, the differences in the organizations indicate the overall structure was a loose combination or hybrid.

CONCLUSION

The following sections summarize the major points of this chapter and how they relate to your business today. For more information on these concepts, search the Internet for these keywords and phrases: *capabilities, decision-making, supply chains, decision metrics,* and *governance.*

Major Points, Considerations, and Lessons Learned

- Under tremendous pressure to negotiate a settlement, Churchill refused. Instead, he took advantage of new, emerging technologies to create a bold and daring strategy to fend off the invasion. You will see how he did this in subsequent chapters.

Best Practices for Your Organization

- Do not let portals be a technology in search of a business problem. Define a business case (expected benefits, costs, and risk), and beware of portal hype.

- View the portal as a tool to achieve a business goal, and not a goal itself. Process improvements do not come automatically with portal implementation. Portals enable business-process redesign.
- Ensure that a governance framework is in place before proceeding with an on demand solution.

Questions You Can Ask Today

At this stage in the project, you should organize your thoughts around the issues and questions listed below.

Articulate the business problem or opportunity:

- What problem are you trying to solve?
- How much pain is it causing in the organization?
- What is the gap between your current and desired capabilities?
- How urgently is a solution needed?

Determine alternative solutions to the problem:

- What different approaches are available?
- What emerging technologies are feasible?

Evaluate the governance framework:

- Is governance in place?
- How does this framework apply to the alternative solutions?

CHAPTER 2

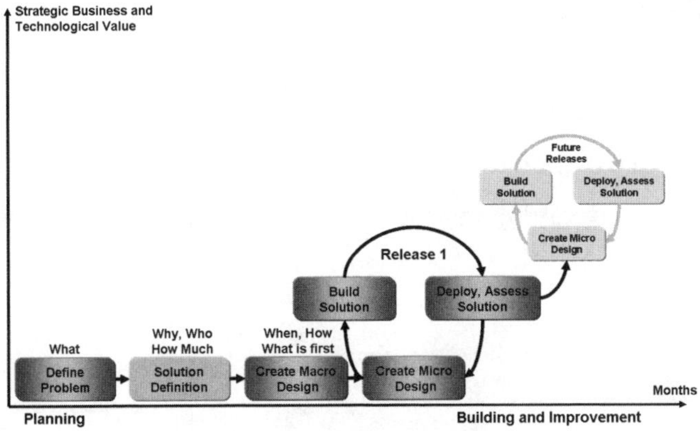

Solution Definition

Never, never, never believe any war will be smooth and easy, or that anyone who embarks on the strange voyage can measure the tides and hurricanes he will encounter. The statesman who yields to war fever must realize that once the signal is given, he is no longer the master of policy but the slave of unforeseeable and uncontrollable events.

Sir Winston Churchill

Chapter Objectives

In this chapter, you learn how to formulate a strategy, define its requirements, assess its impact, and define the operational solution. This set of activities creates a common vision of how the solution will provide the business benefit for the organization. Then, you can make a go/no-go decision about whether to proceed with your project.

The architect uses the solution-definition phase for designing and constructing the solution. It is also used as a baseline in user-acceptance testing, to measure the deliverable against what was planned for, and to define service-level targets. Finally, it forms an important checkpoint at the project conclusion, when the business sponsors sign it off.

When you are done with this chapter, you will be able to define the solution for your portal. With this not these, you will be able to move on to chapter 3, in which you start to define the macro design for reaching your goals.

What Steps Do I Need to Follow?

You go through the following steps (shown in Figure 2.1) to identify your own business requirements:

1. Initiate the solution definition.
2. Formulate a strategy.
3. Define requirements.
4. Assess the impact.
5. Define the operational solution.

To get you warmed up to the subject, let's walk through these steps with Churchill's situation as a backdrop.

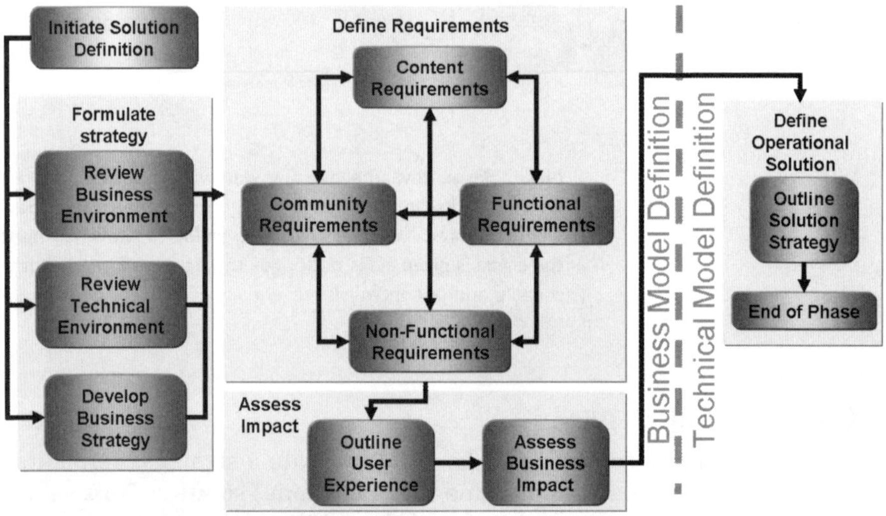

Figure 2.1: Solution definition is conducted in one to three months, depending on the project's size and complexity.

Initiate Solution Definition

The Initiate Solution Definition phase develops a business model of the solution by reviewing the business environment, technical environment, and business strategy. It then defines the community, content, functional, and nonfunctional requirements. From this, the user experience is outlined, and the business impact is assessed. With these activities, you have enough background on the business to begin the technical model. Finally, the operational solution is defined.

FORMULATE STRATEGY

The inherent risks associated with a portal project require a *scoping* phase that consists of reviewing the business and technical environment, and developing a business strategy to leverage this technology. The overall phase creates a business-model definition to support the solution and a strategy for evolving it incrementally and cost-effectively.

Review Business Environment

Before you develop a solution, you need a basic understanding of the organization and the business it conducts by defining commonly used terms and collecting documents. These help define the business context in which the solution must function. You also need to review key business events and a description of the organization. With this information, you can confirm the business interaction model and validate that specific business issues and goals are addressed by the portal project's objectives. The models produced in this chapter are iteratively refined in subsequent chapters.

Define Business Terms

Business units and departments across an organization and its locations can put different meanings to the same words, or different ideas to business functions. You must clarify functional terms through a common glossary to simplify communication, especially when identifying problems. Collect special words, acronyms, and words with new meanings as you encounter them in the project, for later phases when creating support documentation. This requires gathering materials from various business sources, extracting terms that are relevant, and organizing by generic business categories.

For Churchill's architects, the terminology challenge was very symptomatic to the history, culture, and evolution of some of the organizations. Many had grown independently, without a need to interface with other organizations, and they created their own lexicons. This critical problem had to be resolved for the solution to be effective.

Collect Document Inventory

As input to the solution definition, you need to collect different documents and information used across the business processes. Then, you need to evaluate each for document format, processing, quantity, size, and frequency of update, to create a finite set of documents. Some of these documents and information will remain in use with the solution. Others will change throughout its lifecycle to reduce potential duplication.

For Churchill's architects, the challenge lay with the breadth of information and documents that needed to be collected and carefully integrated from the various organizations. For example, information had to be collected from the suppliers of raw materials, the producers of food, the manufacturers of arms and equipment, and the armed forces. This information was necessary for answering questions like the impact of the Axis submarine fleet (the u-boats) on Allied merchant shipping or the effect of a convoy blockade on food or arms supply.

Define Business Context

Based on the business terms and documents collected, you can address the interactions experienced inside and outside of the organization. Diagrams of the enterprise boundary or business area clarify the business relationships among the business entities and processes that create and capture value. These diagrams later aid in determining how a solution will be used.

For Churchill's architects, the challenge lay in clearly identifying and classifying the main areas, made up of organizations and groups. Figure 2.2 shows the enterprise and organizational boundaries and how the armed forces engaged the Axis forces in warfare based on information from the intelligence organizations. Raw materials and production provided the weapons, materials, and food supplies to do so. This model also helped provide input to the content and the organizational change-management plan to support the portal solution.

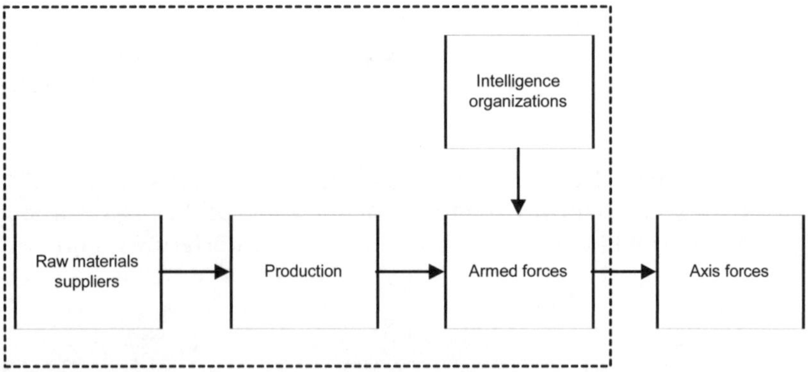

Figure 2.2: The business context diagram outlines the enterprise and clarifies the relationships among the main business entities and processes.

List Business Events

A business event is a stimulus that prompts the business to act. Events determine the points at which interfaces to a solution are needed, how they should be designed, and how the solution should function. This requires listing the events that:

- Trigger the need for information or knowledge
- Occur between the enterprise and the external entities with which it interacts
- Occur internally based on specific conditions or decision-making
- Are triggered by the passage of time (are temporal)

You also need to determine how often the event takes place.

For Churchill's architects, this meant reviewing the key business events shown in Table 2.1.

Table 2.1: Business Events

Business Event Description	Event Type
The demand for replacement equipment because of battle losses	External
Intelligence providing early warning of an imminent air attack	External
The loss of production by the bombing of industrial targets	External
The loss of convoy material and food supplies because of u-boat attacks	External
Inventory levels dropping below the reorder level	Internal
Armed forces withdrawing production of a certain type of obsolete equipment	Internal
Scientific breakthroughs in research and development, or new discoveries	Internal
Troops completing training and maneuvers	Internal
Industrial production milestones, like resource mining or armaments output	Internal
Increases in supply and distribution of supplies like food	Internal
Overdue payments, month-end processing for production targets, stocktaking	Time

Describe the Business Organization

Describing the business organization involves mapping the requirements of your communities, groups, and individuals to the current business processes. This requires understanding organizational structures and units, their reporting relationships, their behaviors and attitudes, and the dominant cultures. It might take time to gain this understanding. It also requires identifying the needed access to information, and the levels of security, by examining internal communities, external communities, and individual users.

For Churchill's architects, the bigger challenge lay in identifying what would be required in waging a total war based on economic warfare, complicated by having to deal with so many disparate entities from within countries, sectors, industries, corporations, organizations, institutions, and groups. This included Allied countries versus those within the British empire; civilian versus military and intelligence organizations; the public versus private sector; commercial versus academic organizations; and industrial production of basic commodities versus armaments. This was further complicated by the intricacies, nuances, and particulars of these entities, each of which carried its own culture and processes. For example, within the armed forces, the Royal Navy considered itself unique, and was reluctant to closely cooperate or share resources with the British Army and Royal Air Force. Fortunately, most of the structures were hierarchical and relatively easy to understand and establish security for, as shown in Figure 2.3.

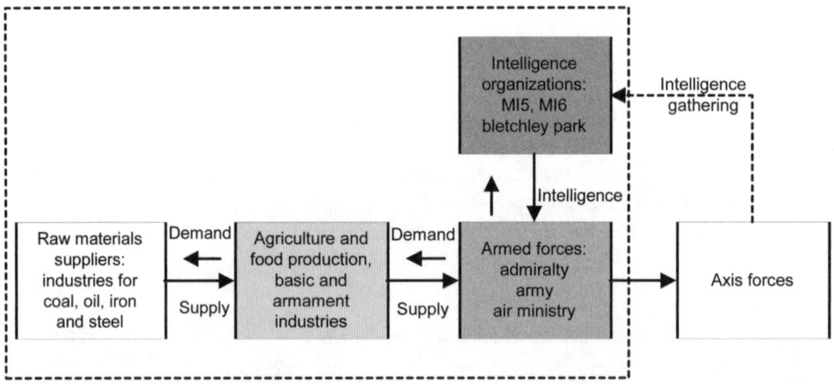

Figure 2.3: The business organizational model adds organizations to the context model. The shading indicates the levels of security—the darker the shading, the greater the security required.

Confirm Current Business (Interaction) Model

Confirming the business model involves clarifying the day-to-day business interactions. You need to look at every aspect of the operation and take into account the various scenarios that might be triggered by an event, or that might trigger other events, and create a workflow. This demonstrates strengths, weaknesses, and areas for improvement.

For Churchill's architects, this required drilling down into the workflow; understanding the interactions between suppliers, manufacturers, and customers; and understanding the impact of events, as shown in Figure 2.4. This model is used to identify bottlenecks and describe the current and future business processes in terms of roles within the business. As the sequence of interactions is completed, the information is collected and stored for the solution.

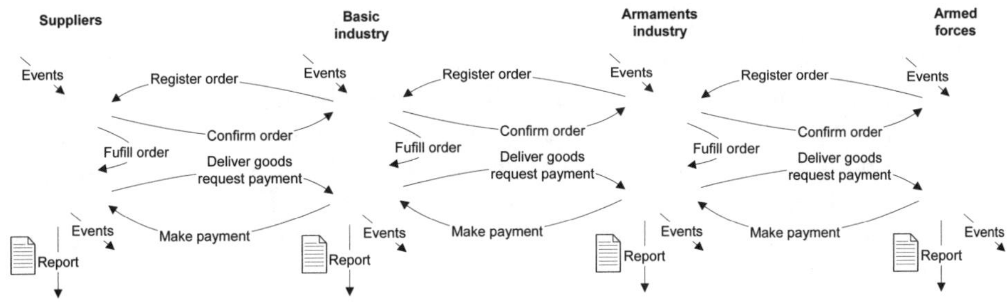

Figure 2.4: The business interaction model describes the workflow for business interactions and the business events affecting the model.

Validate Business Issues and Goals

Business issues, goals, and the organizational direction determine the solution and design and ensure there is stakeholder agreement to the business opportunities that are driving the solution. You need to review the motivations for the project, and then examine the problems facing your organization, the intended strategic and tactical responses, and the goals, objectives, and measurements that address them.

For Churchill's architects, the motivation was based in the short term on surviving the invasion threat and then moving quickly into a position to wage total war, through economic warfare. The enemy had won a series of European victories based on short and sharp engagements. For the architects, the main issues lay in the integration of Allied organizations into communities, and the creation of an effective defense and an overarching and cohesive supply chain. The latter was a daunting challenge considering the large number of organizations, partners, and suppliers, although the motivation of each was high.

Validate Project Objectives

Validating project objectives involves confirming that the executive sponsor and stakeholders agree to the project objectives and on how these relate to the business needs. For this, you need to examine the business problems and the intended strategic and tactical responses, review the project goals, and answer the question, "What are we doing and why?" You need to create a statement of the business problems, technical problems, and opportunities, and clarify and resolve uncertainties and issues.

For Churchill's architects, the goal of the project was to handle information in a timely manner to create an adequate defense and manage the whole supply chain. The key problems lay in understanding all the different entities and unifying the big picture. This required building a federated portal infrastructure that was capable of handling the volumes of information required, all in different formats.

Review Technical Environment

Before you develop a portal solution, you also need a basic understanding of the IT infrastructure and the information exchanges required. You acquire this understanding by establishing the current system context. You can then establish how this ties into the new portal solution. This understanding also provides a baseline for future changes, so a new architecture can be developed.

Review the Current IT Infrastructure

Reviewing the current IT infrastructure involves inventorying the installed hardware base, applications, and technical capabilities in the enterprise and understanding the IT standards and architecture choices. You also need to list the components in the IT environment, documenting the implications of deviating from these standards, the variance process, and components with no established standards.

For Churchill's architects, this meant looking closely into each environment, at how information was created and used. Typically, an environment's operation was manually intensive, using clerks, filers, and sorters. However, new technologies were rapidly automating the way information was collected, categorized, indexed, sorted, stored, and retrieved. For example, punch-card technologies were used for machine accounting systems for central record control and payroll. This greatly simplified paper-shuffling, as each punch card could store 80 variables of data. Records held on punch cards were fed into a machine that mechanically compiled search criteria and results. Other significant office technologies included bank-check sorting/proofing, electric typewriters, and mechanical printing calculators. Conceptually, data processing of 1940 was little different from today.

Establish System Context

Typically, establishing a system context involves a diagram of all the information exchanges between the system and its environment, including all the sources and destinations of content and data. Useful for the build effort, this diagram defines information exchanges with internal and external organizations, like other business processes, service providers, regulatory agencies, and financial institutions. It defines the characteristics of external interfaces with other systems, like files and databases. It also defines external entity relationships and types, and content locations. Finally, it defines the internal aspects of the system, like the number of instances, available access time, type of communications, hardware, operating system, volume, frequencies, and content formats.

For Churchill's architects, the challenge lay with mapping the interfaces and liaisons into the chains of command and individual organizational structures. For example, how and what type of information is exchanged by businesses in the industrial complex, or required by the armed forces? What is the principal method of communication or channel? What information is available, what should be passed back to the portal, and in what format? These information exchanges and data/content sources set the constraints by which the portal would be bound, as shown in Figure 2.5.

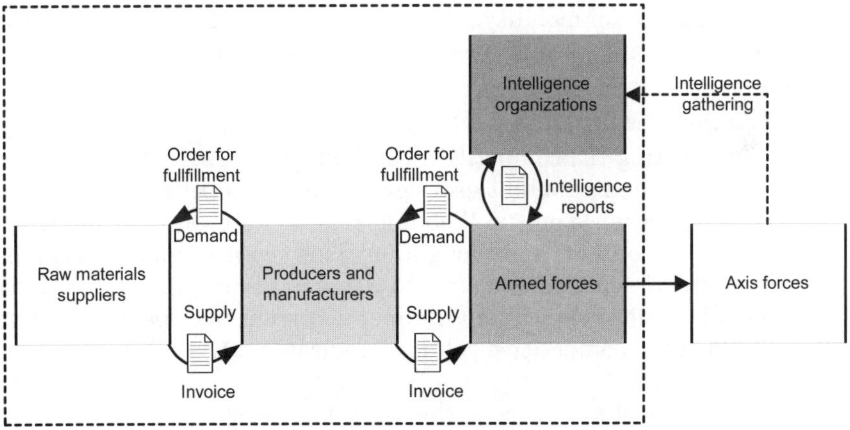

Figure 2.5: The system context model defines the characteristics of external interfaces with other systems and some of the significant information flows.

Develop Business Strategy

Developing a business strategy involves analyzing leading portal practices, the competition, and the organization's business direction, opportunities, and strategy. From this process, you develop options and recommendations on the portal solution's investment areas, based on the contribution that a portal can make to the organization's business goals. This helps prepare an organization and set expectations. It also creates a high-level business process.

Review Leading Portal Practices

In reviewing leading portal practices, you identify potential alternatives, portal archetypes, portal technology, and improvements to the business operation, for later use. Portal success stories highlight the effort required by an organization in the same or other industries, and how that organization executes its processes, policies, and procedures using portal technology and organizes its people to use and support the portal implementation. It also highlights the uses of intellectual capital in the form of content and knowledge management, and how it has improved business operations or finances as a result.

For Churchill's architects, this meant reviewing previous similar situations. The great war of 1918 required a similar undertaking, wherein the government took control of the supply chain and mobilized vast numbers of workers and troops. In fact, this created one of the largest organizations ever created in the UK. However, that business model was hopelessly outdated by 20 years of evolving military and industrial technology and changes in strategy. Tanks and rapid troop mobility, air warfare, the use of intelligence, and total economic warfare were all new factors to consider.

Evaluate Competitive Position

In evaluating the competitive position, you identify the competitor's differentiators in their capabilities, offerings, and competencies. You examine their existing presence on the Web and related applications, and their processes for functions, content, and navigation. This requires visiting competitor's facilities and interviewing customers and users of their applications. This evaluates the business and technical environment, current user perceptions, and the priority levels of the competitive solution environment.

For Churchill's architects, this meant understanding the enemy's situation, activities, and performance. This included understanding the big picture of the supply chain—everything from raw material and resource requirements, to the production capabilities of industries, to the armed forces. This was a role of the intelligence communities like MI5, MI6, and the emergent Bletchley Park code breakers, all under the auspices of the Foreign Office. Churchill also set up a Special Operation Executive (SOE), a resistance and spy network in occupied Europe that could gather information.

Document Strategic Direction

In documenting the strategic direction, you describe the current business, what it aspires to become through a portal solution, the desired state, and the intended transition. This includes understanding the organization's mission, its vision, objectives required to achieve the vision, and the desired state of the business, in both qualitative and quantitative terms. It also includes the areas for which satisfactory results will ensure business goal achievement, alternative portal implementation strategies, releases and quick starts, and business areas where the portal has the most impact on the business goals. The first step in describing your business solution is to articulate the desired output and new capability. Again, let's start by looking at Churchill's desired vision, direction, and objectives in June of 1940.

In the short term, Dunkirk was hailed as a victory. Hitler's hesitance allowed the British to evacuate fully 85 percent of its forces (224,000 troops) and another 123,000 French and Belgian troops. Churchill was aware that the enemy could mount an invasion, but this required air supremacy. The Luftwaffe's 3,500 fighters and bombers outnumbered the RAF's 900 fighters, but through a portal solution with superior intelligence and decision-making (as shown in Figure 2.6), the RAF could target sufficient fighters to offset the threat and conserve numbers. This required gathering enemy intelligence to provide a comprehensive view of the enemy's order of battle, as well as early warning of raids. It also required collecting enough supply-chain information to effectively manage this intelligence, particularly in terms of armaments and fighter production. To achieve this, Churchill needed time. He also had to prepare and strengthen the public's resolve for a fight, so he procrastinated over the enemy's peace offers.

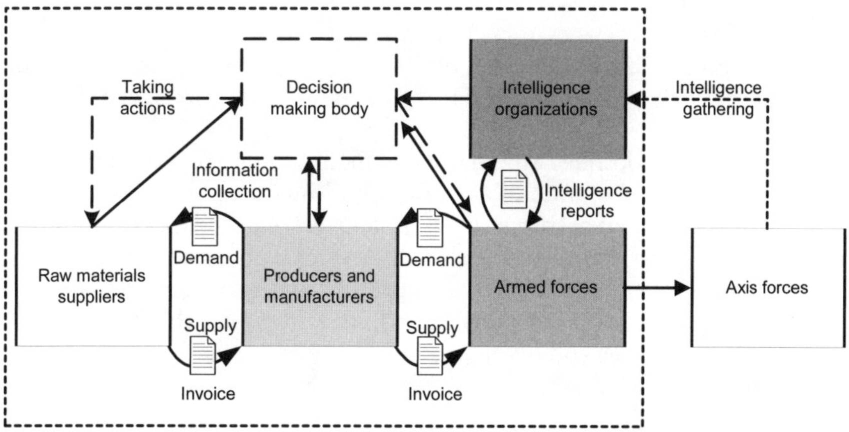

Figure 2.6: The desired business organizational model shows decision-making capability, information collection, and actions taken.

In the longer term, the UK had to wage total economic warfare to defeat a more powerful military giant. This was a massive undertaking that required major organizational changes, such as the creation of various ministries like the Ministry of Economic Warfare. It required using intelligence regarding the enemy's supply-chain and production capability to identify vulnerable industrial targets for bombing. It also required assessing various projects and ideas from across the forces to determine where to do battle and with what resources, so as to cause maximum damage.

Likewise, the business strategy that you pick for your organization must give you a significant business advantage against your competition. For example, you might develop a sophisticated decision-making capability at the core of your business, as shown in Figure 2.7, that analyzes possible actions, lays out the best courses of action, and measures progress towards goals.

Figure 2.7: Decision-making is represented through a cyclical process.

For Churchill's architects, the biggest challenge in realizing the strategy was the scale and complexity of the solution, and whether it would actually work. To verify this required pulling together the various models into a high-level business process model that outlined the workflow, organizational interrelationships, interactions, and business processes. Through this model, shown in Figure 2.8, various envisaged scenarios could be mapped against business events. For example, the model could map how rapid changes in battle and new attacks would be dealt with, or how the resupply of arms, equipment, or pilots would occur.

Likewise, you need to create this model to verify whether you will accomplish your goals. The broad list of principal business processes could include everything from extracting resources, harvesting crops, refining fuels, generating power, undergoing research and development, manufacturing tools and basic commodities, producing food, creating arms, transporting and distributing all the above, supplying populations, and engaging the enemy. The civilian population provides the labor pool for the workforce and the conscripts for armed forces.

For Churchill's architects, the key business processes included managing suppliers (vendors and partners), and procuring goods, services, production, and

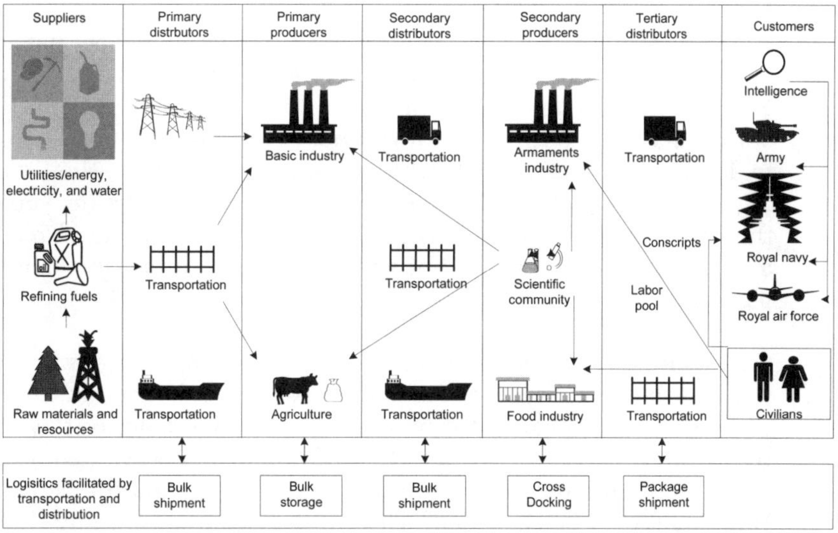

Figure 2.8: The desired business process model outlines the workflow in a giant supply chain.

materials. Resource-management processes included managing the supply chain, production, materials, product lifecycle, distribution, and logistics.

Define Requirements

With the strategy formulated, the next overall phase defines the requirements for community, content, functionality, and nonfunctionality. This is one of the most significant sections of the chapter, as it defines in detail the business aspects of the portal. It determines who will use the solution, for what, and how.

Define Community Requirements

In and between organizations, many informal groups of people or communities meet periodically to share strategically important information and exchange knowledge. Creating communities is important, as people-to-people interactions generate value. From a knowledge and content-management perspective, these communities need organizational support. With the high-level business processes identified, this section examines the target audience, different user profiles, and communities, old and new. The goal is to determine, through use cases, how they will use the portal to undertake their roles in the business process. This also identifies how they will benefit from the portal—its value to them.

Discern Target Audience

In your business, you need to discern the target audience that will use the portal: employees (E), business partners (B), suppliers (S), and customers (C). You also need to determine the portal type (B2E, B2B, B2S, or B2C), the type of information required, and its value. For customers, or B2C portals, you need to define the audience by target segments that indicate their value to your organization and the value that they seek. From the value, you can determine the value propositions that are offered through the portal. This will help create a business case that addresses the tangible and intangible benefits of the portal.

Churchill's architects had to discern the target audience, who the solution was for, and the portal type. Some audiences were self-evident. For example, Churchill and his cabinet were employees, or more accurately executives, and the portal type was equivalent to a B2E today. However, what about all the surrounding organizations, military and civilian, and the population itself? How could they be classified? The answer lies in examining the types of communities and user profiles.

Develop User Profiles (within Communities)

Identify the user profiles within different communities on the basis of their roles within the organization. Different factors determine communities, for example:

- Social or informal networks allow organizations to enable successful communities and create social relationships. These groups naturally collaborate and exchange information, which may be further facilitated by portal functionality.
- The type of information that is released to the community also helps to categorize it.
- Functional requirements differ by the role a community performs. For example, a project-manager community requires access to timesheets, estimating tools, reporting databases, and risk-management tools. A sales-team community, on the other hand, needs access to client-tracking tools, product databases, and marketing-material tools.
- Organizational structures reflect the business and can be divided by products or services, locations, or other hierarchies. Often, customer's business processes define the different roles and communities required.

Churchill's architects had to define the communities and user profiles. This sounds straightforward, but it is not always obvious. It was complicated by the fact that there were many types of organizations and institutions from the government, military, academic, and civilian worlds. Some of the communities could be readily identified, like the war cabinet, government ministers, civil servants, armed forces (army, navy, and air force), special forces, intelligence services, civilian authorities, and emergency services. Churchill's architects created a model of business communities, as shown in Figure 2.9. The size and number of communities was tightly controlled for security and to limit enemy espionage.

Likewise, you will probably identify new cross-functional horizontal communities, like project teams, beyond the obvious, traditional, vertical organizational communities. As a result, the organizational changes that are caused by a portal can be significant, as previously unrelated departments get connected into a community.

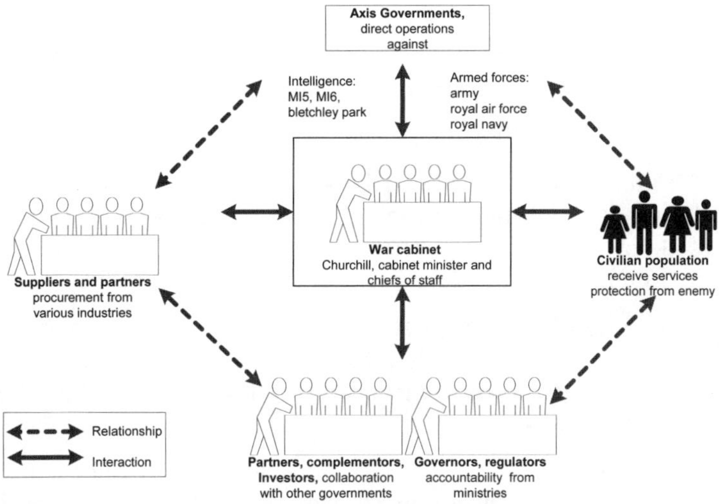

Figure 2.9: The business community model shows the various communities with all potential users of the federated portal. Relationship is regulatory and used for the purposes of compliance.

From the model in Figure 2.9, Churchill's architects could review with Churchill the communities that would have access to the federated portal, and their individual requirements, such as security. This required reviewing the breadth of institutions and organizations. These fell into the main communities of government, armed forces/intelligence, and production/industries. Each of these was vastly complex, and there were many co-dependencies. The armed forces were composed of the national forces, the Royal Navy, the RAF, and the national forces of the Colonies, Protectorates, Mandates, Ireland, and the Dominions. However, these were subordinate to their respective governments' departments before the War Service Ministries. So, the British Army was under the War Office, the Admiralty commanded the Royal Navy, and the Air

Ministry commanded the RAF. This demonstrates the complexity of the organization and what had to be governed.

The roles of the primary community of central government (the war cabinet) included user profiles like the prime minister, cabinet ministers, and ministries responsible for managing all aspects of the war economy. It also extended to the armed forces, intelligence chiefs, and their respective communities, responsible for waging war with the enemy. Some user profiles could traverse horizontally across more than one community, like Churchill and the chiefs of staff (the heads of the three branches of the armed services), scientific officers, and statisticians.

Identify Key Use Cases

A key use case defines how users from communities use the portal and how it interfaces to external systems. Identifying the most important use cases gives a preliminary description of the portal's functional requirements and describes the envisioned capabilities.

The identification of the business community model in Figures 2.9 provided Churchill's architects an insight into the more significant users of the federated portal. These were then grouped into logical communities and mapped to the major business processes identified in Figure 2.8, to include:

- From Storey's Gate, Churchill and his staff, cabinet ministers, and chiefs of staff needed to be in touch with the entire business-process map. This was a principal community that made the overriding decisions.
- From Bentley Prior, the air chief and staff needed a view of enemy activity and forthcoming attacks, the RAF reserve, the production of fighters, and those fighters available.
- At Bletchley Park, the intelligence chiefs and staff required a flow of Enigma information related to enemy activities and the ability to decode, interpret, and distribute it.
- At Whitehall, the ministry of air production required horizontal views of the supply chain, fighter production, and arms manufacturing, as well as the armed forces' needs.
- At Whitehall, the ministries of food, nutrition, and agriculture required horizontal views of the supply chain and food production, as well as military and civilian demands.

These communities are outlined in Figure 2.10 as five major use cases. At this point, you can start to see each of the four portals emerging.

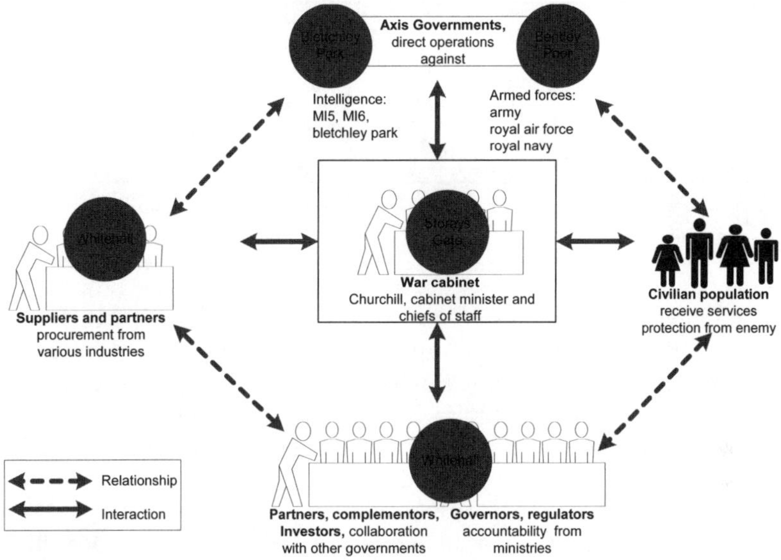

Figure 2.10: Five major use cases were identified, defining how users from communities were to use the federated portal.

With this, you can start to develop the use cases in more detail. This will help organize the menus and functional groupings for the detailed design of user interfaces in chapter 4. Uses cases are numbered consistently and grouped into subject areas to include name, description, and business event.

For Churchill's architects, some use cases were obvious, like that of Churchill and the war cabinet and the priority of certain business events. At this point, only the most critical were identified, as shown in Table 2.2.

Table 2.2: Overall Use Cases

Subject Area	Use Case	Name	Description	Associated Business Event
Collect information	1.1	Ultra information	Information is collected and interpreted for the user.	External; important Enigma signals
Assess information	2.1	Assess situation	The user assesses various situations available.	Temporal (daily, weekly)
Collaboration	3.1	Collaborate with staff	Users collaborate with staff.	Temporal (weekly)

Table 2.2: Overall Use Cases, *continued*

Forecast/plan	4.1	Supply chain	Users forecast demand and plan accordingly.	Internal; event occurring that triggers business rule
Take action/ manage	5.1	Action	User takes various actions.	External and internal

The next step is to define *use-case scenarios* (*UCSs*), which are "instances" that allow the role of each community to be clearly defined in the context of the business process and key business events, the content they access and provide in their role, and the functionality they used to support their role in the process. Scenarios are important to decision-making, especially if rapid and accurate decisions are required.

It is important for purposes of design and usability to describe the situation and to extract the salient points from these scenarios. In the following sections, the key communities and user profiles are closely examined.

Community 1: War Cabinet (Part of Storey's Gate)

Winston Churchill was the principal user and leader of the Storey's Gate portal. As the overall commander-in-chief, he needed to see the big picture. In waging a total war, he was ultimately responsible for the armed forces and their success and the co-ordination and control of defense operations. Therefore, he had to determine how and where the forces should be deployed, which theaters of war would be defended, what would be seceded, and how the enemy would be engaged.

The use cases for this portal are shown in Table 2.3. The war cabinet had to *assess the military situation* (UCS 2.1.1) and required a source for military intelligence or signals that was sophisticated and could show the ever-changing picture of new events. Since battles could be won or lost in a space of hours, information had to be processed in real time so timely decisions could be made. The war cabinet also had to see where new threats might emerge so they could proactively deter them. This was provided by Ultra through Bletchley Park.

The war cabinet had to *assess various projects* (UCS 2.1.2) brought forward from the various departments across the forces. Each idea had to be carefully considered in the bigger picture. Projects had to be coordinated, requiring high levels of collaboration and cooperation between different factions of the forces and their representative military chiefs.

Churchill could influence and *collaborate with his military chiefs of staff* (UCS 3.1.1). He was known to take a healthy interest in the details of war. He had been the Lord Chief of the Admiralty and served in WWI. He continuously *collaborated with his cabinet ministers* (UCS 3.1.2) on many issues, especially the supply chain. Churchill was also in a position to create alliances, treaties, and agreements and *collaborate with allies* (UCS 3.1.3) to bolster the supply chain. For example, he could trade bases with the U.S. for naval destroyers, desperately needed to protect the Atlantic convoys. He was prepared to forge an alliance with the Soviet Union that would put a great strain on his supply chain.

Relative to production, the war cabinet could influence where to deploy production resources and prioritize the types of arms produced. This required the ability to predict demand accurately across the whole supply chain and then to translate this *"forecast" demand* (UCS 4.1.1) into supply- and material-replenishment plans and actions. This allowed Churchill to focus on short-term strategies; for example, he put pressure on the accelerated production of fighters in June of 1940, at the expense of bombers.

Relative to the supply side, the war cabinet had to be aware of distribution and logistics, what had to be *shipped* (UCS 4.1.2) where and why, and whether these were raw materials for production, fuels for industry or armed forces, or food for the population.

Churchill could *take action* (UCS 5.1.1) and appoint ministers. He was not afraid of getting the right man for the job. However, he had a responsibility to his government to collaborate with his inner cabinet and chiefs of staff as he went through a decision-making process.

The war cabinet had to communicate and *disseminate information* (UCS 5.1.2) with various organizations and through different hierarchies. This was done through channels, like memos cascading through the organization. Churchill also communicated through wireless radio with the British population and those of occupied countries.

Storey's Gate portal had to provide an extraordinary level of security. Information from Ultra was so sensitive that sacrifices were made to prevent security compromises. The portal also required a high degree of customization to users like Churchill.

The use cases in Table 2.3 are further detailed through the scenarios in Table 2.4.

Table 2.3: Community 1 Use Cases

Subject Area	Use Case	Name	Description	Associated Business Event
Assess information	2.1	Assess situation	War cabinet assesses various situations.	External, internal, and temporal
Collaborate	3.1	Collaborate with…	Churchill and staff collaborate with various groups.	Temporal
Forecast demand	4.1	Supply chain	Staff forecasts demand and plans the supply side.	Temporal and internal
Take action	5.1	Action	Churchill takes various actions (appointments, communications).	External and internal

Table 2.4: Community 1 Use-case Scenarios

UCS	Termination Outcome	Scenario Summary
2.1.1	Input to decision forum	The war cabinet assesses the battle order and military situation and determines where to focus resources (daily).
2.1.2	Input to decision forum	The war cabinet assesses various projects and determines their priority (weekly).
3.1.1	Decisions made	Churchill collaborates with cabinet ministers (daily).
3.1.2	Decisions made	Churchill collaborates with chiefs of staff (bi-weekly).
3.1.3	Decisions made	Churchill collaborates with allies (weekly).
4.1.1	Forecast completed	Staff forecasts demand.
4.1.2	Supply planned	Staff plans the supply side.
5.1.1	Ministers appointed	Churchill makes ministerial appointments.
5.1.2	Communication sent	The war cabinet communicates with various organizations.
5.1.3	Orders issued	The war cabinet orders the enemy invasion's assembly areas bombed.

Community 2: Bentley Prior (Fighter Command)

The commander-in-chief of Bentley Prior, Hugh (Stuffy) Dowding, faced a desperate situation. The RAF, badly depleted in France, was heavily outnumbered by the Luftwaffe, even though Dowding had pushed hard in peacetime for the development of faster fighters. Fortunately, the British Spitfire fighters were slightly more sophisticated than the enemy planes, and the British Hurricanes could hold their own.

Bentley Prior needed to determine the enemy situation from Ultra intelligence. Specifically, it needed to know the Luftwaffe battle order, when raids were being planned, what the potential targets were, the number of bombers, and the fighter protection strength. The use cases involved are shown in Table 2.5.

Table 2.5: Community 2 Use Cases

Subject Area	Use Case	Name	Description	Associated Business Event
Assess information	2.2	Assess order of battle	Dowding and staff assess incoming enemy raid.	External
Collaboration	3.2	Collaborate with leaders	Dowding's chiefs collaborate with group and squadron leaders.	External
Take action	5.2	Deploy squadrons	Bentley Prior deploys squadrons.	External

The source for military intelligence or signals had to be sophisticated, to assess the ever-changing picture of new events, especially what was being targeted. Bentley Prior staff had to review each Luftwaffe raid to determine whether it was a *raid on airfields* (UCS 2.2.1), a *raid on industrial targets* (UCS 2.2.2), or a *raid on towns and cities* (UCS 2.2.3). Dowding's chiefs *collaborated with group and squadron leaders* (UCS 3.2.1) in determining how to react to each raid.

Bentley Prior's main objective was to keep the RAF operational. Therefore, the top priority was the defense of airfields and radar stations. The radar stations were needed to know where to *deploy precious fighters* (UCS 5.2.1), to conserve strength as best as possible.

In the course of battle, Dowding had to create a perception that there was an inexhaustible supply of fighters by running more sorties per day than the enemy. This put a massive strain on pilots and ground staff. Psychologically, this was very important. Faced by these challenges, Dowding had to rapidly set up a defense structure capable of addressing them. The most critical requirement was for sophisticated operational centers.

The use cases in Table 2.5 are further detailed through the scenarios in Table 2.6.

Table 2.6: Community 2 Use-case Scenarios

UCS	Termination Outcome	Scenario Summary
2.2.1	Input to decision forum	The decision to deploy fighters is based on the size of enemy raids on RAF airfields.
2.2.2	Input to decision forum	Enemy raids on industrial targets determine whether to deploy fighters and anti-aircraft guns.
2.2.3	Input to decision forum	Enemy raids on towns and cities determine whether to deploy anti-aircraft only.
3.2.1	Final decisions made	Collaborate with group and squadron leaders to refine response tactics.
5.2.1	Orders issued	Select and deploy squadrons or anti-aircraft.

Community 3: Intelligence Officers (Part of Bletchley Park)

Bletchley Park consisted of many commands, like the army, air force, and navy, which cooperated and interacted under one roof. Aside from these, it also held a growing team of scientists and cryptographers that were to break the "unbreakable" Enigma using Ultra. The information gained with Ultra was of vital importance to the British and (later) Americans in the strategic planning of the war.

As listed in Table 2.7, the principal role of Bletchley Park was to *provide Churchill and carefully selected staff* (UC 1.3) with military intelligence (through Ultra) that could show the ever-changing picture of new events and provide realtime information for decisions. Although Ultra was operational, its impact was limited and would not be felt until it was scaled up.

The biggest challenge was to prevent the enemy from discovering that *Enigma was compromised* (UCS 5.3.2) and that their signals were being intercepted and successfully decrypted. To maintain secrecy, Churchill ordered that those receiving the information should be kept to an absolute minimum. He appointed Captain Fred Winterbotham as his personal liaison officer to *assess and analyze the information at Bletchley Park* (UC 2.3). Corroborative information had to be gathered from other intelligence sources before Enigma information could be used. This edict was strictly enforced by Churchill to prevent Axis intelligence from correlating any Allied activities with Axis commands sent through Enigma. Information from Ultra was so sensitive that sacrifices were made to prevent security compromises.

In May, during the battle of France, the British were reading most of the Luftwaffe messages. Ultra intelligence was passed on to the appropriate authorities. The most eminent of these was Winston Churchill, who had a special fondness for it. Advanced warning from Ultra that the Dunkirk situation was hopeless promoted advanced planning for the evacuation.

Table 2.7: Community 3 Use Cases

Subject Area	Use Case	Name	Description	Associated Business Event
Collect information	1.3	Ultra information	Intelligence officers handle Ultra information.	External, important Enigma signals
Assess information	2.3.1	Ultra information assessed	Intelligence officers assess and analyze information.	External, Internal, and Temporal
Take action	5.3.1	Ultra to PM	Winterbotham and team deliver intelligence to Churchill.	External and internal
Take action	5.3.2	Enigma compromised	Intelligence officers invoke contingency plans.	External, important Enigma signals

The use cases in Table 2.7 are further detailed through the scenarios in Table 2.8.

Table 2.8: Community 3 Use-case Scenarios

UCS	Termination Outcome	Scenario Summary
1.3.1	Information collected	Analyze Ultra information, provide interpretation, and deliver to Churchill.
2.3.2	Assessment completed	Assess and analyze information.

Table 2.8: Community 3 Use-case Scenarios, *continued*

UCS	Termination Outcome	Scenario Summary
5.3.1	PM received information	Deliver information to PM in a secure manner.
5.3.2	Orders issued	Invoke contingency plans to preserve the secret of Ultra.

Community 4: Ministry for Aircraft Production (Part of Whitehall)

The Ministry of Aircraft Production was created in May 1940 to relieve the air ministry of responsibility for procuring supplies. To meet his short-term goals Churchill appointed Lord Beaverbrook—an outsider and a Canadian, who was opinionated and often ruthless. Aircraft production was critical, and Churchill believed he needed an outsider to handle the politics of such a position. He had long regarded Beaverbrook as a confidant, and now, as a very necessary addition to the war effort. Churchill offered Beaverbrook the post against the advice of King George VI. Churchill had always been impressed by Beaverbrook's vital and vibrant energy, even though they had been at each other's throats on several occasions.

Beaverbrook's main objective was to supply enough aircraft to keep the RAF operational in the defense of Britain. Therefore, his top priority was the manufacture of fighters. The air ministry, which controlled both the fighter and bomber commands, was furious that Beaverbrook leaned towards fighter production over the manufacture of bombers, which were regarded as attack aircraft. Beaverbrook's vision was that by building a superb defense force, the manufacture of bombers could continue at its own pace for use at a later date to their best advantage.

As shown in Table 2.9, Beaverbrook and his staff had to *assess the fighter strength* (UCS 2.4.1) and *production capacity* (UCS 2.4.2). They also had to *forecast upcoming demand* (UC 4.4), so that they could readily meet it. They were faced with several problems involving raw materials and inventory, and a skills shortage.

Meeting the former required not only the ability to handle procurement activities quickly, efficiently, and cost effectively, but also to predict raw material and inventory needs based on collaborative forecasts from suppliers and customers. The aircraft factories had to be able to place accurate orders with suppliers in time, every time; provide accurate details for components and logistics; and accurately forecast demand to suppliers. Suppliers had to handle any exceptions to predicted demand. This required close *collaboration with manufacturers* (UCS 3.4.1) and *allies* (UCS 3.4.2) and the need to share information about order-management processes and practices.

To meet the latter, they had to be aware of production capacity and the scope of the labor pool that was available, including skill levels and training requirements. With conscription in place, not enough male workers could meet the demand, so they had to *forecast the percentage of female workers* (UCS 4.4.2) who could come into the workforce in the required timeframes.

In January 1940, Churchill said, "Millions of new workers will be needed, and more than a million women must come boldly forward into our war industries." In 1940, the Ministry of Labour, under Ernest Bevin, was one of the most important areas of the war economy. Beaverbrook had to operate like an entrepreneur, without regard to procedure and operations.

Table 2.9: Community 4 Use Cases

Subject Area	Use Case	Name	Description	Associated Business Event
Assess information	2.4	Assess various factors	Ministry staff assesses various factors.	Temporal and internal
Collaboration	3.4	Collaborate with...	Beaverbrook and staff collaborate with manufacturers and allies.	Temporal and internal
Plan	4.4	Plan supply and resources	Ministry staff plans supplies and resources.	Temporal and internal

The use cases in Table 2.9 are further detailed through the scenarios in Table 2.10.

Table 2.10: Community 4 Use-case Scenarios

UCS	Termination Outcome	Scenario Summary
2.4.1	Input to decision forum	Assess fighter strength and weekly losses.
2.4.2	Input to decision forum	Assess production against target.
3.4.1	Decisions made	Collaborate with manufacturers and suppliers.
3.4.2	Decisions made	Collaborate with allies and their suppliers.

Table 2.10: Community 4 Use-case Scenarios, *continued*

UCS	Termination Outcome	Scenario Summary
4.4.1	Supply planned	Increase production based on low fighter numbers.
4.4.2	Supply planned	Increase production based on low fuel reserves.
4.4.3	Supply planned	Increase production based on low ammo reserves.
4.4.4	Supply planned	Increase production based on fighter engine parts.
4.4.5	Demand forecasted	Determine requirements for female workers.

Community 5: Ministries of Food, Nutrition, and Agriculture (Part of Whitehall)

Even before the war began, the government had devised a rationing plan to be implemented if it became necessary. This was known as "The Food Defence Plans." The UK was a large industrial and manufacturing country that relied heavily on food imports. Seventy percent of the food it consumed was imported, especially fruit and meat.

As war broke out, the importation of goods into Britain became a problem. Merchant ships could be sunk, overseas food-producing countries were in danger of being occupied or were already under enemy occupation, and goods stored in warehouses could be bombed. Within a week of war being declared, the Ministry of Food in the government was inaugurated.

The UK faced a naval blockade and a potential food crisis. As shown in Table 2.11, Lord Woolton and his staff had to *plan next year's food supply* (UCS 4.5.1), in terms of what had to be imported and what could be produced in the UK. This required an inventory of the current food stock and an understanding of food demands, where shortages would likely occur, and how this would affect the armed forces or other parts of the population. The types of food that would be missing, their nutritional value, the impact of their deficiency in the average diet, and any associated health risks also had to be determined.

The ministry also had to *assess special requirements* (UCS 2.5.1) for certain consumers of food, such as troops fighting in Egypt in the desert, or those being transported on a long journey. Of course, specific groups had to be given a special treatment. For example, pilots returning from overnight missions received full breakfasts.

The ministry had to investigate the supply side of food production in the UK and *collaborate closely* (UCS 3.5.1) with ministers for agriculture and supply. This included looking at other food sources like Canada and the lifeline across the Atlantic, supplied through convoys. The ministry also had to *collaborate closely* with its allies (UCS 3.3.2). Based on all this, the ministry could start to apply the levers available.

Table 2.11: Community 5 Use Cases

Subject Area	Use Case	Name	Description	Associated Business Event
Assess information	2.5	Assess requests	Woolton and staff read special requirements from forces.	Internal
Collaboration	3.5	Collaborate with ministers	Woolton and staff collaborate with ministers.	Temporal
Forecast demand	4.5	Plan food supply	Woolton and staff forecast demand and plan the food supply.	Temporal and internal

The use cases in Table 2.11 are further detailed through the scenarios in Table 2.12.

Table 2.12: Community 5 Use-case Scenarios

UCS	Termination Outcome	Scenario Summary
2.5.1	Input to decision forum	Read special requirements from forces.
3.5.1	Decisions made	Collaborate with ministers of agriculture and supplies (daily).
3.5.2	Decisions made	Collaborate with allies (weekly).
4.5.1	Forecast completed	Forecast demand and plan the food supply.
4.5.2	Supply planned	Plan the supply side.

Categorize and Prioritize Requirements

To review, categorize, and prioritize the community requirements, you create use-case models. These models use "swim-lane" diagrams to graphically outline the use-case scenarios or how the user interacts with the portal. The swim lanes depict the user or actor and his interface into the portal, the interchange of documents and information, and the delivery of functions and services. These models are then compared individually for any commonalities, categorized, and prioritized. This provides useful input to defining the functional requirements. It also helps to rapidly communicate the envisaged scenarios to an executive audience for feedback.

For Churchill's architects, this meant reviewing with Churchill and the war cabinet the use-case scenarios and models, a non-trivial task considering the complexity of each. From this review, Storey's Gate and Bentley Prior emerged with a slightly higher priority.

Define Functional Requirements

Defining functional requirements involves reviewing archetypes. The functional requirements give you the main application functions of each of the federated portals and describe what each does. As a result, all future design decisions reflect the business priorities.

Transfer the Business into Functional Requirements

Once the areas of the business and communities that can benefit from a portal are identified, you need to revise the set of business processes. This activity captures decisions about which business processes will be supported and what functionality will be provided. Functionality is treated as a black box, with the focus on what it does rather than how it is implemented.

Portal functionality often concentrates on how information is moved around the organization so that it facilitates the business processes. Specifically, this includes moving information to and from people or communities, and between people and identified content repositories.

Churchill's architects turned the business requirements into the functionality of a federated portal. The main functions, based on the use-case scenarios and models, were to provide the following:

- Intelligence (military and civilian) based on time-sensitive information that could be either reactive or proactive
- A decision-making forum
- Communication channels

Shortly after assuming the office of Prime Minister in May 1940, Winston Churchill visited the cabinet war rooms at Storey's Gate, to see what preparations had been made to allow him and his war cabinet to continue working if enemy bombing made it impossible to stay above ground. Churchill said, "This is the room from which I will direct the war." This well-hidden site, whose location and purpose was known to only the most privileged, was to operate around the clock every day of the year, from the start to the end of the war.

Likewise, your project must turn the stated business requirements into functional requirements. These are the main functions of the business solution and what it does, through its interfaces, transactions, and information. For example, you need to determine how the portal interfaces and communicates outside of itself, how it handles transactions and their processing, and how it maintains and exchanges information.

The federated portal's functions and features had to be defined for the people who would use it, like Churchill, his war cabinet, and their immediate staffs. Other organizations also connected in, from both military and civilian outposts.

Introducing Archetypes

The functions and features of a portal can be very complex. To simplify the requirements process, therefore, *archetypes* are used. An archetype is a collection of information or architectures that provides examples of previous portals and various combinations of functionality. This simplifies the possible portal implementations and identifies implications, constraints, and benefits in later phases. You start with an industry archetype (pattern) that has similar business processes to what you need, as shown in Figure 2.11.

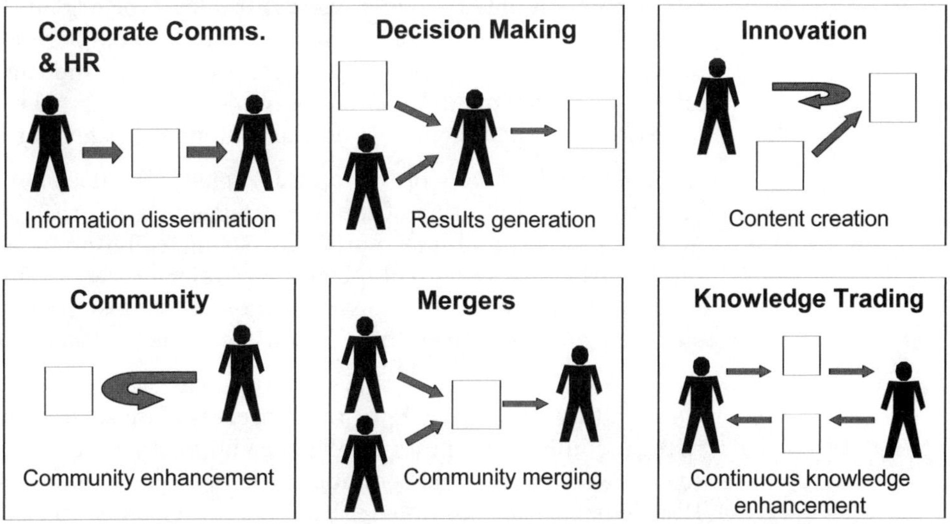

Figure 2.11: Archetypes, concepts, and models are used to define functions for portals.

Archetypes are useful because they allow you to explore and conceptually "test drive" the solution definitions. Working at a pattern level provides a quick means of identifying the basic functional requirements explicitly, then mapping them onto the particular business process requirements. The requirements from the use-case scenarios for the portal are compared against each archetype in the library to find similarities and learning lessons.

Each archetype differs by the functions it provides, the communities it serves, and the content it organizes:

- *Corporate-communication archetype*—This archetype emphasizes supporting employees in their work through effective communication, information provisions, and appropriate tools. These are provided in a personalized way, so employees can make informed decisions and provide maximum benefit to their organization. This archetypes is on a more personal scale than the decision-making archetype, discussed next. The results do not typically flow back into the portal, but the preferences are captured. For Churchill's architects, this archetype had some relevance when information was being passed from Storey's Gate, the master portal, to the other federated portals.
- *Decision-making archetype*—This archetype emphasizes making complex decisions and forming action plans. It enhances decision-making through the right information in the right place at the right time, and decision support tools.
    - Enhanced decision-making allows decision makers, under pressure, to go straight to the required information and not hunt for information and waste valuable time and energy. It allows for urgent decisions, without the availability of the full facts, instilling a high level of confidence that the information is accurate, up to date, and complete. It addresses taxonomy definition and implementation, and content insertion into the taxonomy and the content management system.
    - Decision support tools provide simulations of the decision results, statistical manipulation of input and output data for the decision making process, and information gathering, collation, analysis, and presentation/modeling tools. These also offer process definition and recording, collaboration support such as meeting support or brainstorming aids, and tools that instigate actions for the decisions.
    - For Churchill's architects this archetype was relevant for Storey's Gate and Bentley Prior. Both these processed massive amounts of real-time information into intelligence for decisions making. The results were routed and communicated to their relevant communities. Decisions varied with urgent situations, when sometimes making a decision was more important than getting the answer perfect first

time. Others dealt with very large, complex decisions, when it was imperative to get it right first time with no second chance. The former was important to Bentley Prior, the latter to the Storey's Gate.

- *Innovation archetype*—This archetype emphasizes generating, capturing, sharing, improving and leveraging ideas within a single community or across many communities. This archetype is very focused on gathering information, browsing and searching, locating expertise, and collaborating to form and build on ideas. It is for portals enabling knowledge generation, enhancement, and use. For Churchill's architects, this had some relevance for Whitehall and the manufacturing communities that required the free flow of ideas for improving the quality of equipment, combined with the tools to capture these ideas and enable them for further development and use. The starting point is a very simple portal with limited functionality that allows people to communicate. For example, this might use a newsgroup-type approach or chat facilities.
- *Community archetype*—This archetype emphasizes creating and developing communities, enabling them to flourish and providing inputs to improved business results. Information dissemination forms a core part, as does collaboration and online help. This archetype also accentuates personalization, user roles, and access rights for appropriate information and services to support community participation. For Churchill's architects, this had a lot of relevance for Beaverbrook, who was trying to rapidly scale up a specialist, niche organization into a broader fighter-producing capability. This required pulling together a host of manufacturers and producers into a cohesive community that could function as a team. There were many different user roles and individual users.
- *Mergers archetype*—This archetype emphasizes assisting diverse communities to develop a common understanding and merge into one effective community. Portal users need to work with information that is meaningful to them, while sharing it with others who might see it differently. This develops a common understanding of the information meaning, so the separate communities no longer exist. The complexities of taxonomy, content management, and personalized content delivery are the main focus of this archetype. For Churchill's architects, this had a lot of relevance for Woolton, who was trying to meet the overwhelming food demands of a nation under siege. Across the supply chain, many disparate and complex communities interacted, resulting in the issue of moving content in and out of the taxonomy when different communities joined or left the organization.
- *Knowledge-based trading archetype*—This archetype emphasizes getting the right, authorized information to the right people from a wide range of sources and within time constraints. It is largely about secure, fast

turn-around knowledge transactions, and it is less dynamic than other archetypes. It also deals with information dissemination, rather than directed information flows, where experts accumulate and analyze information to publish their findings. Consumers of this provide feedback and request information, which creates a flow of knowledge back to the experts who transact with these consumers. For Churchill's architects, this was relevant to Storey's Gate in helping Churchill and his staff increase their understanding of Ultra information. This community needed access to intelligence experts and tools to best interpret the information presented to them. The Ultra information was very sensitive, so strict security controls had to be enforced. Speed was also critical, so that the knowledge transactions were based on up-to-date information, the source was accurate, and the intelligence experts performed valid analysis.

Business Model and Application Functions

This step expands the archetypes and functions into even more detail. You need to identify application functionality in the following four areas, listed in increasing levels of sophistication:

- User
- Analytical
- Content-management
- Presentation

The User application functionality moves information around the organization between people, communities, or content repositories to facilitate business processes:

1. *Access and publishing information* is held in content stores, databases or other file systems, and applications. Publishing enters information into an organizational content repository to make users' "tacit knowledge" (the knowledge in peoples' heads) explicit.

2. *Collaboration* exchanges information between communities and captures agreed consensus in either realtime or non-realtime. Realtime (asynchronous) functions involve phones, teleconferencing, same-time connect, and virtual meetings. Non-realtime (synchronous) functions involve team rooms, email, newsgroups, and shared folders.

3. *Learning* delivers approved information to users and helps apply it to their roles:

   - Reference information allows users to search through content individualistically.

- Self-help information provides structure for topic-specific information, like frequently asked questions and user guides.
- Online courses provide structured learning through a defined syllabus undertaken at the user's pace.
- Taught courses provide an online tutored environment and allow a tutor to monitor and guide the learning process.

4. *Workflow* ensures business processes are supported by the users' application. *Document workflow* forwards information to the next person in the process. Documents can be quite small, including small transaction records. *Process workflow* accesses application-integration workflow with back-end transactional systems, as used by automated business processes.

For Churchill's architects, User application functionality was vital to all the communities as a means of moving information around the organizations, between individuals and communities. Access to information and realtime collaboration was vital to Churchill and the war cabinet for decision-making, as it was to the Whitehall ministries managing disparate groups. Access to experts was equally important, to increase the value of basic information and usage. Workflow was also very important to Whitehall for dealing with complex business processes in the supply chain. Learning was important to all communities in getting their staffs up to speed on the operational aspects of the portals.

You also need to consider the four types of knowledge generated by the User application functionality:

1. *Potential knowledge*, or tacit content, has high value. It is turned into different types of explicit content, knowledge assets, and sustainable benefits.
2. *Emerging knowledge* is used at least twice in collaboration, or the informal sharing of documents and information. The benefits of reuse are achieved, but the information is not part of the organizational knowledge base.
3. *Approved knowledge* is used several times. It is endorsed by the organization as acceptable and is distributed broadly as guidelines or best practices.
4. *Mandated knowledge* is a set of standards and processes carried out by all users. This knowledge is reused by many people and is embedded in the workflow.

As the collected knowledge in an organization evolves through steps A to D, its reuse and value increases, as shown in Figure 2.12. In addition, as the level of functional sophistication increases, the volume and diversity of knowledge decreases by 50 percent.

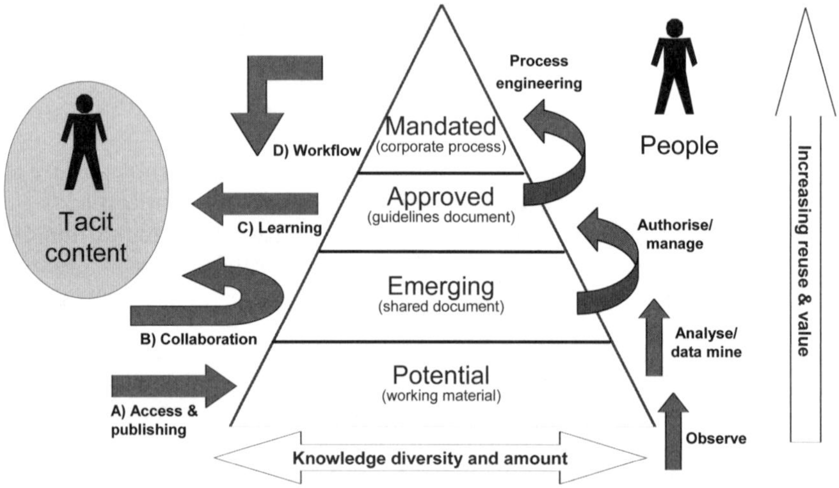

Figure 2.12: User application functionality, A to D on the left, moves information around the organization, increasing its reuse and value. People on the right interact with the generated knowledge.

For Churchill's architects, potential knowledge existed in the form of Ultra messages. As this knowledge was interpreted and better understood, it became emerging knowledge. Approved knowledge existed after Storey's Gate had digested it and endorsed it for distribution, combining it with knowledge from other sources. Bentley Prior and Whitehall ran their procedure-based operations on mandated knowledge embedded in the workflow.

The Analytical application functionality operates on the content within the portal, analyzing it and structuring it automatically. It includes the following:

- *Expertise location* monitors individual or group interests and creates indexes for areas of expertise based on the publishing history of related topics and documents retrieved or inserted. Topic and community affinities are linked to these.
- *Personal network identification* disseminates very tacit information through individuals to other interested parties. Tracking the collaboration identifies the individuals and promotes them as contacts for new types of information.
- *Web-site analysis* examines metrics for visits (hits) to the portal content structure and feeds this back to the designers to improve the portal's effectiveness.

For Churchill's architects, expertise location was important to all communities, in particularly Storey's Gate and Bletchley Park, which required interpretation of complex information. Personal network identification was important to Whitehall, as best practices would be passed quickly to interested parties to improve manufacturing productivity.

The Content-Management application functionality manages the authoring and publishing of documents to external communities, especially through B2C and B2B portals. Organizations require an overall content-management strategy not decided by individual communities. This functionality includes the following:

- *Authoring* creates new documents and is usually part of the infrastructure. It differs from publishing in that authoring generates or edits documents or records for organizational content, while publishing identifies documents to the portal and puts them into use.
- *Publishing* makes the authored content available through the portal. An authorization process is followed when moving content from development to production.
- *Configuration management* tracks changes to the published content, allows reversion in case of error, and provides accountability for changes.
- *Workflow* supports content management, allowing authors to change and forward documents on to managers for authorization, and then allowing publishers to install the documents.

For Churchill's architects, this functionality was extremely important to Storey's Gate. Authored documents had to be published in a very controlled way to the federated and external communities, through a workflow and with complete accountability. For example, documents had to be published to allied governments, but any documents falling into enemy hands could cause enormous damage.

The Presentation functionality identifies how the content is delivered to the user:

- *Presentation components* provide access to certain content or functionality on a user's desktop. They are part of the user interface, to be reused across communities.
- *User personalization* involves standardized business processes that require the same application software (and presentation components) across communities and its members. People need to ensure that the content aligns with their roles in the business process. This requires manager-setup and rule-based personalization, as well as the following.

- *Role-based personalization* modifies presentation components to meet community needs. For example, a project manager accesses a project team room, and a salesperson accesses a marketing team room.
- *Individual personalization* modifies presentation components to reflect a user's job requirements. It is essential for employees. For example, project managers can identify their projects, and salespersons can specify products of interest from a marketing database.
- *Device personalization* allows users to interact with different presentation components according to the device used. For example, in a wireless phone or PDA, the smaller screen is unsuitable for displaying normal browser graphics and text, so the content is converted by transcoding.
- *Notification* alerts someone when a significant business event occurs. It uses email, same-time messages, or a specialized "alert" component on the browser.
- *Subscription* provides users with new or changed information about a specific topic on a regular basis (time-triggered).

For Churchill's architects, some aspects of the Presentation functionality were important to all communities, like personalization of information to specific roles in the organization. When dealing with realtime information and decision-making, individuals need to take action promptly to prevent bottlenecks in the overall business process. Presenting information, whether cascading orders through a hierarchy or notifying individual commands, was very important to Storey's Gate and Bentley Prior. Intelligence from Bletchley Park could only be disseminated in an extremely controlled and secure way, similar to a subscription mechanism. Notification was important to all communities, but it was absolutely critical to Bentley Prior, which had to respond immediately to events like raids.

Outline the System Function Model

The system function model identifies the automated system functions required to support the business requirements, the flow of information between these functions, and the automated functions and data stores that are needed. For Churchill's architects, this model was created specifically for the supply chain, to collect information for reporting and indicator purposes. This model is refined and presented in chapter 3.

Define Content Requirements

In the context of content requirements, content includes all forms of information (such as images, documents, emails, Web pages, audio, video) and how it is stored or accessed within the portal. This phase assesses the content, outlines a logical data model, and produces a process/data-usage matrix. It combines information about technology, user characteristics, learning behaviors, and psychology with data analysis and classification. It establishes the context and the views of content that make it accessible and give it value.

Churchill's architects were faced with the problems of having to assess what content was necessary and useful to the federated portal. As in today's world, they were faced with content overload.

It is important not to organize the content around an organization's structure, for example by business units. Instead, plan the content, its structure, and the supporting functions to meet the user needs or the business objectives. Otherwise, the classification and navigation will be cumbersome and frustrating to the user.

Content Assessment

You need to assess content from four perspectives:

1. *Content value* is determined and prioritized according to the business need of each community. For example, Ultra content from Bletchley Park was of paramount value to Churchill. Both Ultra and radar content were critical to Bentley Prior. Production numbers were critical for Whitehall.
2. *Content availability* is identified both by type and by user/community to meet the necessary benefits in the business case. This identifies and classifies the sources, formats, owners, content elements, and access requirements. It also includes conditions of use agreed upon with each content provider. For example, content from the supply-chain manufacturers varied in sources, format, and owners, and its use had to be negotiated by Whitehall.
3. *Content architecture* is prerequisite to manage the high content growth in a portal. It is determined by the publication hierarchy or classification structure, which relates to the following:

   - Topology of the site, context, general site map, and expected vitality
   - Common vocabulary for core lexicon and definitions
   - Classification and labeling for grouping, organizing, indexing, and schemas
   - Content structures/descriptions, like news briefs, product information, and summaries
   - Navigation that builds the classifications, indices, and cross-references, and the mechanisms or the specific types of content

- Content delivery plan, which describes the content placed on the site
- Content migration required for legacy content

4. *Content processes* are reviewed to determine whether robust enough to select, assign, create, publish, measure, and maintain content and for the new solution.

For Churchill's architects, all content processes were important to all communities because of the need for managing realtime information and decision-making. Consistency within the portal federation required a common content architecture.

Outline Logical Data Model

The logical data model captures knowledge of the organization's existing business information structures and the way information is processed, in a standard format. A portal does not necessarily need a logical data model, but it is very useful in creating a normalized data inventory. Churchill's architects created a data model to identify and collect indicator information, which was very specific data from the supply chain. The model was under the auspices of various ministries responsible for the supply chain. This model is refined in chapter 3.

Outline Process/Data-usage Matrix

The process/data-usage matrix makes explicit the dependency relationships between the process model processes (see Figure 2.8) and the data of the logical data model. The relationship and mutual dependency of these two matrix views is documented so they are appropriately reflected in greater detail. This ensures that a community's content is synchronized with the processes it uses. Churchill's architects had to create this model to support the development of management reports from the supply chain. This model is refined in chapter 3.

Define Nonfunctional Requirements

Nonfunctional requirements are not related to portal functions and what the portal does. Instead, they define operational characteristics like security and safety, reliability, availability, performance, and maintainability. This section identifies these characteristics and the community expectations for the final portal implementation. Nonfunctional requirements are incredibly important to a portal. This is where you could lose your shirt.

Runtime Properties

For your portal, nonfunctional requirements related to runtime properties include availability, safety, security, and system management. A portal has to be secure, stable, and continuously available, so the requirements have to be carefully considered.

For Churchill's architects, this meant reviewing with the communities their requirements related to security and safety, availability, performance, and maintainability. The federated portal had to be secure because if the enemy had any knowledge indicating that Enigma communications were compromised or insecure, there would be grave repercussions. In fact, many lives depended on the federated portal, so it was life-critical. The information had to be trustworthy and accurate. Availability was also very important. The portal was also mission-critical; if it were unavailable, the hub of operations and all the federated portals would be severely affected.

The nonfunctional requirements for performance required Churchill's federated portal to provide timely information. As soon as information was available, it had to be distributed and presented to the right people in the organization. It also had to be maintainable, so changes could be made to equipment, processes, or the organization. These requirements had to be carefully considered, as every ongoing change had an impact on the quality of intelligence and decision-making. These also affected functions like communications.

Likewise, the nonfunctional requirements for system performance and capacity have a far-reaching impact on operations. The system has to perform with redundancy. With portals, user response is absolutely critical.

Non-Runtime Properties

Requirements based on "non-runtime" properties include scalability, portability, maintainability, environmental factors, and evolvability. A mistake in defining nonfunctional requirements can have a significant cost impact on the project budget, far more reaching than a mistake in the functional requirements.

For Churchill's architects, these properties were essential. For example, the scalability of Bletchley Park was necessary to decode the increasing volumes of all the available Enigma signals. Portability was needed so that when Churchill had to travel and meet Allied leaders around the world, he had access to information and models. Evolvability was needed for Bentley Prior and its operation to rapidly face new and changing situations.

Service Levels

For portal nonfunctional requirements, you need to define the runtime properties for performance, capacity, and availability, and set baseline targets for service output. These are subsequently used for developing SLAs (service-level agreements) and SLOs (service-level objectives).

For Churchill's federated portal, nonfunctional requirements also defined service levels for the runtime properties like performance, capacity, and safety, and set baseline targets for operation and service output. For example, redundancy had to be built into the number of fighter airfields and radar stations, as these were top targets for destruction.

Constraints

With portals, constraints must conform to any technical standards in place, as well as to business standards like geographical location.

The constraints for Churchill's federated portal started with defining physical size specifications. This was mandated by the limited space available, for example, in Storey's Gate. Other functions were mandated by geography. For example, Bentley Prior had to exchange information rapidly between headquarters and operations centers in the field.

Assess Impact

The overall process of assessing impact outlines the user experience, assesses the business impact, and ensures that expected organizational change is addressed. It ensures due diligence in the project. This is the last section before the technical model definition.

Outline User Experience

The process of outlining of the user experience articulates the kinds of interactions the user ought to have with a federated portal. Preferably, the user experience is positive and meets the objectives of the user. This process is driven by the use-case scenarios that help frame the overall experience expectations. This also prepares for usability design and testing. Typically, customer portals focus on supporting the brand experience, where the channel upholds the customers' experience with the brand that is symbolic of the organization. This is less important with employee portals, unless the employees face the customer.

For Churchill's architects, this was important for user adoptability and sustained usage. It was also very critical in a decision-making environment where rapid decisions had to be made, shown in Figure 2.6. A poor user experience would undermine the ability to complete these activities successfully.

Assess Business Impact

A portal automates processes and integrates workflow, pushing information and resources between communities. This has a major impact on a business and the current organization. This section measures this organizational impact and verifies the project feasibility by creating a cost/benefit analysis.

Organizational Impact

Assessing the organizational impact addresses two primary objectives:

- Gauging the level of organizational change likely with a new portal and the organization's ability to cope with this change
- Understanding the business processes affected and their overall positive contribution to the business goals when automated

Almost all of Churchill's federated portal was new, with the exception of some existing facilities that required integration. The organizational change was significant. For example, under Beaverbrook, the civilian workforce had to be very flexible to changes in shifts and aggressive production schedules. Military personnel also had to adapt to the novelty of a large number of female staff.

Throughout the portal implementation, you need to maintain business as usual by constantly assessing the business and organizational impacts. A review of the environment determines the organization's ability to accommodate changes. It requires identifying the impact on individual elements of the business, preferably through metrics, and determining where adjustments need to be made to ensure acceptable productivity.

For Churchill's architects, this meant reviewing critical elements of the supply chain that would be most affected. For example, certain points in resource/supply, manufacturing, and transportation would be stretched to a breaking point. This would also require understanding the personal skills-enhancements needed.

Create a Cost/Benefit Analysis

Portals provide opportunities for improving the organization from the customer, supplier/partner, and employer perspectives. However, some portals are easier to justify than others. For example, a *customer portal* focuses on tangible benefits related to improvements in sales, and therefore revenues and profits.

An *employee portal*, on the other hand, focuses partly on intangible benefits related to productivity gains from time savings, like average door-to-door time of processes, average idle time of processes, and time for information search and retrieval. It also looks at the costs for the provision of information and the number of processes supported by the portal that are executed in the portal. Employee benefits include increased productivity, decreased costs, satisfied employees, easy-to-find information, easy-to-use applications, and reduced decision times. As a result, the analysis is somewhat more complex and should establish the types of metrics required.

A *supplier portal* focuses on tangible benefits related to cost savings through reduced procurement costs, average inventory of goods, and average duration/costs of negotiation process.

A *decision-making portal* falls in between these three portal types, with both tangible and intangible benefits.

Churchill's architects probably did not go through a formal costs/benefit analysis, but they were still under pressure to make the right choices. After all, the limited resources available to Churchill had to be wisely applied, in a very short timeframe. Once the costs are determined (as discussed in chapter 3), the costs/benefit analysis can be completed.

Define Operational Solution

The overall process of defining an operational solution unifies all the plans, procedures, and approaches into a road map for the project in the longer term, over several releases. The primary objective is to create a technical model definition to support the federated portal solution.

Outline Solution Strategy

The solution strategy defines a testing strategy, maintenance and support, metrics, service levels, and configuration procedures. It refines the impact analysis and defines plans for deployment, release, and static testing. Effectively, this lays out all the key plans for a solution strategy.

Define a Testing Strategy

The test strategy is a high-level description of the test activities for the implementation, so they conform to a standard. The test strategy expressed by the testing objectives includes the following:

- Assessment of the business and technical risk
- Test focus areas, the critical attributes of the federated portal
- Levels of tests, based on known standards and what is needed to meet quality criteria
- Types of tests to consider, related to business or structural functions
- Organizational responsibilities based on project deliverables
- Entry and exit criteria defined for different levels of importance to the project's success
- Any technology, tools, or strategies relevant to the project

- Any organization or business-unit metrics or strategies relevant to establishing the portal's success, such as data from employee surveys and focus groups on usability, satisfaction, and perceived value

For Churchill's architects, testing was critical for determining the integrity of the solution. Decision-making in realtime requires accurate information, with little room for error. The level of risk was reduced by taking information from several sources for corroboration. In addition, the testing timeframes for Churchill's architects were very short, measured in weeks, thus requiring extra resources and increasing the risk.

Define Maintenance and User-support Approach

Identifying the required strategies that best satisfy the community requirements requires the development of a high-level plan for supporting the processes, major tasks, schedules, skill levels, and estimated resources. For Churchill's architects, this meant looking at the mission-critical elements of the portal that required high levels of support to maintain continuously high levels of services. The Bentley Prior operations centers and the radar stations were two such elements.

Metrics and Service Level Agreements

SLAs are critical to establishing expectations for infrastructure support and for assuring the ongoing service quality. SLA experts should begin to establish goals for service quality and implement these during the build stage. SLAs should be adjusted continually for additions and changes in business or technical goals and services[1].

Churchill's architects had to establish SLAs throughout the portal for a number of critical elements. Bentley Prior had to scramble fighters within a specific timeframe to be effective; Ultra intelligence had a limited shelf life to be really useful; supply-chain information could affect production schedules.

Refine Impact Analysis

Any new information that alters the portal effect on the organization is noted. That is where the impact to the organization is significant. Any enterprise information that is not ready to be deployed via a portal will have a negative impact. Also, new functions like personalization cause changes in business processes and induce new processes.

Churchill's architects had to assess the impact and repercussion of the portal on the forthcoming air battle. The worst-case scenario if the portal was not

[1] Source: Business-to-Employee Initiatives: Managing Implementation, Gartner Oct, 2002.

effective was the battle would be lost, resulting in the bombing of cities and civilians, followed by invasion.

Set Up Configuration-Management Procedures

Throughout development, the portal is reconfigured to perform specific tests, run user scenarios, test performances, and add new technologies. Procedures ensure that all changes are recorded so they can be backed-out at any time. They provide tools for controlling changes and allow everything to be verified via auditing and reporting.

For Churchill's architects, this meant that the rapid portal changes needed to be carefully recorded through configuration-management procedures to ensure a controlled back-out plan. This was important for testing the federated portal, specifically for Bentley Prior, which underwent incessant testing.

Sketch Deployment Plan

Portals are deployed over a number of releases as the community, function, and content vary. For each, you need to do the following:

- Choose the pilot community members.
- Identify the sequence for which the portal is installed for each community. It is wise to deploy at business-unit level first, but scale across the enterprise rapidly.
- Verify the installation procedures that execute prior to the cut-over.
- Identify deployment responsibilities for each person, organization, and subcontractor.
- Specify the deployment communications materials.
- Identify deployment responsibilities for acceptance testing, rollout, and assessments.
- Agree who is responsible for maintenance and daily portal operations.
- Specify deployment-completion criteria.

For Churchill's architects, this meant selecting the communities for deployment. This was based on priority use cases and communities. In the short term, community 5, the ministries of food, nutrition, and agriculture (part of Whitehall), were moved out of initial deployment.

Sketch Release Plan

Based on the solution, the release plan scopes and divides the work into manageable units and provides an understanding of the deliverables for each release. The cost/benefit analysis further refines the plan. Communities need to provide feedback to the plan so the project team better understands what is required.

The release plan involves assigning required capabilities from the use cases to individual releases and then estimating delivery schedules. In iterative releases, the portal functions are ranked according to the risk, complexity, and technology issues. The plan also reviews the exposure of the technical structure and its impacts on architecture. In each release, the phases, activities, and tasks are estimated.

Churchill's architects could only guess what content was going to be useful. The plan was created in an incomplete state, with the understanding that it would have to be rapidly refined through the project releases. The plan broadly delivered three releases that:

1. Laid the foundation with a basic release that established and proved the portal infrastructure and created new processes for service delivery and content management
2. Expanded the reach with a release that recognized key events, migrated existing content and services, and integrated applications
3. Enhanced capabilities with a release that completed migration of existing content and services

The architects had to work in a compressed timeframe and deliver a number of releases quickly, based on the use cases.

Sketch Static Test Plan

Static testing involves the detailed examination of deliverables against what was planned. It ensures that defects are found as close to their source as possible and fixed early in the project lifecycle by comparing the characteristics of a work product to an expected set of attributes, experiences, and standards.

In creating the static test plan, Churchill's architects documented the inspections, walkthroughs, and reviews necessary to validate that the requirements had been met. The plan indicated whether these tests were to be conducted on a timed basis, by phase, or at the completion of certain deliverables.

Conclusion

The following sections summarize the major points of this chapter and how they relate to your business today. For more information on these concepts, search the Internet for these keywords and phrases: *Project Management Institute, financial business case, supply chain, service levels,* and *metrics.*

Major Points, Considerations, and Lessons Learned

- Churchill had to map out a global view of the supply-chain and business models as input to a portal solution.

Best Practices for Your Organization

- Recognize that organizational changes caused by a portal are significant. Previously unrelated departments get connected, and new functions like personalization cause changes in business processes.
- Address organizational and process issues early, as these are critical for the effective implementation of portals.
- Establish metrics for measuring and evaluating project success.
- Identify new cross-functional horizontal communities, like project teams, beyond the traditional, vertical organizational communities.
- Realign business processes to the required changes.
- Select archetypes, carefully making sure that each is explored in context of the use cases.
- Connect business applications and experts to increase the value of basic information and usage.
- Provide employees with unprecedented personalization.
- Ensure customer or B2C portals focus on the branded experience. This is less important with employee or B2E portals.
- Ensure the portal has strong community interactions (people-to-people linkage).
- Implement at business-unit level and scale across the enterprise rapidly.
- Outline and refine a business case or cost/benefit analysis as a critical step in the creation of your portal.
- Ensure that content is assessed for its value and availability and is matched to the community.

Questions You Can Ask Today

At this stage in the project, you should organize your thoughts into the following categories and ask the questions listed:

Formulate a strategy:

- What strategic options are available?

- What emerging technologies are available and should be considered?

Define requirements:

- How does the new capability look?
- What are the key requirements for communities, their functions and content, and nonfunctions?

Assess the impact:

- What is the business rationale and justification for the solution?
- What is the likely impact on the business and organization?

Define the operational solution:

- What is the strategy for testing, support, and deployment?
- What is the release plan?

CHAPTER 3

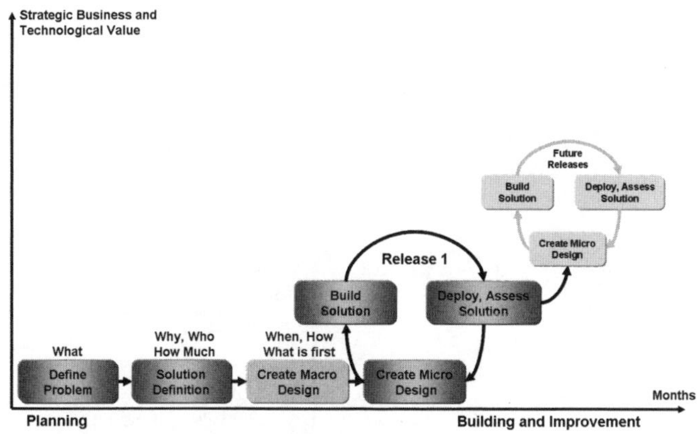

Create Macro Design

One ought never to turn one's back on a threatened danger and try to run away from it. If you do that, you will double the danger. But if you meet it promptly and without flinching, you will reduce the danger by half.

Sir Winston Churchill

Chapter Objectives

In this chapter, you learn how to refine the business problem and model and turn the solution design into one that can be built. For this, you justify the solution value and create a business justification for informed investment decisions. This is the first pass at understanding the technical details of the portal. Macro design addresses the overall, solution-wide issues that ensure a robust architecture, which promotes flexible releases. Figure 3.1 outlines the major activities of macro design.

When you are done with this chapter, you will be able to refine the architecture and macro design for your portal. With these, you will be able to move on to chapter 4, in which you start to define your micro design, a subset of the macro design.

What Steps Do I Need to Follow?

You go through the following five steps to identify your own macro design:

1. Initiate the macro design.
2. Refine the business models.
3. Create a conceptual design.
4. Select a pilot for deployment.
5. Complete the operational solution design.

To get you warmed up to the subject, let's walk through these steps with Churchill's portal as a backdrop.

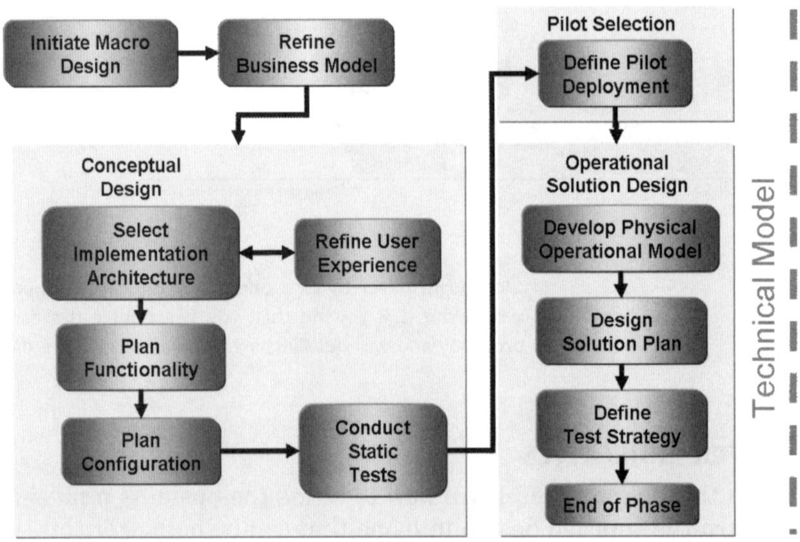

Figure 3.1: Macro design revolves around conceptual and operational designs.

Initiate Macro Design

The macro-design phase develops a technical model of the solution. The technical model combines conceptual, component, and operational models with an implementation release plan. It is important to spend time in macro design addressing design issues that affect every release. The standards, guidelines, and architectural deliverables developed in this phase minimize long-term development cost and reduce rework between releases.

Today's business marketplace is characterized by constant change. Organizations need flexibility in their systems to accommodate this change. Macro design achieves this, through the delivery of the releases, by developing a robust user interface and architecture.

The project team must go through this chapter with due diligence, pay attention to the granular decisions required, and ensure that the appropriate escalation mechanism is in place to form a steering committee. Problems caught at this stage are significantly simpler and less expensive to fix than those found later in the project.

Churchill was a minister during WWI, so he knew the ordeals a wartime government had to face. To maintain his vision, he had to keep his eye on the big picture. He was resourceful and pragmatic, and provided the right encouragement for his team to "get on with it" and deliver the required solution. This was a long and arduous process, which required discipline. Likewise, you will need to maintain your concentration on these tasks within your organization.

REFINE THE BUSINESS

The overall process of refining the business models builds on the requirements and analysis work discussed in chapter 2. It completes the business picture and adds several important business-process and data models.

Complete the Business Models

To complete the business picture, you refine the business organizational model, the metadata architecture, the process/data-usage matrix, the system function, and the logical data models. For Churchill's architects, these models were particularly important for the Whitehall federated portal, which aggregated information from many disparate sources and systems. In the following section, this portal will be used as an example for the development of these models.

Refine the Business Organizational Model

Early in chapter 2, you developed the business organizational model (shown in Figure 2.6). With the community, content, functional, and nonfunctional requirements complete, you can now refine this model, adding these requirements as input.

In June 1940, it was apparent that an invasion of Britain would only be successful with dominance of the skies. Therefore, for the immediate releases, the federated portal had to support an air battle—the "Battle of Britain" as it was later known. The government focused the majority of its resources and materials on achieving this aim. The business organizational model was adjusted to reflect this aim, as shown in Figure 3.2.

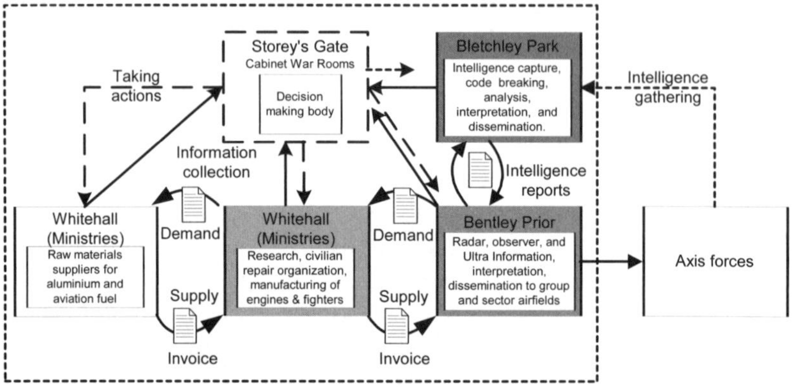

Figure 3.2: The business organizational model was customized to face an air war. Storey's Gate integrated disparate organizations into a cohesive supply chain to support Bentley Prior.

For Churchill's architects, this meant reviewing all the elements (organization, technology, and process) that were critical to Bentley Prior, primarily pilots, fighter aircraft, ammunition, fuel, and supporting facilities. A number of facilities were already in place, while others would have to be developed. The Luftwaffe's superiority in the overall number of planes indicated that the likely strategy would be a battle of attrition, in which the Luftwaffe would hope to draw out as many RAF fighters as possible. Bentley Prior's strategy countered this by sensing raids well in advance, flying repeated sorties, providing well-coordinated repair facilities that could get aircraft quickly back into service, and rapidly recovering downed pilots. Dowding pressed for investments in the Observer Corps (volunteer sky watchers), new operations centers through all levels of Fighter Command, and all-weather runways.

Within Whitehall, Beaverbrook brought the functions delivered by RAF Maintenance Command under the control of the ministry of aircraft production. These included storing, distributing, repairing, and salvaging of aircraft, and restoring them to operational standard. The Directorate of Aeronautical Inspection also covered the defense of aircraft factories, the inspection of all material and equipment, and the delivery from the manufacturers' premises of new aircraft to squadrons. Dowding needed information related to all these elements, as well as proactive intelligence on the enemy intentions and the order of battle. This would come from Bletchley Park.

Refine the Metadata Architecture

Metadata is a term that has many definitions. Simply put, it is data about data, or a single source of data. It is created by removing all duplication and redundancy from the architecture.

For Churchill's architects, the focus was on the supply chain and the information from this set of business processes that could be used to manage it effectively. Today, database schemas would be designed based on the supply chain and used in creating a data mart. A *data mart* is essential for managing a lot of data from disparate systems and functions, providing rapid access to this information, and data mining to support decision-making.

Refine the Logical Data Model

The logical data model is refined to ensure that it is compatible with the final business requirements and the use-case scenarios developed in chapter 2. The model, based on the metadata architecture, comprises a high-level information structure that identifies the major entities, attributes, and relationships in the supply chain. An *entity* is a person, place, thing, concept, or event that is relevant to the business. Entities are composed of *attributes*, which cannot be decomposed. This model inventories all the entities about which it needs to store facts.

Churchill's architects required management reports and indicators based on the activities within the supply chain, as shown in Figure 2.8. These were defined by three views:

- The supply side of the supply chain represents the activities to plan quickly and efficiently, manufacture, and leverage all the partners. For Churchill, this included everything from the procurement of materials, parts, and subassemblies, to the manufacture of fighters in the plant.
- The demand side of the supply chain represents the activities to meet the demands of the customer—namely, shipping the manufactured planes to RAF depots.
- The end customer of the supply chain represents the activities to coordinate and distribute the fighters and supplies to squadrons at fighter stations and airfields.

The model shown in Figure 3.3 was under the auspices of Whitehall and its ministries.

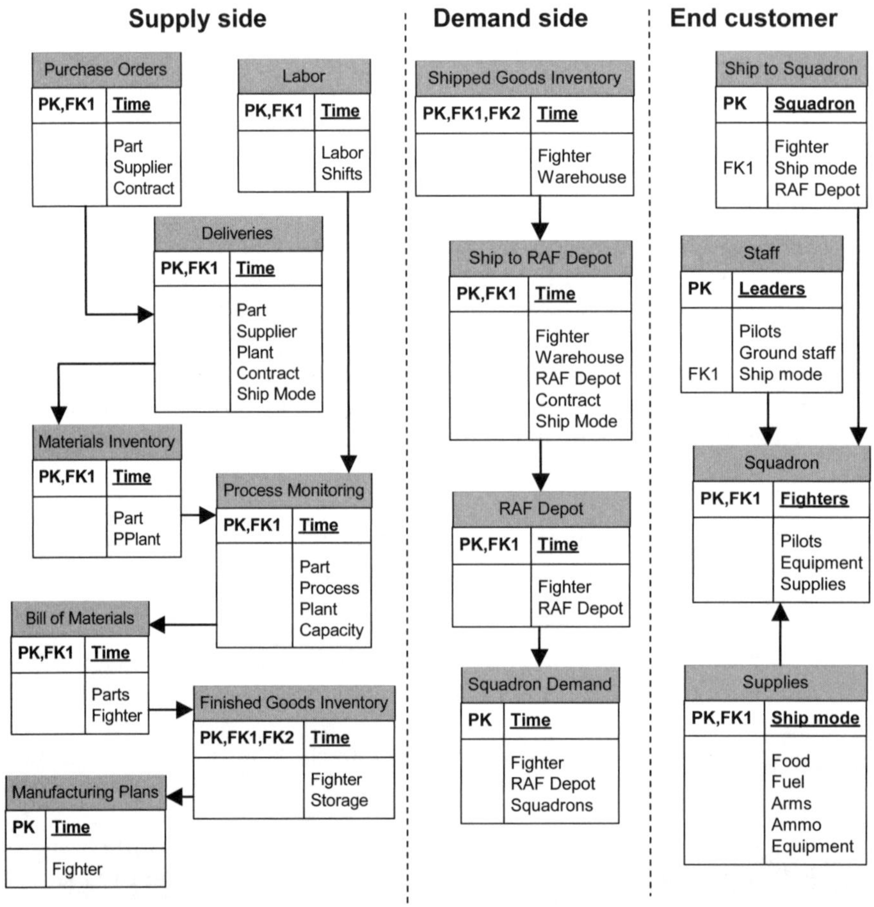

Figure 3.3: The logical data model of the supply chain shows the supply, demand, and customer views. Each box is an entity, shown with its attributes (primary and alternate keys, PK and FK).

Refine the System Function Model

The system function model is refined based on the general functions of the supply chain and establishes their interfaces. As input, it uses the business interaction and process models, Figures 2.4 and 2.8. Churchill's architects concentrated on these functions and their respective interfaces to create the model shown in Figure 3.4.

For Churchill's architects, this model was useful for identifying the key interactions that were used to monitor progress through the supply chain. This

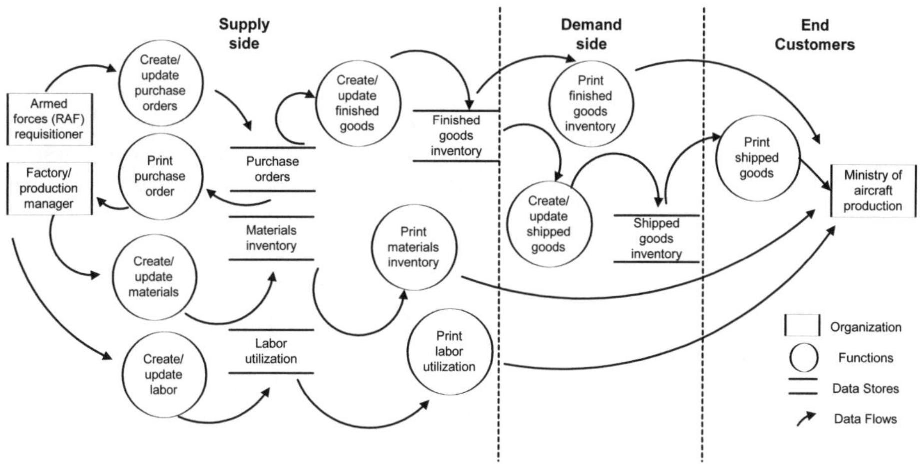

Figure 3.4: The system functions model for the supply chain shows the flow of information from the requistioner to the shipment of goods.

began with the RAF requisitioner's initial purchase order and ended with the delivery of fighters to the airfields.

Refine a Process/Data-usage Matrix

The logical data model, Figure 3.3, contains the entities information. The system functions model, Figure 3.4, contains the major processing structures, made up of functions. Table 3.1 combines these two models to create a matrix for the supply chain. It documents all data flows from the systems functions model, between a process and a data store, in the matrix. It references the key logical data-model entities in the matrix and ensures that they have at least one interaction with a process.

Table 3.1: The Process/Data-usage Matrix

	Data sources				
Process (Functions)	**Purchase orders**	**Materials inventory**	**Labor utilized**	**Finished goods inventory**	**Shipped goods inventory**
Update	RUD	RUD	RUD	RUD	RUD
Create	C	C	C	C	C
Print Information	R	R	R	R	R
Record Transaction	R	CRUD			R

The matrix lists the principal processes and entities in the system, where each cell identifies how its corresponding process uses data. It uses the standard *CRUD* notation (*Create*, *Read*, *Update*, and *Delete*). With this matrix, Churchill's architects could plan and select the required information from the envisioned data stores to monitor and manage the supply chain. For example, monitoring materials inventory was essential because of the supply-side interruptions caused by the u-boat blockade. This required measures such as the recycling of old materials to increase production levels.

Conceptual Design

The conceptual-design phase creates a portal model by looking at the future releases of the portal at a more granular level. The model is required by sections in this chapter that address the global user interface and architecture.

The functionality required in today's portal solutions means greater complexity. This can be simplified with implementation architectures, rather than the integration of applications, reviewed in the subsequent section.

Select Implementation Architecture

"Conceptual design" means selecting an appropriate implementation architecture, rather than designing a conceptual architecture. You do this by developing an architectural overview and identifying stereotypical interactions.

The implementation architecture takes account of the infrastructure, content-specification constraints, and support functionality. It defines how to select products and components that can be readily integrated into it. It represents an architecture that defines the major application design and the integration standards. It ensures release flexibility and cost-effectiveness by providing a consistent approach to common design problems. It saves time and effort by simplifying application integration.

For Churchill's architects, the release plan specified four unique communities that could be created as four separate portals: Storey's Gate, Bentley Prior, Bletchley Park, and Whitehall. However, the solution required a more integrated approach of broad user access and the sharing of services and information among portals. Churchill or the war cabinet could enter and interact with any one of the portals. In addition, Storey's Gate had a greater hierarchal status, collecting information from and making decisions for the other portals, which were peers. In effect, Storey's Gate was a "super portal" sitting on top of the federated portals unified into an enterprise, as shown in Figure 3.5. Access to any federated portal was independent of the super portal, with sideways access available.

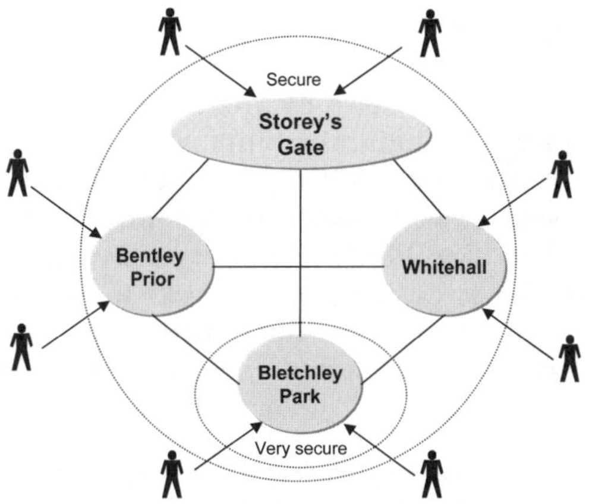

Figure 3.5: Storey's Gate was a "super portal" sitting on top of a federation of portals unified into an enterprise.

Develop Architectural Overview

Evaluating the high-level architectural options available creates a vision for the portal. The architecture overview provides an enterprise view of the federated portal, and the business and systems capabilities required, as shown in Figure 3.6. It indicates the general scope and scale of the functionality to be integrated. It is built on the use-case scenarios, existing infrastructure and content specifications, and nonfunctional requirements. The architecture overview also identifies the common services provided through the portal and their originating service providers.

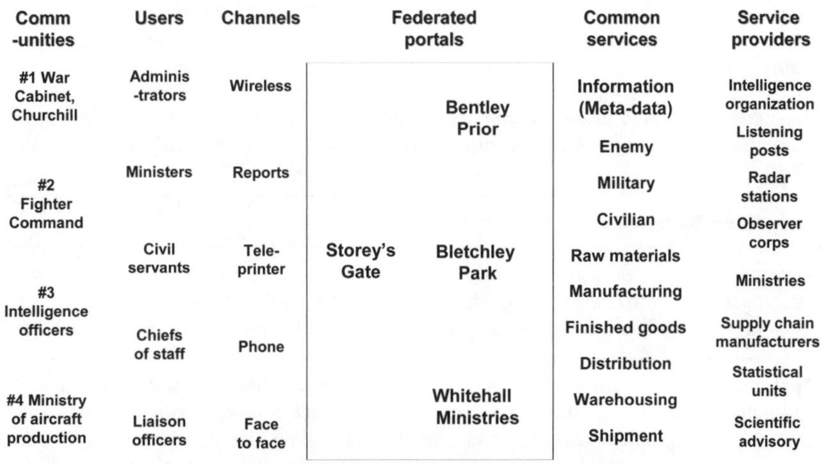

Figure 3.6: The architectural overview diagram outlines from left to right the communities, users, channels, federated portals, common services (combined basic services), and service providers.

Identify Stereotypical Interactions

After you identify the common types of interactions within the federated portals, they can be addressed by architectural patterns. This approach increases the uniformity and maintainability of the design, and reduces costs. You need to look for repeated characteristics in the federated portal, such as transactionality, persistence, workflow, and user interface behavior. The architectural patterns taken from libraries, based on architectural assets and industry standards, are used as basic building blocks to refine the solution objectives, the high-level participants, and the nature of interactions, as shown in Table 3.2. Each pattern is self-contained and provides the minimum end-to-end interactions necessary to implement and automate a business process.

Table 3.2: Business and Integration Patterns

Pattern	Description
Business Patterns	
Self-service (User-to-Business)	Addresses internal and external users interacting with a business to view or update data and enterprise transactions.
Collaboration (User-to-User)	Addresses interaction and collaboration between users, specifically teams who work towards a joint goal. Examples include email, bulletin boards, newsgroups, instant messaging, team rooms, and online meetings.
Information Aggregation (User-to-Data)	Allows users to access and manipulate data aggregated from multiple information sources. It captures large volumes of data, text, images, and video, and uses search and data-mining tools to extract useful information and manage documents.
Extended Enterprise (B2B)	Addresses the interactions between business processes in separate enterprises, like solutions with programmatic interfaces to connect inter-enterprise applications.
Integration Patterns	
Access Integration	Addresses designs that access one or more patterns, particularly from multiple channels (devices). It integrates common services to support a consistent user interface. The services include device support, presentation, personalization, security, and administration.
Application Integration	Integrates multiple business patterns, applications, and data. It provides seamless execution of applications and data access to automate new business functions. Reliable application integration, whether stovepipe, packaged software, or custom, requires replicable patterns consisting of process integration of functional flow processing between applications, and data integration for applications.

The applicability of the business patterns from Table 3.2 to Churchill's portal include the following:

- Self-service—A junior minister might collect various recent transactions and metrics related to arms production, labor utilization, and distribution. The minister would be able to update reports with the data and information.
- Collaborative—Target communities leverage information from the federated portals to turn it into valuable intelligence. This requires secure communities made up from disparate groups like experts, duty officers, scientists, administrators, and technologists who could collaborate productively on many projects during the war effort.
- Information aggregation—Communities had to leverage vast amounts of data and make sense of it. The scale of this was enormous, as it pertained to not only military data, but also civilian data related to the population and industrial data related to production for the war effort. This was required for both the UK and its allies. Of course, this data also had to be collected for the Axis as well, to build up an accurate picture of enemy capabilities.
- Extended enterprise—Decisions at the top level, by Churchill and the war cabinet, had to be cascaded and communicated to a complex hierarchy of military, industrial, and civilian organizations. These federated portal interactions required programmatic interfaces to interconnect them.

The applicability of the integration patterns from Table 3.2 to Churchill's portal include the following:

- Access integration—This was a key part of coordinating intelligence into a decision-making environment for hierarchical decision-making. Churchill and the war cabinet could carefully examine new opportunities, those in progress, and projects.
- Application integration—A portal will affect the business processes and will also pull and aggregate data from existing applications.

For Churchill's portal, Table 3.3 shows the relative importance of the selected patterns (on a scale of high, medium, and low) for each portal and its subsequent user groups.

These patterns were integrated with the architecture overview enterprise view, Figure 3.6, to create the "IT system" view of Churchill's portal. This view clarifies how Churchill's federated portal needed access and application integration and new application functionality. This also included the requirements for a

Table 3.3: The Portal/Patterns Matrix

Pattern	Storey's Gate	Bentley Prior	Bletchley Park	Whitehall Supply-chain
Self-service	H	L	L	M
Information Aggregation	H	H	H	H
Collaboration	H	M	M	M
Extended Enterprise	M	M	M	M
Access Integration	H	H	H	H
Application Integration	H	L	M	L

cross-federated approach to security, administration, and management, thus reducing future development costs.

Refine User Experience

Refining the user experience involves creating a user prototype from several of the use-case scenarios. A prototype is a trial model of the overall solution. It is used to resolve risk and refine requirements by creating a user-verified design on paper that is iterated through the project. The process walks through the use-case scenario and outlines the pencil-and-paper renderings that depict content, layout, and flow, demonstrating how the prototype depicts the behavior of the interface. This provides an opportunity to refine the experience that the organization is looking for with the user. For example, it might be looking for ease of use and understanding, responsiveness and accountability, or convenience and control.

Churchill's architects used tools to create a prototype of several of the use-case scenarios to provide a way to explore designs and test them iteratively with users. A prototype provides a more tangible interpretation than analysis diagrams. Therefore, it solicits a more clear specification. For example, with Storey's Gate, critical information had to be presented to the war cabinet and Churchill for decision-making. The information that had to be incorporated was derived from other federated portals, so it was varied. Paper walkthroughs of hand-drawn sketches outlined what the user might see and do, as shown in Figure 3.7. Put together, these sketches show how the portal works in a given situation.

For Churchill's architects, the user experience varied across the federated portal between communities. For example, the Storey's Gate user experience was grounded in decision-making, so it required both ease of use and understanding, and it had to be responsive and accountable. At Bletchley Park, the principal user experience was to provide security and trust.

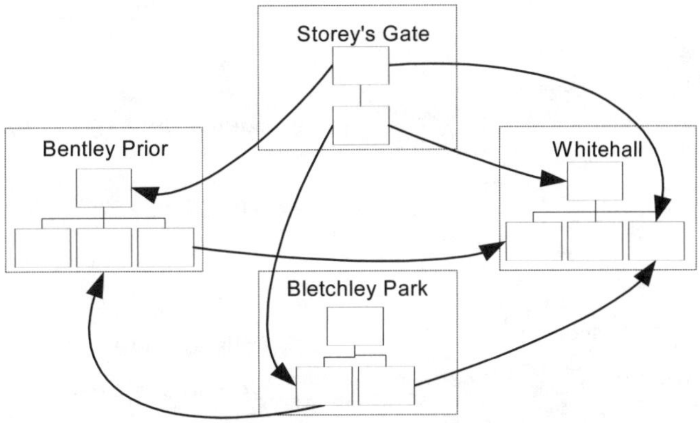

Figure 3.7: User prototyping describes content, layout, flow, and the behavior of the interface.

Plan Functionality

The functionality of what the portal will do, defined in chapter 2, is refined by developing a functional component model. This starts the process of evaluating and selecting the products and technologies to meet the required functionality. This is done for all the releases defined in chapter 2.

Note that this step maps portal *components* to the selected business and integration patterns. Components are specific functions that describe the entire hierarchy of software or hardware/software, their tasks, interfaces, and relationships, and how they collaborate to deliver the functionality required in the use-cases scenarios.

The functional component model highlights how the application and technical parts of the portal are related and the interactions of lower-level software components, including their protocols, interfaces, usage, and dynamic behavior. This helps decompose large or high-risk software components.

For Churchill's architects, a functional component model was defined for each of the four federated portals. Figure 3.8 shows a generic model for all the portals, with the business logic layer for Whitehall. The model maps business-model functionality onto the functional components and products, to determine the implementation architecture suitability.

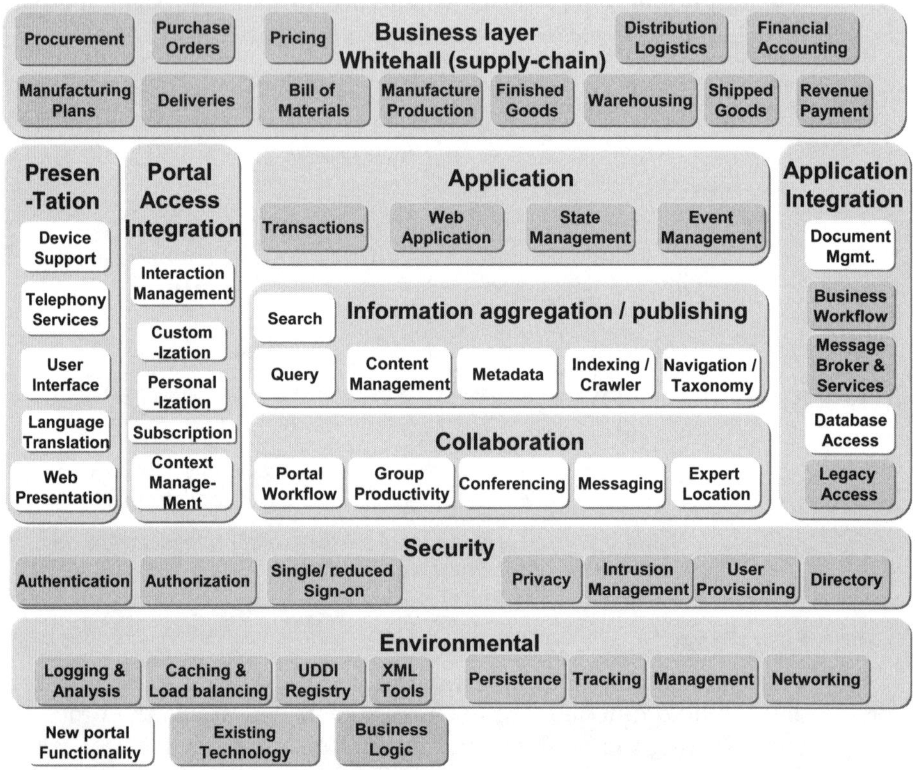

Figure 3.8: The functional component model for the Whitehall portal maps the components to business and integration patterns. These layers are further defined in Table B.1, in appendix B.

The functional component model helps define how the whole portal functionality is structured across the releases, and how the major functional parts communicate. This ensures that the releases are developed consistently. Components are determined by whether they can be purchased as a product, a binary unit of functionality, or are distinct from the applications that they enable.

The model has a number of benefits. Primarily, it reduces complexity and simplifies the design of large and complex portals. It also defines the boundaries between reusable parts. Overall, it provides enough detail to estimate and plan releases, and allocate the first release-design work. This helps organize the development project.

You are now ready to define the components to be placed on the operational model. These will be executed and managed on the target platforms. (For descriptions of these components, see Table B.1 in Appendix B.)

Plan Configuration

Planning the configuration involves configuring community topologies, developing a content-management system, and developing a logical operational model. Most of the information presented so far has concentrated on the functional requirements of the portal. The operational model reflects the nonfunctional requirements that drive performance, availability, and the operational architecture design. It will have a significant impact on the choice of portal framework and products used. If not undertaken properly, it could have a significant financial impact.

Configure Community Topologies

A topology creates a hierarchy of portal users. In configuring the community topology, you need to review the communities established in Figure 2.9 and 2.10, as well as the use cases and their priorities.

For Churchill's architects, the community topology for the Storey's Gate federated portal is shown in Figure 3.9. It outlines the hierarchical structure of commands.

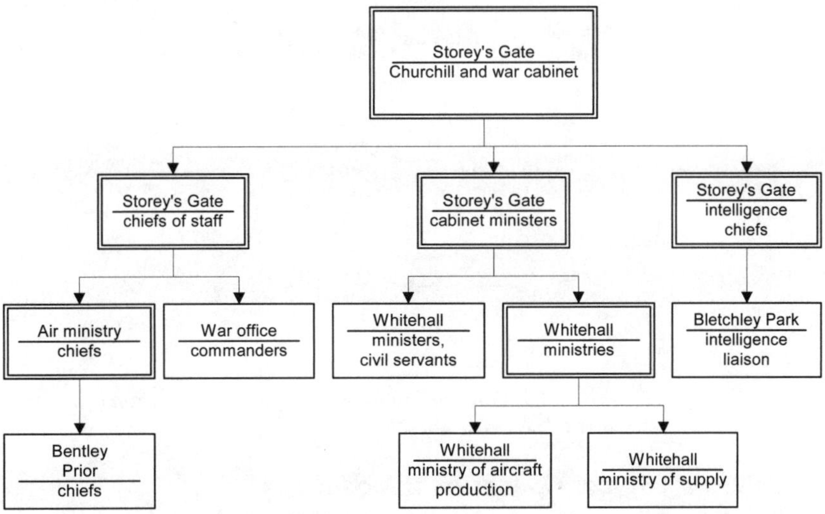

Figure 3.9: The community topology for the Storey's Gate federated portal outlines its hierarchy.

Develop Content-Management System

You determine how the organization manages the current knowledge and content base by determining where information is located, how it is organized, and how it is managed. This process results in a plan for the management of this content, which determines what is captured, categorized, and included in the federated portal. It also determines whether any procedural or organizational changes need to be instituted to support use and maintenance.

A content-management plan includes ways of gathering nonelectronic content; eliminating or consolidating content; and determining audience-content requirements and gaps, key processes and associated tasks, and roles and responsibilities for managing the content. It requires establishing and configuring content connector interfaces. It also determines content constraints and, very important, determines primary policies and guidelines for governing content, as shown in Figure 3.10.

For Churchill's architects, data was available from numerous sources in many different formats, including spoken communication, written documents, files, and photographs. Data had to be extracted, transformed, and loaded into something for it to be useful information, metadata that was accurate and timely. It could then be stored, refreshed, and readily accessed by various target audiences using query and search techniques.

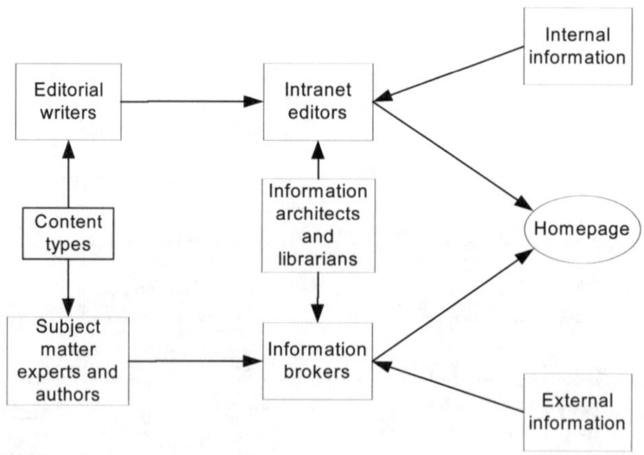

Figure 3.10: Content management governs the promotion of content into the federated portal.

Develop Logical Operational Model

The logical operational model describes the technical architecture of the portal through a series of *nodes*, which are logical units that deliver specific types of processing. The model is developed iteratively from the communities, use-cases scenarios, models, service-level requirements, architecture overview diagram (Figure 3.6), functional component model, and the nonfunctional requirements that the portal is expected to fulfill. The model includes the following:

- The topology and geographic distribution of the portal, the node definitions and their network connectivity, and where and how users and external systems interact. Table B.2 in appendix B, describes each node and the components (hardware, software, and data) that run on it to meet the service-level requirements like performance, availability, security.
- A transcoder, which helps transform data from one format to another.
- The edge node, which provides load-balancing and intelligent routing.
- Input to the physical operational model (shown in Figure 3.13), which represents the actual physical computer systems.

For Churchill's architects, a logical operational model was defined for each of the four federated portals. Figure 3.11 shows a generic model for all the portals. The technological limitations are identified, but the detailed choice of technology is not.

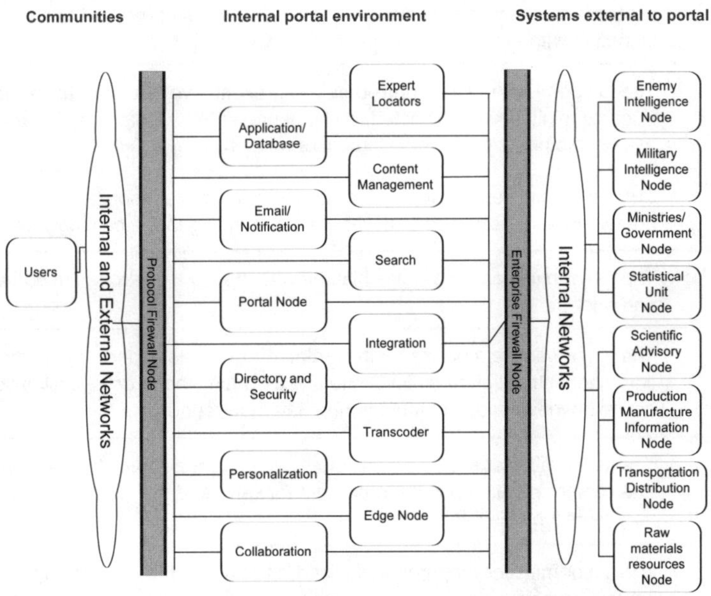

Figure 3.11: The logical operational model outlines the portal nodes, their functions, and the nonfunctional requirements. The nodes are further defined in Table B.2 of appendix B.

Technical Walkthroughs

Technical walkthroughs describe the business activity flow and interactions of a user with the portal, based on use-case scenarios and models. They confirm technical details related to the nodes and their connections, as shown in Tables 3.4 and 3.5 and Figures 3.12 and 3.13. For example, they indicate whether nodes are split or merged, the routing of connections between the nodes, and the technology products that implement the nodes and connections. This confirms whether technical components handle communication and coordination across nodes, that end-to-end service-level requirements will be satisfied, and that the logical operational model supports all planned releases.

In the following tables, technical walkthrough 1 is taken from use-case scenarios UC 2.4 in Table 2.9, and technical walkthrough 2 is taken from 2.2, 3.2, and 5.2 in Table 2.5.

Table 3.4: Technical Walkthrough 1

Step	Description
1	The junior minister from the ministry of aircraft production enters the Whitehall portal and presents his identification and password. The minister, graded at a medium security level, is signed in with the date, time, and reason for his visit.
2	The junior minister is recognized as a representative of a specific ministry portfolio. Someone from his ministry was expected, so he is presented a "role-based" package, for his eyes or the eyes of his peers only, from Churchill's office (Storey's Gate).
3	The junior minister is instructed to research a complex topic and produce a report that is to be presented and discussed at a war cabinet meeting in the coming week.
4	The junior minister familiarizes himself with the work environment so he can conduct research and analysis.
5	The junior minister collects metrics related to various aspects of fighter production, labor utilization, and distribution to airfields. He makes a few phone calls, customizes specific data feeds, and examines various manufacturing data and reports.
6	The junior minister sees new mail notification from his ministry and reads the latest dispatches. The cabinet meeting has been brought forward, and the report is required tomorrow for preliminary review by his minister.
7	The junior minister prepares an initial draft of a report by integrating research information and content carefully.
8	The junior minister finds the scientific and production experts and books a meeting to review the draft with them.

Table 3.4: Technical Walkthrough 1, *continued*

Step	Description
9	The junior minister initiates workflow activity for typing up the report and passing it across to his team members for review, update, and approval.
10	The report is given a security grading and delivered to a select and personalized list "for their eyes only" at Storey's Gate.

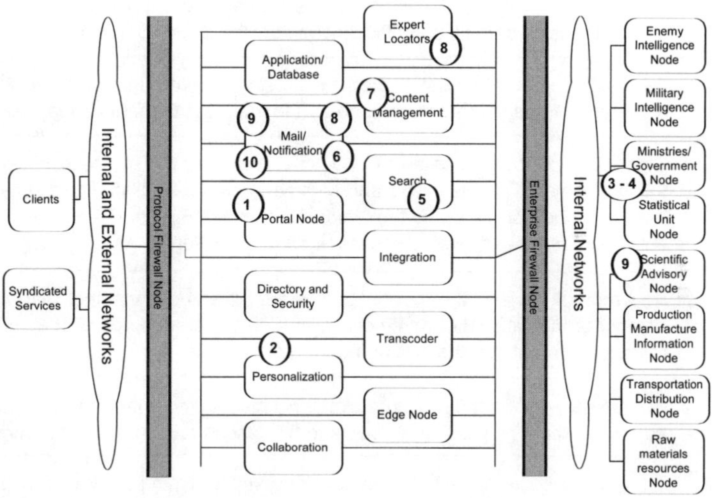

Figure 3.12: Technical walkthrough 1 is based on use-case scenario 2.4.

Table 3.5: Technical Walkthrough 2

Step	Description
1	Air Chief Marshall Dowding enters the portal (at Storey's Gate) and presents his identification and password. Dowding, graded at a top security level, is ushered in immediately.
2	Dowding receives a package, for his eyes only, and is ushered into Churchill's private room. He is given the daily and weekly reports on Fighter Command actions to review while waiting for Churchill. He calls Bentley Prior to get information on the latest enemy activity, through observer and radar reports.
3	Churchill picks up the daily Ultra report from the Special Liaison Unit (SLU). He calls Captain Winterbotham, liaison officer for Bletchley Park, on the secure scrambler phone to walk through the report. He learns that bombing raids planned against specific sector airfields will continue that evening and through the week.
4	Churchill arrives and takes Dowding to the map room, where the duty officers walk through the latest situation report. The officers share concerns about prolonged damage to sector airfields in the southeast. Churchill and Dowding review the latest indicators.
5	Back in his office, Churchill shares his latest Ultra information with Dowding. They collaborate on a strategy to use fighters from Group 12 to intercept the forthcoming raid.
6	Churchill and Dowding complete the collaboration and enter the cabinet war room to meet with the war cabinet. The ministers and commanders are waiting. The discussion focuses on the production reports prepared by the junior minister and Fighter Command. The fighter factory's output is compared to the latest losses. It shows a widening gap.
7	Beaverbrook reviews the report. He lays out several options, including the scaling down of bomber production. After much discussion, this is agreed upon. Churchill suggests that further resources be put into the civilian repair organization.
8	Churchill draws the meeting to a close. He instructs that the map-room indicator model be adjusted accordingly and that orders to be passed to commands for immediate actions.
9	The cabinet secretary initiates workflow activity for typing up the minutes and orders of the day. These are passed on to the respective ministers and staff in the communities.

In summary, the operational model is a representation of a network of computer systems, their associated peripherals, and software (systems, middleware, and application). The model assesses the viability of portal implementation, the geographical distribution and the operational complexity, with some early cost estimates. It describes users at various locations who perform use cases that access data, using the necessary components, and satisfy nonfunctional requirements and constraints.

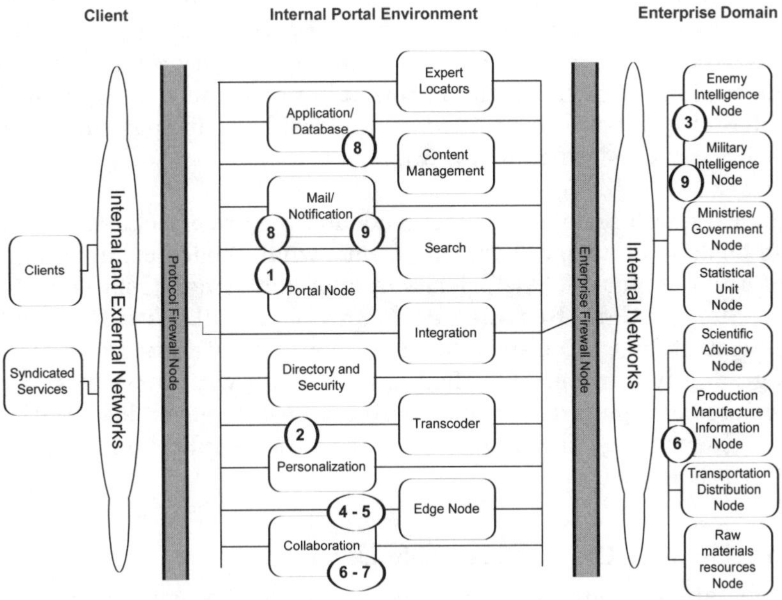

Figure 3.13: Technical walkthrough 2 is based on use-case scenarios 2.2, 3.2, and 5.2.

Conduct Static Tests

Static testing tests all the requirement, analysis, and architecture work. Static testing differs from dynamic testing in that it tests on paper rather than with physical systems. It uses techniques like walkthroughs, inspections, reviews, checklists, and mapping. The purpose of static testing is to find defects early in the project.

For Churchill's architects, this was particularly important for Bletchley Park. Before the complex processes could be automated, they had to be deemed robust enough. Therefore, they needed to be carefully scrutinized on paper and determined to be successful.

Pilot Selection

Pilot deployment scopes how much of the portal functionality and content will be rolled out at different points in the project. A *pilot* is a subset of the finalized delivery. It differs from a prototype in that it explores and tests designs and experience.

Note that this section determines which communities are a part of the roll-out, as set out in the solution definition. The releases follow a broad functional-release strategy, which controls the number of community users affected by the solution and monitors their acceptance of the solution. This reduces the risk by gradually introducing community reliance on the portal. When working with the communities, it is important to design for the support of different types of user profiles, and to design "learnings" into tools to reduce experienced users' time for training.

Churchill's architects, under tremendous time pressure, had to look at what could be done in a very short timeframe, what needed completion, and what could be put off. The priority of pilot deployment related to Bentley Prior, Storey's Gate, Bletchley Park, and Whitehall. With Bentley Prior, the release strategy was geographically driven. The operations center network was gradually introduced to the fighter groups, with those closest to the French coast deployed first and those furthest deployed last. With Whitehall, the urgency was getting information from the supply chain—specifically, fighter production.

Complete Operational Solution Design

The operational-solution design phase develops the physical operational model and designs the solution plans for the next three chapters. Effectively, this sets the shape and justification of the project.

Develop Physical Operational model

The physical operational model specifies the intended physical implementation of the logical operational model—the "builder's view." Like a construction blueprint, it organizes all the information about the portal in the physical world and refers to specific types of computers, networks, and software.

The logical operational model is transformed into a physical operational model by applying physical constraints. For example, it shows the specifications for a node in an actual physical location, and all the required attributes like electrical power, or concepts like *tiering*. Tiering re-architects the environment into three tiers that are geographically dispersed across data centers to avoid local disruptions and cope with Internet congestion. Single-server failures are accommodated as transaction requests are redistributed. This enables *sideways scalability* of selected components to improve availability and security. It also allows for security zones to be set up across the portal.

The physical operational model also provides performance and sizing estimates for use in the later development phases. It provides an opportunity to avoid complexity, strive for simplicity, and focus on manageability, operability, and ease of use.

For Churchill's architects, a physical operational model was defined for each of the four federated portals. Figure 3.14 shows a generic model for all the portals. This model played an important role in highlighting the operational responsibility for the infrastructure's first- and second-level support, and in determining how to protect the portal and meet SLAs. It shows that availability was maintained by eliminating single points of failure through replication and redundancy, failover links, and independent scaling.

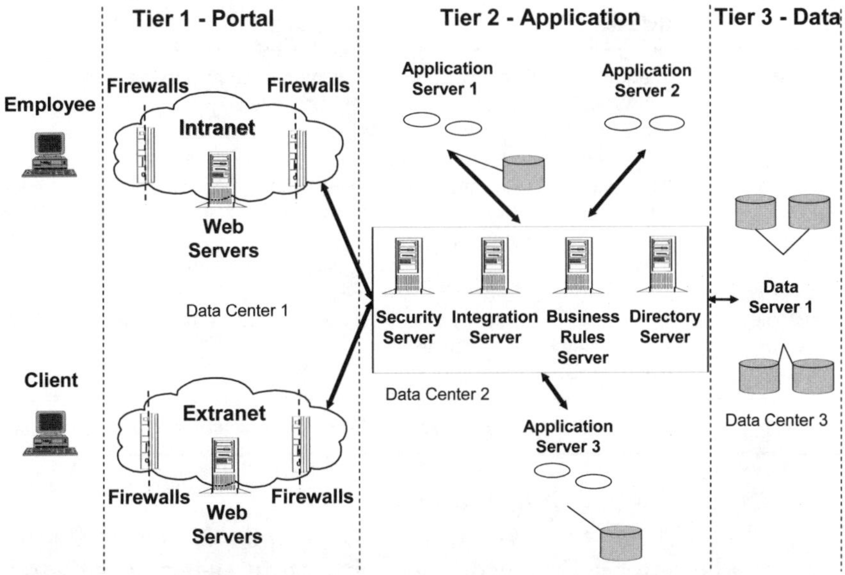

Figure 3.14: The physical operational model is structured for high availability. Tier 1 manages the portal and its interaction. Tier 2 manages the applications. Tier 3 is an intermediary for data access.

Design Solution Plan

The solution plan refines the release plan and the cost/benefit analysis. The plan is encompassing in its scope and is a driving factor for the progress of the project. It completes a more detailed breakdown of the costs and the business justification initiated in chapter 2.

Refine Release Plan

The release plan developed in chapter 2 is expanded by creating various executable plans, such as test, training and user support, and deployment. Each plan has a cost, list of tasks, schedule, and list of resources associated with it. The release plan defines the number of releases and assigns functionality, architecture, and user experience to each of them. It also carefully ensures that the functionality and content for each release can be met by the project.

The prevailing situation of urgency for Churchill's architects would have accelerated the release-completion time from two or three months to one month. The releases are listed in Table 3.6.

Table 3.6: Release Model

Strategy for Releases

	Release 1	**Release 2**	**Release 3**
Storey's Gate	Integration to Bletchley Park and Whitehall; use cases 2.1, 3.1, 4.1, 5.1	Full integration to Bentley Prior and Storey's Gate	
Bentley Prior	Integration of operations centers, radar, observers, and Bletchley; use cases 2.2, 3.2, 4.2, 5.2	Integration to Anti-Aircraft Command	Integration to Bomber Command
Bletchley Park	Integration to Storey's Gate and Bentley Prior; complete manual procedures	Automate manual procedures	Scale up automation
Whitehall	Integration to Storey's Gate	Complete indicator model	Use cases 2.3, 3.3, 4.3

Refine Cost/Benefit Analysis

The cost/benefit analysis can now be completed, as costs for the components can be better determined. The type of portal determines the return that an organization can realize from deploying it, whether it is internal to employees or external to customers, suppliers, and partners.

Experience with enterprise portals, B2E, has shown there are many challenges in creating a cost/benefit analysis. Typically, the indirect benefits are more significant than the direct benefits, as shown in the cost/benefit model in Figure 3.15. Since these are somewhat intangible, it is important to carefully determine how they link to an organization's revenue and profit. Organizations need to take into account both direct and indirect benefits to understand the true value of the portal's return.

To help you identify the detailed cost/benefit analysis, Table 3.7 outlines the benefit categories, formulas, description, and portal type. The benefit categories included cost savings, increases in productivity, business velocity, and intellectual capital.

Category		Year 1	Year 2	Year 3	Total
Expense	Server	($9,600)	($38,000)	($45,000)	**($92,600)**
Expense	Network	($40,000)	($250,000)	($250,000)	**($540,000)**
Expense	Content	($43,000)	($400,000)	($400,000)	**($843,000)**
Expense	Software	($509,000)	($130,400)	($110,400)	**($749,800)**
Expense	Labor	($986,000)	($2,200,000)	($2,100,000)	**($5,286,000)**
Indirect Expense	Consulting and Training	($1,277,000)	($1,050,000)	($650,000)	**($2,977,000)**
Direct Benefit: Cost	Travel Savings	N/A	$333,333	$333,333	**$666,666**
Indirect Benefit: Customer	Improved Customer Experier	N/A	$5,544,000	$6,098,400	**$11,642,400**
Indirect Benefit: Efficiency	Expertise Location	N/A	$41,250	$41,250	**$82,500**
Indirect Benefit: Efficiency	Improved Information Access	N/A	$1,485,000	$1,930,500	**$3,415,500**
Indirect Benefit: Efficiency	Streamlined Publication Proc	N/A	$41,250	$41,250	**$82,500**
Indirect Benefit: Learning	New Employee Productivity	N/A	$1,425,600	$1,425,600	**$2,851,200**
	Total	**($2,864,600)**	**$4,802,033**	**$6,314,933**	**$8,252,366**

Figure 3.15: In this cost/benefit table for B2E, the indirect benefits are more significant than the direct benefits.

Table 3.7: Cost/Benefits Analysis

Cost Savings

Category	Formula, Value	Description	Type
Infrastructure consolidation	# of servers + software + networks	Consolidate Web sites and duplicate infrastructure.	B2C, B2E
Training	# of users in new roles * weeks of acclimation * ultimate revenue contribution per week * reduction factor	Reduce travel and time through e-learning, decreasing traditional costs by up to 80%.	B2E
Staff saving and headcount	# of automated processes * hours saved by employee per process per week * # of users * cost per hour	Provide self-service tools, such as a human-resource tool.	B2E
Research library	# of users * hours saved per week * user cost per hour	Consolidation and centralization of research reports into one location saves time in searches, duplication, and subscriptions costs.	B2E
Standardization		Less training time is needed.	B2E

Table 3.7: Cost/Benefits Analysis, *continued*

Increase in Productivity

Category	Formula, Value	Description	Type
Highly functional and accurate search engine	# of users * hours saved per week * user cost per hour	Improve ad hoc organization-wide search capability and sort through the immensity of information and sources.	B2C
Best practices library	# of users * hours saved per week * user cost per hour	Disseminate process improvements rapidly to employees across the organization.	B2E
Disseminating critical information	# of users * hours saved per week * user cost per hour	Some pieces of information, like outage alerts, require very rapid dissemination. Alert notification does not disturb work, but pushes information when appropriate.	B2E, B2B
Efficient distribution of Information, better communication	# of users * hours saved per week * user cost per hour	Cascading communication through numerous managerial layers is inefficient. Provide accurate, timely, and consistent way of communicating across organization.	B2E, B2S
Sharing applications/resources	# of users * hours saved per week * user cost per hour	Individuals access public-wide applications considered unique to one group or line of operation, like directories, phonebooks, time-off figures, and people-locator services.	B2E, B2B

Increase in Business Velocity

Category	Formula, Value	Description	Type
Decision-making	Subjective value to decision maker; may include # of users * hours saved per week * user cost per hour	Improve overall decision-making across the organization by monitoring key alerts/events for unusual changes. Provide better, more informed, and more timely front-line decision-making for both employees and customers.	B2E, B2C
Facilitate document sharing/creation	May include # of users * hours saved per week * user cost per hour	Through a collaborative process and workflow, improve project execution and individual productivity through better document sharing or reuse, and creating new documents.	B2E, B2B
Better visibility into the supply chain	Value in improved supply-chain	Provide the ability to hone in on problems and make better decisions.	B2S, B2B

Table 3.7: Cost/Benefits Analysis, *continued*

Increase in Business Velocity

Category	Formula, Value	Description	Type
Unified view of disparate departments: better organizational efficiency	# of departs embodied as communities in portal * average communications cost-savings per unit	Prevent the balkanization of departments, which interact more intuitively and efficiently.	B2E

Increase in Intellectual Capital

Category	Formula, Value	Description	Type
Collaboration	# of customers visiting portal for support * percentage that would have called instead * cost of answering call	Customer collaboration drives more efficient customer service, leading to better-satisfied customers.	B2C
Disaster-recovery plans	Time saving minutes	Based on protecting lives and organizational assets, provide this information in a timely and accurate way.	B2C
Communities created around common areas of interest	(# of users * hours saved per week * user cost per hour) + (# of employees * attrition-rate * reduction factor * cost of acquiring & training new employees)	Individuals share ideas; functional interest groups can hold forums. Employees become more connected to their organization by having a direct say. This improves employee morale, satisfaction, productivity, and retention.	B2E, B2C, B2B
Standardized collaboration mechanism	# of users * hours saved per week * user cost per hour	Provide faster deployment of resources to a project, including external people. Projects touch diverse groups that require regular communication. Collaboration allows for team-oriented capabilities beyond boundaries.	B2E
Common directory and organizational chart	# of users * hours saved per week * user cost per hour	Determine who people are, what they do, and how they can help, beyond contact info, name, and function. This improves employee productivity, employee knowledge, and intellectual capital, and reduces the costs of sharing information with remote teams and finding experts.	B2E

As you go through the cost/benefit analysis, identify solution-success indicators, benchmarks of current and targeted measures, and alternatives for reducing the risk. The completion of chapter 3 provides an estimate of the direct and indirect costs based on the operational models. The cost/benefit analysis is readjusted. Finally, the use-case scenarios are reprioritized, as shown in Table 3.8.

Table 3.8: Prioritization of Use-case Scenarios

Cost/Benefits Analysis

Portal	Categories	Value	Rationale
Storey's Gate	Collaboration, decision-making	H	The most critical player
Bentley Prior	Decision-making, collaboration	H	In the short term, absolute priority
Bletchley Park	Dissemination of critical information	H	Critical in the short and long terms
Whitehall (aircraft)	Decision-making, dissemination of critical information	H	One of the key players in the short term
Whitehall (food)	Decision-making, dissemination of critical information	L	Important, but in the longer term

Define Test Strategy

The testing approach is defined for all the releases of the portal implementation. This test strategy is used to determine the number, types, and specifications of tests. These tests, in turn, are used to verify that the system is defect-free and that it meets the organization's requirements. In defining the test strategy, you also determine who will do the testing, where, and how. This requires the use of the table shown in Table 3.9, with the cost justifications, schedules, and change process.

Table 3.10 is the main document for testing. It outlines why the test is being undertaken, along with its objectives, overall strategy, and documentation. Based on the predefined test strategy, the extensive tests performed could include stress, performance, regression, security, and operational.

Churchill's architects needed to define a strategy for testing the effectiveness of the portal. One of the overall priorities was the scrambling of fighters in time to meet the attackers. So, this particular test would be critical to Dowding and Fighter Command.

Table 3.9: Test Depth Table

Factors to Consider	Definition
Test environment(s)	The extensiveness of the simulated test environment required
Cost justifications	Based on direct and indirect benefits and costs
Test plans	The types and increasing levels of testing, iteratively progressing through unit, integration, system, acceptance, and operability
Business impact of change	The business operations or functions affected
Deadlines	The hard and soft dates for the change
Schedules	Any external project dependencies that might exist
Resources	The test team's organization, skill level, and time requirements
Expected results	The outcome of the tests and how the test is measured
Change strategies	Small, medium, large, or emergency changes

Table 3.10: Test Plan Table

Factors to Consider	Definition
Testing purpose/objectives	Scope and summary: breadth, depth, and length
Documents related to the test	Descriptions, references, and links to other locations.
Test concepts (overall strategy and approach)	Test philosophy; verification methods; test levels and extensiveness; organizational roles (who carries out the tests)
Verification requirements	Test criteria, personnel, and verification standards
Requirements/test summary	Expectations for testing, output, and variances
Types of testing	The battery of tests, as unit, integration, and system
Verification testing	Verification personnel and standards (not left to developers)
Acceptance testing	Acceptance personnel and criteria
Control/reporting procedures	How the results will be communicated

Conclusion

The following sections summarize the major points of this chapter and how they relate to your business today. For more information on these concepts, search the Internet for these keywords and phrases: *architecture*, *functional requirements*, *nonfunctional requirements*, *functional component model*, *logical operational architecture model*, *manageability*, *operability*, *reliability*, *redundancy*, and *e-business patterns*.

Major Points, Considerations, and Lessons Learned

- Churchill's architects created a comprehensive architecture for the four federated portals.

Best Practices for Your Organization

- Leverage a metadata architecture and logical data model to improve the provisioning of data.
- To avoid conflicts, create a portal architecture to simplify the management of services.
- Work closely with suppliers and partners to identify process-integration opportunities in designing a supply-chain portal.
- A successful portal implementation requires an easy-to-use presentation framework and a robust and scalable integration infrastructure. The former provides a single, easy-to-use interface for constructing a portal that is tailored to the needs and interests of the user. The latter enables the presentation framework to search and categorize data in a variety of formats, integrate with existing applications, and provide collaborative capabilities, all within a secure environment.
- Configure communities into topologies.
- Carefully plan the content and its management.
- Use technical walkthroughs of the architectural models (static testing) to verify that the architecture addresses the use-case scenarios.
- Include five basic portal services: topic hierarchies, search, personalization engines, links, and news services. (See appendix B for more information.)
- Build security zones for access into the portal.
- Build the portal geographically, to avoid local interruptions and cope with Internet congestion.

- In building portals:
    - Remove any single points of failure.
    - Avoid complexity and strive for simplicity.
    - Consider manageability, operability, and ease of use.
    - Consider mass customization.
    - Anticipate future requirements.
    - Design "learning" into tools to reduce experienced users' time for training.
    - Design to support different types of user profiles.
    - Define end-to-end availability, along the paths of critical transactions.
- Leverage architectural patterns for common types of interactions to increase the uniformity and maintainability of the design and reduce costs.
- Use architectural models to better understand the relationship between functions and the software components required.
- Ensure your team goes through this part of the project with due diligence. Problems caught at this stage are significantly simpler and less expensive to fix than later in the project.
- Ensure your team pays attention to the granular decisions required and that the appropriate escalation mechanism is in place to a steering committee.
- Avoid under-investing in nonfunctional requirements. A mistake in defining nonfunctional requirements is far more costly than in functional requirements.
- Carefully determine the portal functionality and content for each release and make sure these can be met by the project.
- Determine the risk of deployment. For example, deploying an employee portal to 100,000 users increases the risk of failure. The repercussive costs of deploying an incomplete portal to all the employees could be far greater than the capital invested.
- Ensure you complete a cost/benefit analysis for your portal that considers both sides of the ROI equation. Employee portals affect both sides of the ROI equation by lowering expenses through the elimination of "information intermediaries" and increasing revenues by getting closer

to customers and partners. A portal will also provide an increase in performance and usability to existing applications.

- Develop an action plan to remove or contain the project's risks and increase the probability a project succeeds, typically at the end of the macro and micro designs.

Questions You Can Ask Today

At this stage in the project, you should organize your thoughts into the following categories and ask the questions listed:

Refine the business model:

- Does the business model show the business picture and important business-process and data models?

Work on the conceptual design:

- Does the conceptual design include a technical risk assessment by business service of how the portal is designed to meet the nonfunctional requirements?

Work on the pilot selection:

- Does the view of the pilot have a definition of when functionality and content will be rolled out within the releases?

Complete the operational solution design:

- Does the design outline the physical models, business rationale, and justification for the project?

CHAPTER 4

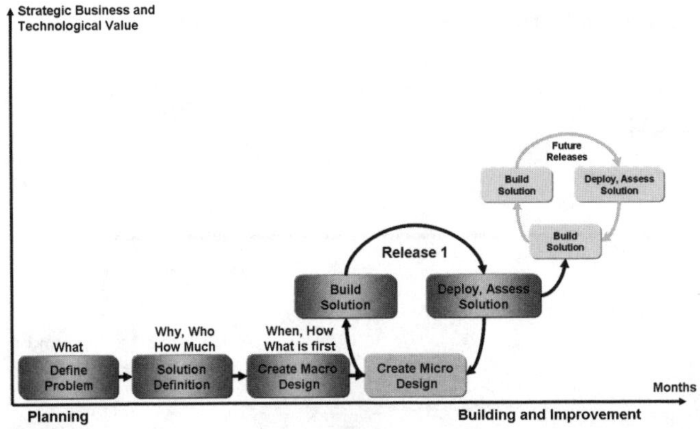

Create Micro Design

Never hold discussions with the monkey when the organ grinder is in the room.

Sir Winston Churchill

Chapter Objectives

In this chapter, you learn how to create the detailed design for the portal, user interfaces, functions, content, and architecture. This will prepare you for the build cycle of a specific portal release. Each release cycle starts with the micro design, which transforms the business model into a design by running selected use-case scenarios through an "object-oriented" development phase. The business model is transformed to a level of technical detail that can be implemented by adding architectural and implementation components (hardware and software). This finalizes the design before the build phase.

When you are done with this chapter, you will be able to define the micro design for your portal. With this, you will be able to move on to chapter 5, in which you start to build the portal.

What Steps Do I Need to Follow?

You go through the three steps shown in Figure 4.1 to identify your own business requirements:

1. Initiate micro design.
2. Prepare the detailed design.
3. Plan training and development.

To get you warmed up to the subject, let's walk through these steps with Churchill's portal as a backdrop.

Initiate Micro Design

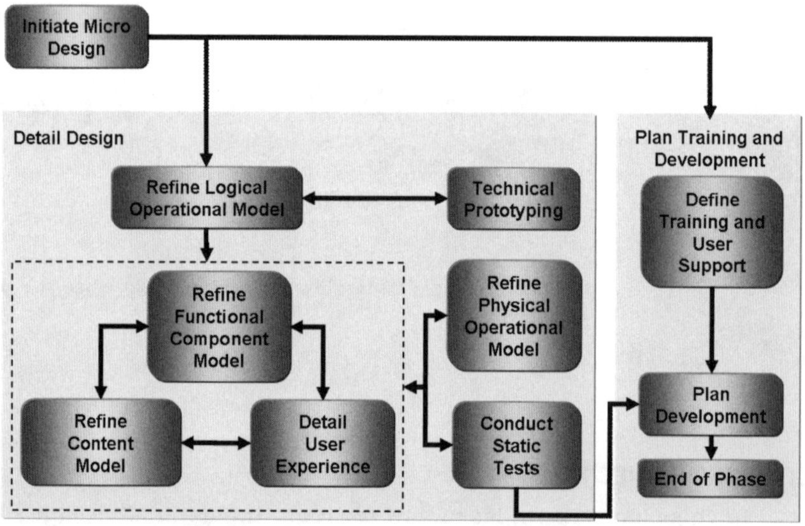

Figure 4.1: Micro design is the first phase of an iterative release.

The micro-design phase is repeated for each release of the portal. This differs from the solution-definition and macro-design phases, which are done only once. The micro design drills down on a specific release and refines many of the same deliverables as the macro design, but to a greater level of detail.

The micro design binds the analysis and interactive models (from user interfaces) to a specific implementation platform and creates a physical portal model that details the operating systems and computers used. Designing these models in parallel reduces the overall complexity.

For Churchill's architects, the micro design focused on all the elements that were critical to Dowding and Fighter Command in the ensuing air battles. These were primarily the operations centers, fighter aircraft, pilots, and supporting facilities like radar and the observer corps.

DETAIL DESIGN

The overall process of detail design refines the logical operational model based on the availability of technologies. It then iterates through the following three activities until the design and usability objectives are reached:

- Refine the functional component
- Refine the content models
- Detail the user experience

This phase also completes the requirements, interactive modeling, and analysis modeling for the release. During this phase, it is important to focus on the functions, components, and experiences that the users want and need, not simply those that the designers want them to use.

Refine Logical Operational Model

Refining the logical operational model includes updating the model, finalizing nonfunctional requirements, completing technical prototyping, completing a viability assessment, and evaluating and selecting computer products and technologies. The operational model is refined to a detailed level required for implementation based on the availability of products and technologies.

Update Logical Operational Model

The logical operational model is updated based on the detailed technical walkthrough in chapter 2. It is further refined to specify the required technical software components that run on each node, so they can be installed and run on physical computer systems. However, before these components are included in a new version of the functional component model, their nonfunctional requirements need to be reviewed. Some of these requirements should be tested through a prototype.

Churchill's architects reexamined the technical walkthroughs to determine any changes to these and the logical operational model. This was based on the priorities of tests, deployment, and releases.

Finalize Nonfunctional Requirements

The nonfunctional requirements are reviewed for each operational model node defined in chapter 2, identifying any particularly demanding ones. Then, the overall nonfunctional requirements are finalized for the first few releases.

For Churchill's architects, this meant reviewing the nonfunctional requirements related to security, availability, redundancy, maintainability, and performance, as shown in Table 4.1.

Table 4.1: Nonfunctional Requirements Table

Requirement	Federated Portal Most Affected by Requirement
Security	For Bletchley Park, security was critical because if the enemy had any indication that Enigma was compromised, the operation would be nullified.
Availability	For Storey's Gate, availability of information was critical. This information had to be presented to the right person for decision-making in a timely manner.
Redundancy	For Bentley Prior, built-in redundancy was critical, in the number of fighter airfields and radar stations built. These were top targets for destruction.
Maintainability	For all four portals operating in a dynamic environment, maintainability was important, with many continuous and incoming changes needed.
Performance	For Bletchley Park, performance was critical because Enigma code that could not be broken in a specific timeframe would lose its value. For Bentley Prior, performance was critical in the ability to handle information traffic and the potential overload of information. For all four portals, user performance and productivity were very important.

Technical Prototyping

A technical prototype is constructed based on the chosen technical components. This is done not only to analyze any particularly challenging nonfunctional requirements, but also to uncover areas of unknown complexity and any new critical technologies. This allows the architects to evaluate alternate strategies for achieving the results with the existing technical software components and reduce the overall risks. With a prototype, perfection is not a priority; practicality is.

A prototype is initiated as the risk is uncovered, preferably early in the project. It explores the technical challenges of the products, the development of any software code, and other significant issues. Prototypes are used to:

- Clarify technical requirements and feasibility in the context of the architecture
- Assess the technical viability of the design of a specific component

- Verify the compatibility of a component with other parts of the solution
- Secure buy-in from executives, or involve end-users in the design
- Determine portal service-level characteristics

Projects with areas of technical uncertainty or complexity might require several prototypes to reduce the risk of encountering technical problems. Although undertaking a prototype is time-consuming, its value far outweighs its costs. Prototyping can be either evolutionary or throw-away, one which incorporates results as refinements and is used to test a design concept, even though it might not be used in production.

Churchill's architects had the opportunity to create several technical prototypes to solve various nonfunctional challenges across the federated portals. For example, one challenge was the ability to handle information traffic at Bentley Prior without affecting the performance of the portals. The most complex and risky problem was at Bletchley Park. Specifically, the code-breakers needed to break Enigma codes rapidly, in the 24-hour window before the Enigma keys changed. This required isolating that particular day's ring setting and wheel order, but doing this by hand was incredibly laborious. The Bletchley team could partly automate the process by building electromechanical machines, or *Bombes*, that could break the Enigma code much more quickly. Bombes helped the code-breakers determine whether plain-text "cribs," clues from previous messages, were actually in use.

Since the bombes were critical to Bletchley Park, their creation became the technical prototype. For Churchill's architects, the prototype lessened the risk of project failure by providing an insight into unforeseen technical problems. It also allowed the Bletchley Park team to learn and explore this new technology. Finally, it determined the technology's feasibility and estimated costs.

Evaluate and Select Products and Technologies

Vendor products and technologies are evaluated against criteria based on the solution functions and on the technical specifications taken from the operational model. The vendor's software is evaluated using a score sheet. The scores for each function are averaged as input for the final product and technology recommendations.

For Churchill's architects, the technical prototyping proved the viability of the automation of the Bletchley Park's code-breaking processes. This was only a first step, however. The real challenge lay in rapidly scaling up the number of bombes in production. For this, the architects had to evaluate alternate strategies for achieving the results with the existing technical components. Following vendor evaluations, the rapid manufacturing of the bombe machine was deemed feasible and was outsourced to the British Tabulating Machine company at Letchworth. A similar evaluation process was followed for the other federated portals.

Refine the Functional Component Model

The functional component model is refined and expanded for each of the federated portals. This process reexamines individual components and then refines and integrates them. It also completes the business logic layer for the model and addresses questions about the federation and whether any of the functions can be shared. Finally, it determines what the completed functions and the functional component model look like, so it can be presented as a report. The final section presents the detailed design and states the completed functions and functional component model from Churchill's federated portal.

Reexamine the Components

Since the initial definition of the functional component model (in Figure 3.8), a number of activities have been completed. This section reviews the more significant of these, including the finalized use cases and scenarios, archetypes, application functions, business patterns, logical operational model, technical walkthroughs, nonfunctional requirements, technical prototypes, and release strategy. It uses all these as input. It reexamines each component within each layer of the model. It selects the components that are required for each of the federated portals. Typically, only a few are needed in a layer. Finally, it prioritizes the most important components based on common usage and on the completion of the most important business activities within the business processes addressed by the portal.

For Churchill's architects, the most important components, prioritized on just common usage, were metadata for Whitehall, security (intrusion management) for Bletchley Park, and conferencing for Storey's Gate. When prioritized on the completion of the most important business activities, Bentley Prior's early-warning and squadron-deployment systems were critical. This functionality was based on event-management and tracking, and on passing information to the operations centers for decision-making. All the related and supporting components for this functionality were given top priority.

Complete Detailed Design of Components

Completing the detailed design of components determines the source of the components: whether they already exist in the environment, need to be acquired, or must be developed from scratch. (A *component* encapsulates software that reduces complexity and improves the development quality.) For existing components, this step determines whether further development, customization, or configuration is required, and the extent of this. It then designs the components in greater detail prior to the build phase and provides input to the development plan. This step also identifies reusable components or those that may be shared. These serve several of the federated portals, like a component for search. With existing components, the technology is already proven.

For Churchill's architects, functions like research and the metadata used for the supply-chain indicators were common to both Whitehall and Storey's Gate. However, in other cases, similar functions could not be readily shared because of security or privacy constraints.

Integrate Components

Components are independent and not restricted to any particular technology, so they need to be integrated. Integrating components involves determining the interrelationships and communication between them, the ways they interact and collaborate to deliver the required functionality, and their individual responsibilities. This is based on the dynamic behavior of components and the likely combinations of components within or between layers of the model, taken from the various use-case scenarios and technical walkthroughs. This process also defines the component collaborations for important use-case scenarios, determines how the components interface, and provides guidance on how to integrate these interfaces.

For Churchill's architects, technical walkthrough 1 from Table 3.4 determined how a user navigated across the functions of the Whitehall portal and determined what data was transferred with the user and exchanged between the components within the information-aggregation layer. In another example, at Storey's Gate, collaboration and decision-making were very closely related; data was transferred between the two layers of the model, collaboration and information aggregation.

Complete Business Logic

Completing the business logic completes the business layer of the model and the unique business-logic functions. These are critical to the functioning and processing for each of the federated portals. These components are unique, generally not shared between portals, and differentiate organizational portals.

For Churchill's architects, it was relatively easy to determine the business-logic functions by examining at a business level the responsibilities of the communities using each portal. For example, procurement of aircraft materials and manufacturing were the unique responsibilities of the ministries in Whitehall, while the operation of aircraft was unique to Bentley

Prior. Similarly, code-breaking was completely unique to Bletchley Park, as was international collaboration with external communities to Storey's Gate.

Address Federation Questions

At this point, you need to look at some of the common portal services related to a federated portal and the levels of federation required by the portals. Federation is important in organizations where multiple portals exist for different business purposes. These can highlight the lack of integration between existing business systems or sites. For example:

- At the simplest level, the portals are loosely coupled. A federated content catalog publishes information, allowing each portal to be located by a federated search. Each portal has a common look-and-feel and behavior. Layout and navigation are as consistent as possible.
- At the next level, a federation search finds content across the federated portals. Information is freely exchanged between portals. Federation metadata shares the tagging of content, and federation standards are in place.
- At the next level, the user can access applications and portlets across the federated portals. The user's identity and preferences are carried to local portals, and portlets/components are registered for use across the portals.
- At the highest level, portals are tightly coupled. The user readily navigates the applications and portlets across the federated portals, where the common user identity and attributes are shared. Users are exposed to specific application functions based on role and are unaware that they are moving across portals. There is no wrong door or misdirected navigation.

For Churchill's architects, some functions had more relevance than others. The figures below further describe the more important functions, such as content-management (Figure 4.2), search (Figure 4.3), and single authentication (Figure 4.4). The figures show "before" views on the left and "after" views on the right.

Single enterprises or shared content management require centrally established and managed policies and processes. Churchill's architects were faced with vast amounts of content that needed to be organized for distribution to users based on their roles and security profiles in their organizations. Managing content across the portals for common services had its advantages, like efficiency, reduced duplication, and costs. However, it also creates challenges, like security.

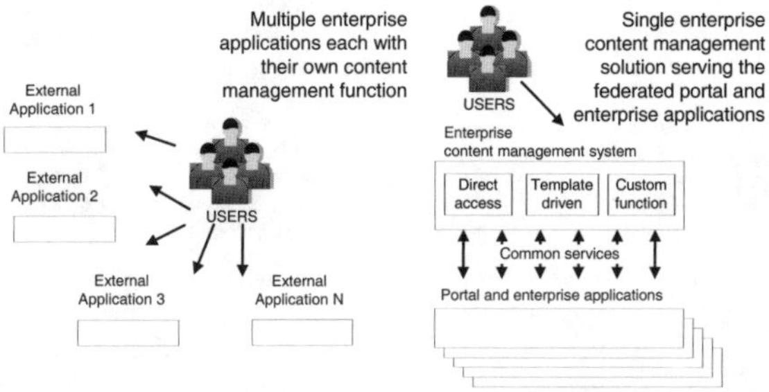

Figure 4.2: The content-management capability crosses many applications.

A single federated search ensures that multiple content repositories can be readily searched across the portals. Churchill's architects used indexes for searching in locations where large repositories of information existed, such as the Whitehall ministries and the index room at Bletchley Park. A federated search would have been very useful to the Storey's Gate communities, in collecting intelligence for decision-making.

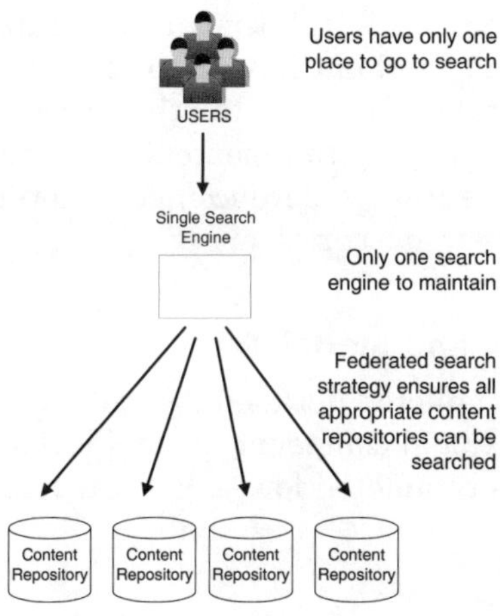

Figure 4.3: A federated search is completed.

Most multiple-enterprise applications have their own unique approach to authentication and authorization (access control). Where all applications access a common directory, authentication system, and policy service. The access models need to be granular to cover cross-authentication to different portals.

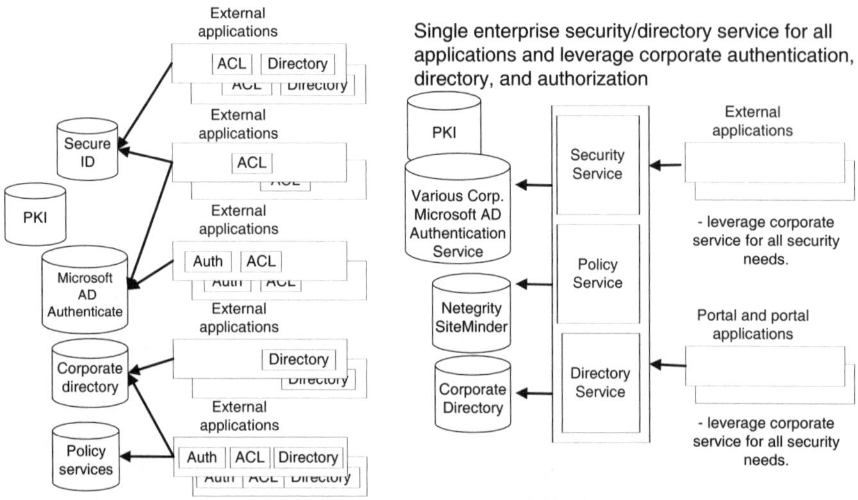

Figure 4.4: Single authentication of a user crosses portals.

Churchill's architects had to deploy single authentication and authorization for users like Churchill, his War Cabinet, and his high-profile staff members. Once inside the federated portal, they needed rapid access everywhere they were authorized to go, without having to reestablish their authorization credentials with each portal or function. In other words, they needed to use functions and models without having to repeatedly sign on. This is a challenge in a federated portal model, as user preference needs to remain with the user as he or she moves from portal to portal.

State Components and Model

Finally, the completed detailed design of the functions is stated, determining what the functional component model looks like so it can be presented as a report. This is completed for each of the four federated portals in the following sections.

Storey's Gate Components and Model

Churchill's architects created the Storey's Gate super-portal as a secure, bombproof government headquarters. Located in a vast bunker beneath Whitehall, it housed a complex village, a network of narrow passages, and tiny rooms. The complex processed vast amounts of aggregated information from the federated portals for decision-making. It accommodated key organizations like the chiefs of staff, Home Defense, Cabinet secretary, and Joint Intelligence Committee. The three most important rooms, or functions, in the complex were the cabinet war room, the map room, and Winston Churchill's room.

The *cabinet war room* was the center of the collaborative and real-time decision-making environment. It was based on the decision-making archetype from Figure 2.11. The room was used for meetings of the prime minister, coalitions of ministers from Parliament, the War Cabinet advisers, and chiefs of staff for the armed forces. Its design included a U-shaped table for the ministers and a rectangular table for the chiefs of staff. Churchill occupied the large seat at the center of the room with a world map behind him, as shown in Figure 4.5. The room was the principal facility for conducting the war, bringing together specific ministers and chiefs of staff.

The *map room* was the center of the event-tracking environment, feeding information to the cabinet war room. It was based on the corporate communication archetype from Figure 2.11. Presentation, information aggregation/publishing and application, and security were all important layers, as were content management and analytical application functionality.

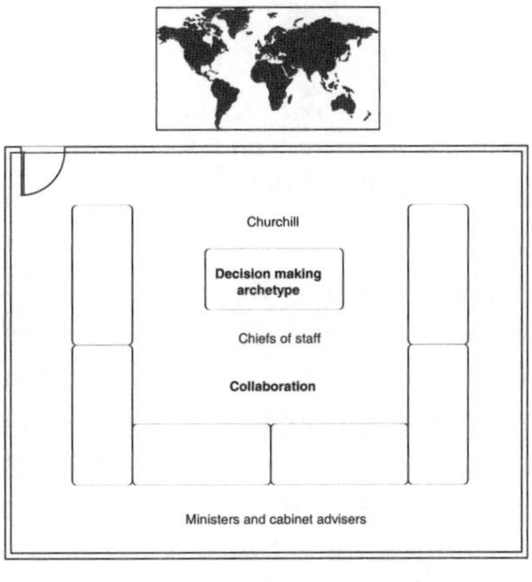

Figure 4.5: The cabinet war room was the largest room in the Storey's Gate complex and the inner sanctum of British government. It provided collaboration and decision-making functions.

The room was critical to the portal, the hub of Storey's Gate, as shown in Figure 4.6. Access to the map room was strictly controlled. The walls were pasted with large-scale maps of the world and all major theaters of war. The changing fronts were updated in real time following key events like enemy movements and battles. This provided an executive "dashboard" to the war, a wealth of information on the order of battle, troop movements, enemy positions, and industrial production capacity that was an important input for decision-making. The map room was also a collaboration room between the three military arms, and a communication hub with links to their various command headquarters through the colored telephones in the center of the room, the "dawn chorus."

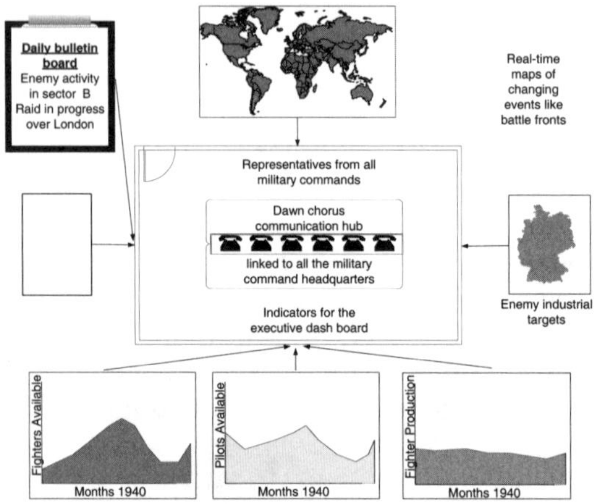

Figure 4.6: The map room aggregated information in the real-time maps, and acted as the communication hub for Storey's Gate.

Winston Churchill's room was important as a individual collaboration and decision-making environment. It was based on the decision-making archetype from Figure 2.11. This multifunction room was very significant to the complex. First, it was situated next to the map room, which gave Churchill ready access. Second, it provided a bedroom for Churchill that was more comfortable than anywhere else in the complex. Third, it was set up so Churchill could broadcast his messages to the world. Finally, he had a private room where he could collaborate with heads of state, politicians, and military figures.

Storey's Gate also included secondary rooms (functions) to support the three main rooms:

- The *transatlantic telephone room* housed the secure hotline between Churchill and Roosevelt. Conversations were enciphered and sent by radio waves to Washington.
- The *map room annex* gave extra space to the planners and housed the telephone switch to allow secure communications between federated portals.

- The *dock* in the sub-basement had small dormitory rooms that extended the full length and breadth of the building. It provided living quarters for the administrators.

The remaining rooms housed the following:

- The Joint Planning Staff responsible for planning, assessing, and reviewing projects
- The broadcasting equipment to deliver Churchill's wartime speeches to the world
- The telephone exchange for all the communications within the portal
- The office administration and typing pool, which prepared minutes and reports that had to be copied and disseminated within hours, day or night
- The emergency offices for the secretary to the Cabinet, private secretaries, and headquarters for Home Forces, responsible for defense against enemy attack and invasion
- The staff responsible for the daily upkeep, supply, maintenance, and security of the portal, which held the keys for full access to all the rooms in the complex
- The mess, where members of the senior staff and the War Cabinet office could socialize

Bentley Prior Components and Model

Churchill's architects and Dowding shaped Britain's air defense through an RAF Fighter Command portal. At the heart of this was Bentley Prior's operations center, a top-secret hub of defensive air operations and the nerve center of the whole organization.

The *Bentley Priory operations center* was the center of a real-time decision-making environment. It was based on the decision-making archetype from Figure 2.11. It also was an early-warning system, feeding information to other operations centers. Collaboration, presentation, information aggregation publishing and application, and security were all important layers, as was content management and analytical application functionality.

The operations center aggregated information and events, processed them, and displayed them on the map table shown in Figure 4.7. As enemy planes took off, they were tracked on this real-time model, reflecting every change. Enemy raids were plotted through positioned counters, representing formations.

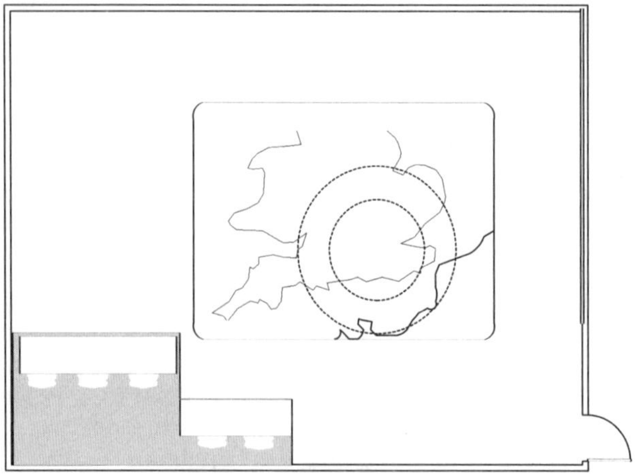

Figure 4.7: The operations center at Bentley Prior was dominated by the central map table.

This information was then disseminated through the command structure, which divided up the country into groups. Each group had a station and commanding air officer, and was further divided into sectors with stations (headquarters) and surrounding, smaller fighter stations/airfields. Backing these up were the radar stations, observer corps, barrage balloon units, anti-aircraft regiments, and searchlight units, all critical sources of information.

The *individual group and sector operations centers* had many of the characteristics of Bentley Prior, with an event-tracking and decision-making environment. The centers were expected to have the most activity, even though Bentley Prior was at center. The headquarters saw the overall picture of events, whereas group levels saw only what pertained to the groups. However, the sector level was where the final decision went out to the individual squadrons and pilots.

The *radar stations* formed a defense network along the southern and eastern coasts, from Land's End to the North Sea, as shown in Figure 4.8. They consisted of two types of complementary stations: the crude Chain Home Radar Direction Finder and the more sophisticated Chain Low. The latter could pick up high-flying enemy aircraft at 30,000 feet and up to 150 miles away. The former had a shorter range, but could pick up low-flying enemy aircraft. Both operated on pattern recognition.

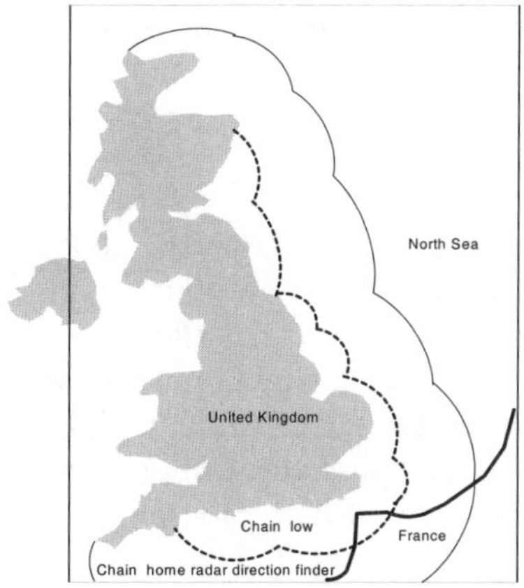

Figure 4.8: Over 50 radar stations identified incoming raids and alerted the operations centers to these events.

The *observer corps*, made up of civilian volunteers, identified and assessed the enemy aircraft strength, from 1,000 observation posts, based on silhouette or pattern recognition. The corps could only track aircraft detected by the radar stations. Observer information was aggregated by the corps center and then by Bentley Prior, from which it cascaded down through its hierarchy.

The *barrage balloon command* operated 52 squadrons across the country, creating a barrage of huge balloons that protected towns and cities, as well as targets like industrial areas and ports. They protected everything at ground level from the threat of low-flying dive-bombers. Set at heights of up to 5,000 feet, they would force aircraft to fly high, limiting their accuracy and bringing them within range of the anti-aircraft guns.

The *anti-aircraft command,* under the army, was divided nationally into seven divisions, but linked to fighter command groups. Its primary role was to protect the aircraft manufacturing industry and support the fighter command. Anti-aircraft fire was more effective in daylight than at night, as the incoming bomber streams were in closer formations. At night, the aircraft were very widely spaced, with a 1:50 chance of a hit. The *searchlight units* were closely linked to the anti-aircraft command.

The *operational training units* were responsible for pilot training. The number of available pilots was a continual problem for Dowding. Pilot training took three months and was limited to pilots under 30. Dowding brought Allied pilots into the RAF squadrons, as well as volunteers from the Commonwealth and countries under Axis occupation.

Bletchley Park Components and Model

The Bletchley Park portal was based on the knowledge-based trading archetype from Figure 2.11. It enabled secure knowledge transactions with other portals.

Bletchley Park was a large, multispecialist organization at the center of the code-breaking operation, located just outside of London. The organization had to operate in total secrecy so that the enemy would not deduce its existence by reading counter activities or by penetrating the organization directly. Therefore, Bletchley Park had to be in tight control of dissemination of top-secret intelligence. Keeping the Enigma decrypting secret outweighed any temporary advantages gained by acting on its intelligence. To achieve this, some basic rules had to be followed:

- Bletchley's existence was kept totally secret.
- Staff could not be put in a position that could lead to their capture.
- The use of the code word *Ultra* was strictly forbidden.

The Bletchley Park operation was structured into three functions:

- The *Y*, or wireless intercept stations, dotted around Britain
- The code breakers (*hut 6*) located at Bletchley Park and in selected places close by
- The intelligence section (*hut 3*) located entirely in Bletchley Park

Before May 1940, Bletchley Park was a fledging operation, run manually. It had to be organized, automated, and rapidly scaled up to be effective so that it could process the volume of expected Enigma traffic.

The *Y stations* formed an important information-aggregation environment. Without them, Bletchley Park would have been deaf, dumb, and blind. The stations were in four locations and specialized in wireless traffic from the three different services and from other countries that could provide useful intelligence. The stations listened and recorded enemy radio messages and sent them to Bletchley Park to be decoded and analyzed.

Huts 3 and *6* were the center of the collaborative and analytical environment. Information dissemination and security were important layers of the model, as was content management and analytical application functionality.

The Enigma decrypt teams worked in hut 6 to produce the raw decrypts from the ciphers, which were then aggregated by the team in the neighboring hut 3, the heart of the operation at Bletchley. The main task was to evaluate the raw decrypts from hut 6, extract the given intelligence for Churchill and his staff, ministries, and commands, and turn the deciphered messages into intelligence reports. The dissemination of information was controlled by the intelligence section in hut 3.

Whitehall Components and Model

Churchill's architects and Beaverbrook shaped aircraft production through the Whitehall portal based on the mergers archetype from Figure 2.11. Diverse communities were helped to merge and to act as one. Some of the more predominant functions of Whitehall are listed below. The first two were closely aligned to Bentley Prior and its demand for fighters.

The *ministry of aircraft production* was at the center of fighter production and the supply chain. It was the heart of the collaborative and decision-making environment and based on the decision-making archetype from Figure 2.11. The organization was responsible for managing the procurement of supplies, the manufacture of aircraft, the inspection of the finished aircraft, the distribution of these aircraft to squadrons, and the defense of aircraft factories. Information aggregation and publishing were absolutely critical in providing decision-makers the necessary views of this supply chain.

The *Civilian Repair Organization (CRO)*, based on a community archetype, was a system of workshops that had to quickly accommodate and repair damaged aircraft. Storage areas had to be organized where spare parts from destroyed aircraft could be systematically stored and retrieved whenever needed. The CRO was transferred to Beaverbrook when Churchill appointed him minister.

The three functions below were similar to each other, in that they aggregated specialist information for the Whitehall community. They were based on the innovation archetype from Figure 2.11:

- The *Statistical Advisory Section* built up by Churchill at the start of the war was combined with the Central Economic Intelligence Service of the War Cabinet in May 1940. In the early part of the war, many government statistics were extremely confusing, conflicting, and incomplete, making it difficult to get an overall picture of what was happening. It became a life and death matter to change this.
- The *Social Survey Department* was established to conduct surveys on the economy, social topics, and questions relating to wartime morale. It supplemented data from existing surveys of public opinion. Churchill's architects needed regular feedback from the general population.

- *Scientific units* advised Churchill mainly on the new scientific and technological possibilities in most branches of the wartime economy. It was important to investigate the application of science to air warfare.

Detail User Experience

Detailing the user experience includes completing the following:

- Release use-case scenarios
- User interfaces at the level of detail required for a specific release of the portal
- Interface constraints
- Usability requirements

It is important to keep usability simple for the user, to maximize the portal's effectiveness.

This phase defines how Churchill's architects completed detailed user interfaces for each of the federated portal. The finalized interfaces indicated how the user experience would look across the federation.

Complete Release Use-Case Scenarios

The use-case scenarios from chapter 2 and the strategy for releases shown in Table 3.6 are closely examined. Then, they are completed iteratively, based on input from the component and content models.

Churchill's architects verified the release timing of the use cases for each portal based on the availability of content and components.

Detail User Interfaces

The user interfaces are defined at a detailed level. These are presented in the form of text, graphics, and tables on paper or screenshots on Web pages. This clarifies the portal's functionality, size, complexity, and look and feel, and supports its development. A user interface is something difficult to get right the first time. It needs to be iteratively tested and modified based on feedback. The output is an interactive model.

For Churchill's architects, with the completion of user prototyping, detailing the user interface was particularly important for each of the federated portals, but for different reasons. Complex interactive models were used by staff to understand and predict how the real-time situation around them was changing:

- The *map room* in Storey's Gate was at the core of the decision-making process, where real-time information models tracked the changing world through real-time events. Complex decisions had to be made rapidly, based on these representative models. Therefore, the models had to be incisive, intuitive, and represent different views, so the repercussions could be readily understood. Passing visitors to the map room, like advisors or high-ranking military chiefs, had to rapidly absorb and comprehend these models.
- Whitehall's *Ministry of Aircraft Production* was at the heart of the supply chain for fighter production. The ministry had to analyze and manage the supply-chain data to meet specific production targets. This data was also a source of indicators for other portals, like Storey's Gate.
- The *operations centers* were a part of the Bentley Prior hierarchical structure. They were made up of a few large group stations and many small sector stations interlinked into the headquarters. They required a high level of conformity and consistency to facilitate information-handling and the movement or transfer of staff. Information at the headquarters provided a big-picture view of the order of battle. Subset views were required at the corresponding stations beneath the headquarters. In each center, the map table was identical.
- Bletchley Park's *hut 3* was at the heart of a very complex operation. With thousands of incoming messages, traffic analysis had to determine and recognize patterns quickly. This had to be reflected in a model that provided intelligence and value.

Storey's Gate Map Room Indicator Model

The map room had to present different types of content and indicators; the latter were of particular importance. Indicators were of a high priority because they were carefully selected to provide early warning of a challenging situation or a specific event, so timely, proactive decisions could be made. This was critical in battle situations. Indicators varied from the supply chain and industrial production to the availability of fighters and stockpiles of fuel, as shown in Figure 4.9.

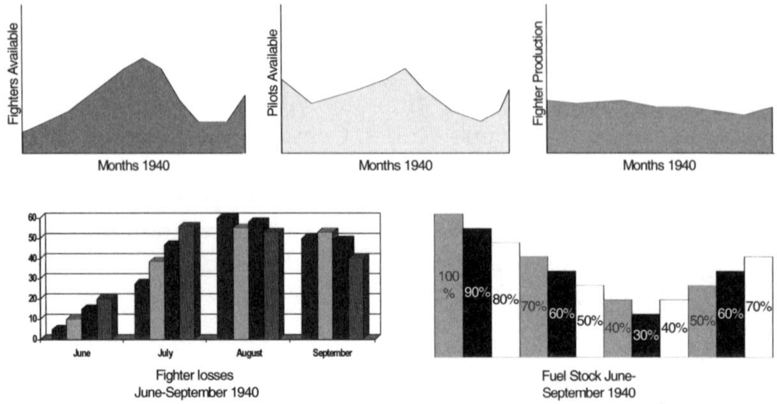

Figure 4.9: The user interface for the map room showed indicators from the air ministry, ministry of aircraft production, and Bletchley Park.

Whitehall Ministry of Aircraft Production Indicator Model

The model was, in fact, the superset of supply-chain indicators from which the map room's indicators were extracted. It presented content and indicators specific to the industrial production of fighters and the overall supply chain. Here, detailed decisions were made on the rate of fighter production.

Bentley Prior Operations Centers Map Model

In a user interface, *objects* represent things like files, folders, and phones from the real world. The relationships among the objects specify how user tasks are supported and grouped, reflecting how users see the overall application. This helps the designer represent the objects in the interface, e.g., whether in the same menu or behind the same buttons, or in the interface.

The fighter operations centers were to have one of the most elegant user-interface models in the entire portal. The purpose of the model was to map a visual representation of the skies above Britain. The map table used objects, or counters, to show the location of friendly and enemy aircraft on a scaled map of the British Isles. The counters on the glass-covered table were color-coded, as shown in Figure 4.10. A red *F* on white background was for friendly aircraft, a black *X* on yellow meant unidentified, and a black *H* on yellow was for hostile aircraft. The enemy counters representing formations were of three different colors: yellow, red, and blue. These corresponded in five-minute intervals to the amount of time the counters had been on the table, according to the operations room's clock (also colored yellow, red, and blue).

When positions of the same aircraft were given by two stations, greater reliance was placed on the accuracy. As new reports were received, a colored arrow for each raid was changed. The situation was updated, so that all the information on the table was no older than fifteen minutes. As a result, the model provided a snap shot of real-time events, giving the decision-makers the information they needed to manage the movement of fighters. They could position and group fighters at the required operational heights.

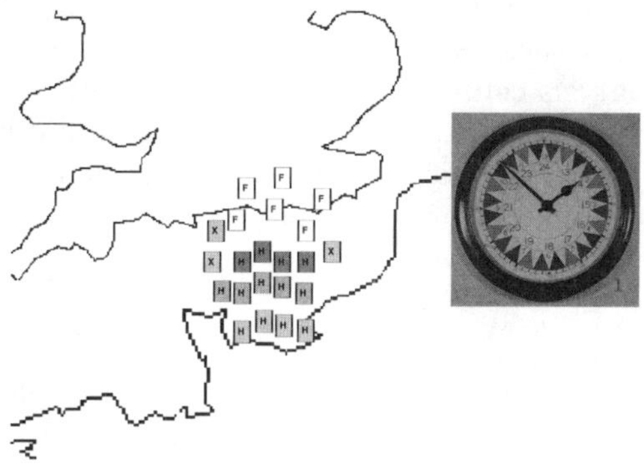

Figure 4.10: The operations center's map model recorded details of enemy raids, and the squadron intercepting them. The color-coding was synchronized to give "five-minute snaps" of the battle.

The group operations centers had a second user-interface model: the tote board shown in Figure 4.11. Named after the horse-racing tracks "Totalisator" board, it had dozens of electric lights that ran the full length of a wall. These indicated squadrons in contact with the enemy, and those disengaging to refuel and rearm. It also indicated the operational state of readiness of squadrons held in reserve that were "available" in 30 minutes, at "readiness" in 5 minutes, or at "cockpit readiness" in 2 minutes, as well as what was in the air.

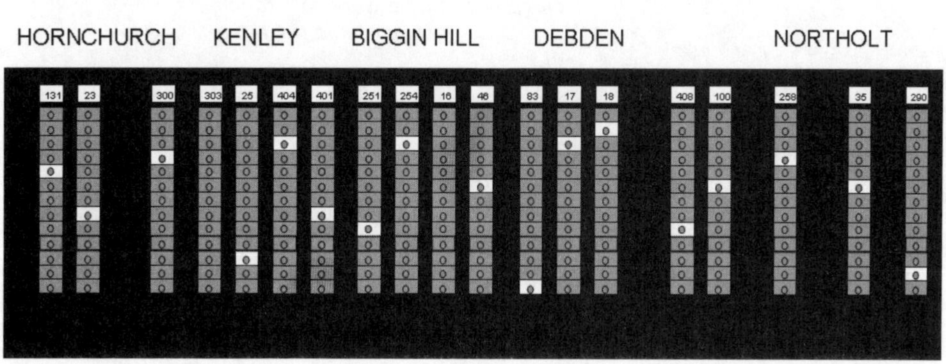

Figure 4.11: The tote boards indicated squadrons and fighter readiness across the operations centers within a group.

The sector operations centers had a direction finder room that obtained the positions of the fighters from radar stations and a situation map like that of group operations, but smaller.

Bletchley Park Traffic Analysis Model

There was also value in studying the "externals" to the Enigma traffic—not the content of the message, but the message lengths, radio frequency, source or network (each used a unique daily setting), and time of broadcast. Traffic analysis could be used to predict the text of some parts of the enciphered messages. As a result, intelligence could be gained on the order of battle, stations communicating, and sometimes, intentions. The model was represented with colored pencils that charted the various networks, as shown in Figure 4.12.

Figure 4.12: In the traffic analysis model, batches of incoming Enigma messages were sorted into corresponding networks of stations, providing intelligence on the order of battle.

Complete Release Interface Constraints

Completing interface constraints involves examining security, access, and disability constraints and determining solutions to address them.

For Churchill's architects, the constraints of primary importance for all the interface models were security, privacy of information, and understandability of information. The latter was closely related to the decision-making processes that had to be acted upon promptly based on the information presented.

Define Usability Requirements

The usability attributes are those features that facilitate the portal's ease of use, like interaction/navigation, screen layout, and affective or aesthetic appeal. To meet the ease-of-use expectations, you need to guide developers on user-interface design and performance standards for usability evaluations and define scenarios for test plans and testing. You also need to consider the following ease-of-use features:

- *Tailorability*—Customize the interface and its components to suit users based on work style, personal preferences, and experience level.
- *Efficiency*—Minimize steps, simplify operations, and enable the quick completion of tasks.
- *Integration*—Automatically execute tasks that cross functional boundaries.

It is important to ensure the features and functions are not too tightly coupled to the user interface. The interface can then be rapidly changed to improve the user experience. From the requirements, user interface guidelines are put in place so the design is consistent across the federated portals, to reduce "relearning" when users move through different portals.

Refine Content Model

The content model is refined along four paths: value, availability, information architecture, and process. Content is the life-blood of a portal. Therefore, time needs to be invested in refining the content model. It also should be refined to match the functional requirements, not organizational hierarchies.

Content Value

You need to determine the content value for each community group and prioritize it accordingly. Content should be selected to drive user adoption. For example, radar content was critical to Dowding, while supply-chain and manufacturing-production numbers were critical to the ministries (specifically for Beaverbrook). Ultra content from Bletchley Park was of paramount value to Churchill, as well as content from other portals to provide the bigger picture.

In 1940, many government statistics were extremely confusing, conflicting, and incomplete. It was difficult to build an overall picture of what was happening. For Churchill's architects, the Whitehall portal leveraged the statistical advisory section. This content was very important for providing advice on the economics and possibilities, looking into most branches of the wartime economy.[1]

---

[1] Source: *War, Economy and Society* 1939-1945, Alan S. Milward, Penguin Books Ltd., 1977.

Content Availability (Identify Sources of Data/Content)

Content availability is identified both by type and by user/community. Both are required for the business case. A plan identifies and classifies content sources, the conditions of use, and a list of requirements that each content provider needs to agree with. Content providers need to understand the granularity of information and the numerous ways it can be accessed.

You need to determine the characteristics of each content source—its type (for example, voice, data, or text), owner, placement, organization, structure, timeliness, veracity, lifecycle, creation methods, and management. You need to determine from community groups the current availability of content, where it is, its format, who owns it, its accessibility, how frequently it is updated, the rate of content growth, the access performance considerations, and whether its presentation varies based on classification, external configuration, or contractual relationship. You also need to assign ownership for it.

For Churchill's architects, the content was aggregated from many sources as listed below:

- *Whitehall*—The ministries aggregated supply-chain reports and indicators based on weekly statistics or specific business-event triggers; established stock, turnover, and production figures for hundreds of parts related to fighters, weaponry, ammunition; and estimated completion schedules. This information would be stored (populated) in a supply-chain data store. The reports included tables showing the trends for each item over a period of several months. The existing monitoring of raw materials was developed into full-scale bookkeeping, encompassing all raw material suppliers, dealers, and users. Producing these statistics required cooperation between several civil and military authorities.
- Bentley Prior—Information aggregated from the following sources gave early-warning information for sensing incoming raids:
    - Radar information related to the perceived enemy position, direction, height, and estimated strength was aggregated by crews operating in the low- and high-level stations. This information was phoned directly to the radar operation's command rooms or headquarters. This had a filter room where sightings and detection information could be aggregated, analyzed, and sorted out. The information was then passed onto the filter room at Bentley Prior headquarters for further processing. The radar stations and observer corps covered nearly ninety percent of Britain's coastline.
    - Observer corps information was aggregated on to the observer corps center (HQ), which in turn informed the sector station filter room and the group and Bentley Prior operations centers.

- Ultra information sources for the RAF would normally be of a strategic nature, indicating the size of a raid, the incoming fleet, and the type of planes. It would be passed to Bentley Prior, not directly to groups as transactions. The admiralty and bomber command would also eventually have direct links with Bentley Prior.

This type of early-warning information is critical to on demand solutions. One of the challenges is to determine where to place probes. Another challenge is how to discern signals from noise.

- *Bletchley Park*—This required the input of intercepted wireless messages from Y stations, which were aggregated for hut 6. These needed to be logged and carefully stored by date. Hut 6 would undertake codebreaking techniques to produce decrypts. These would then be passed onto hut 3 and the intelligence section, which had the authority to translate messages into English, determine how to best use them, and where to pass them on.
- *Storey's Gate*—Information was aggregated from all the above organizations. It was also generated from within the cabinet war rooms. This information took many forms, including extracts from the minutes and papers of top-level conferences, minutes and telegrams by Churchill on military matters, letters from the Foreign Office, and situation reports.

Content (Information) Architecture

The content's architecture is essential to managing the high content growth typical to portals. The following elements need to mature over time:

- *Topology* defines the portal context and map and its expected vitality by range, breadth, and depth. It determines parent, sibling, offspring, and peer sites that require linkages and have independent information architectures. It also determines the defined purposes, audience information, business objectives, hit rates, growth rates, transactional needs, and key measures.
- A *common vocabulary* is necessary for effective information architecture, as the core lexicon and definitions are used by all content owners, authors, and designers. A common vocabulary avoids misunderstandings, delays, and general semantic confusion.
- *Classification and labeling* is also known as grouping, organizing, indexing, and schemas. Sample classifications include hierarchical, alphabetical, chronological, geographical, topical, task-oriented, and audience-oriented. From these, the content is grouped logically to allow site navigation and access to content. You also need to do the following:

   - Determine what content is at the highest site levels, based on the audience and task priorities and the time users are willing to search for it.
   - Provide alternate content-access indices (cross-references, links, synonyms, antonyms, or homonyms) to offer quick paths to information lower on the site structure.
   - Determine the informational elements of the site and a page.
- Content *structures and description* defines group classifications, such as news briefs, product information, and summaries. Determine each group's attributes, values, and relationships, and how they are established and maintained. For Churchill's architects, the organization of content included arrangement files that were divided into policy and strategy, including relations with allies. Specifically, within Storey's Gate, these files were prepared like dossiers on major defense and political issues. The file series were set up by the deputy secretary of the War Cabinet.
- *Navigation* determines the mechanisms or devices best suited to the delivery of users tasks, related to the content types. Possible navigation mechanisms include:
   - *Global navigation* is inherited from a parent level and is consistent across all siblings and progeny.
   - *Hierarchical navigation* is the path the user is expected to follow to execute specifically identified tasks sequentially.
   - *Contextual navigation* offers an alternate path to content and is entered once the user has identified content interest, dependent on alternate indices.
   - *Supplemental navigation* offers specialized alternate paths to content, with retrieval mechanisms like site maps, tables of contents, and user-type specific guides. Site maps categorize content and applications access based on intuitive associations.
- *Content delivery plan* determines the content for each site, page, section. It also defines the content structures and elements, and the attributes for the selected content, like views and versions. This is not the design of the page, but a layout of the content that is required.
- *Content migration* determines how the existing static content is transformed for a dynamic environment. It also determines how it is identified, extracted, converted, transcoded, classified, and indexed within the information architecture, through templates, style sheets, guides, and other tools.

Indicator Model or Dashboard

A portal can be used to support an executive dashboard that provides a mechanism to monitor the business activities and output. The dashboard drives qualitative improvements, reports performance against goals, establishes priorities, identifies ways to improve performance, highlights flaws in the operation, and ensures sustainability. However, the most difficult task is to determine what to measure. For example, financial measurements, like net profit, do not provide good steering information because these *lag indicators* reflect the past. They only prove that an organization exists, not what it is doing.

Churchill's architects created a dashboard of key indicators that could provide a real-time pulse by which Churchill and his cabinet could read the war, understand battle situations, and determine short-term needs. They could then communicate with the respective commanders, and influence them in the control and performance of the supply chain and production. These lead indicators had to recognize events, like changes in battle fronts, that had a direct effect on the supply chain. Successful indicators would influence the future success of the organizations and their ability to deliver quality and innovation. Measuring these provided a balanced overview of the performance of the supply chain and its influence on battle situations, as shown in Figure 4.13.

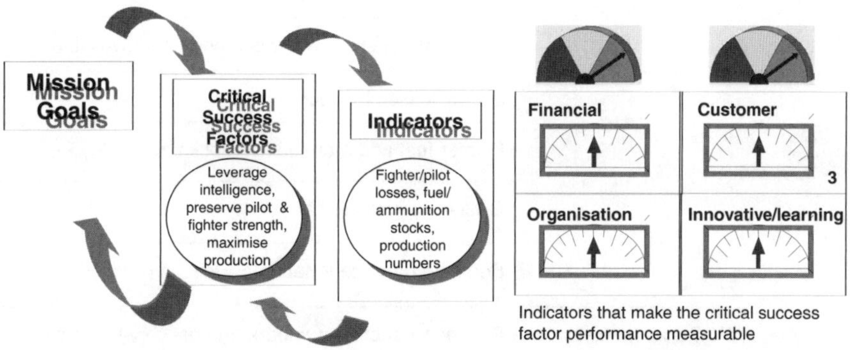

Figure 4.13: The indicator model ties the mission and its goals to the indicators. It links the critical success factors to the key performance indicators to translate the strategy to the operation.

With these indicators, Churchill could ask some very important questions: Could the supply chain be sustained efficiently and economically? For how long? Was the financial picture healthy? Were the costs too high to be sustainable? Was bankruptcy possible?

In today's business world, an effective dashboard structures the indicators to reflect both the macro and micro views. One approach is to use a *balanced scorecard* to balance the financial, organizational, customer, and innovation perspectives. It is worked out iteratively from the organizational strategy to determine which data is needed to measure where the organization is going, and what is required to get it there. The strengths of the scorecard are that it uses measures on every level, is applicable for everyone in the organization, puts order to complexity, and helps communicate and reflect the organizational strategy.

In your organization, you can create an executive dashboard, useful for senior and mid-level managers, using a Web-based analytics application and a data mart. For Churchill, the indicator model provided information on the overall picture through events like changes in battle fronts and the performance of key elements of the supply chain, as shown in Table 4.2.

Table 4.2: Churchill's Overall Indicators

Source	Lead Indicators (Supplied Daily)
Bentley Prior Fighters	Fighter losses by squadron
	Number of sorties flown
	Pilots lost versus new pilots trained and available
	Enemy losses by aircraft type
	Fighter fuel and ammunition stocks available
	Civilian casualties
	Bombing damage to factories, loss in production
Whitehall (ministry of aircraft production)	Fighter production numbers and delivery to airfields
	Key fighter-component production numbers and inventory
	CRO repair turnaround in timeframe
	Fighter imports from Canada
	Anti-aircraft production numbers
Bletchley Park	Indicators of enemy order of battle
	Enemy plans or intentions

Design Data Mapping

Data mapping focuses on the data sources and identifies what data is required for the indicators, where it is located, and most important, its condition and quality.

Churchill's architects created a "source-to-target" data map that defined how the source data, found within the supply-chain and manufacturing environments, was transformed and converted to the indicators. They used the overall indicators from Table 4.2 to determine a description of the target column. Through the process, business rules were identified and documented—for example, how the data was produced, when, and its format.

Refine Physical Operational Model

Refining the physical operational model determines what you have in place and what is left to do. The physical model design is based on updates to the logical operational model, the functional component model, the content model, changes in the nonfunctional requirements, or changes in the IT infrastructure.

Churchill's architects had, at this point, a very clear understanding of the requirements for the physical operational model, as shown in Figure 3.14. Some of the physical facilities were already in place, as shown in Table 4.3. This is a common condition when existing infrastructure elements are incorporated into a project.

Table 4.3: Physical Operational Model Characteristics

Categories	Storey's Gate	Bentley Prior	Bletchley Park	Whitehall
Organization	◔	◓	◓	◕
Processes	◔	◓	◔	◕
Data processing	○	◔	◔	◔
Data storage	○	○	◔	◔
Facilities	◕	◕	◓	●
Networks	◔	◔	○	◓

Not in place - deployed

○ ◔ ◓ ◕ ●

The physical operational model provided Churchill's architects guidance regarding what had to be completed in the build phases. For example, some of the facilities at Bentley Prior were partially in place, but had to be completed by adding watertight and blastproof doors, a large network of telephone cable, and signaling equipment in the filter room. In the field, new sector and fighter stations had to be completed. Network communications had to be established between the existing operations centers of command and fighter airfields, through trunk cables and teleprinters. External communications to radar stations and Bletchley Park were also required. The former required laying trunk ducts and repeater stations. The latter required the set up of processes.

Conduct Static Tests

Static or paper testing is conducted to test requirements, architecture, and models, in the same way as in chapter 3. Identifying potential problems at this point in the project is far more cost-effective than identifying them during full dynamic testing, discussed in chapter 5. Defects are found close to their source and earlier in the project, before they are passed on to the next stage.

Table 4.4: Static Test Plan

Phase in Project	Storey's Gate	Bentley Prior	Bletchley Park	Whitehall
High-level design	M	M	M	M
Detailed design	H	H	H	M
Program modules	H	H	H	H
Test plans/cases	H	H	H	H
User documents	M	M	M	M

For Churchill's architects, static testing could be applied to different activities in the phase and at different levels of depth. As shown in Table 4.4, they were prioritized as high, medium, and low.

Within the federated portal, the characteristics of some of the infrastructure elements' blueprints provided a tangible presence that lent themselves well to static testing. One example would be completing a walkthrough of the Storey's Gate map-room blueprint. However, the primary focus was the scrambling of fighters, and this could only be tested dynamically.

Initiate Master Test Plan

The completion of the static test plan provides very useful input to the test strategy and plan defined in chapter 3. The completed use-case scenarios are used as input to set up test cases. The usability and ease-of-use requirements also define test scenarios for the test plan. Finally, the master test plan is adjusted and initiated.

Plan Training and Development

Defining training and support requirements produces plans for the development undertaken in chapter 5. This is the time to ensure the support staff are prepared to receive and support the solution.

Define Training and Support

The purpose of this phase is to gather the requirements for the tools that the staff will need to support and maintain the portal. Typically, the tools include a users' guide for some of the more complex models, an operations manual for the more extensive processes, and the support of application and maintenance fixes and upgrades. Relative to Churchill's portal, Table 4.5 shows some of the user education and training needs, prioritized as high, medium, and low, and the overall training time in months.

Table 4.5: Training and Support

Org	Function	Training (Specific to)	Tools	Level	Months
Storey's Gate	Chiefs of staff	Decision tools	User guide	H	1
	Defense committee	Decision tools	User guide	H	1
	Senior aides	Interpret information	Ops manual	H	6
	Duty officers	Map room model	Ops manual	H	3
	WREN administration	Administrators	User guide	M	1
	Security personnel	Access to areas	Ops manual	M	1
Bentley Prior (Fighter Command Ops centers)	Ops room controllers	Map/tote models	Ops manual	H	3
	WAAF (Women's Auxiliary Air Force) administrators	Map/tote models	Ops manual	H	2
	Security personnel	Access to areas	Ops manual	M	1

Table 4.5: Training and Support, *continued*

Org	Function	Training (Specific to)	Tools	Level	Months
	Radar technicians	Radar technology	User guide	H	1
	Observers corps	Plane identification	User guide	M	1
	Code breakers hut 6	Crack Enigma	Ops manual	M	6
	Intelligence officers hut 3	Protect Ultra security	Ops manual	H	6
	SLU officers	Ultra dissemination	Ops manual	H	6
	Administrators	Enigma traffic analysis	User guide	M	4
	Security personnel	Access to areas	Ops manual	M	1
Whitehall	Ministers	Ultra intelligence	User guide	H	2
	Junior ministers	Indicators	Ops manual	M	2
	Civil servants	Indicators	Ops manual	M	1
	Administrators	Indicators	User guide	L	1
	Security personnel	Access to areas	Ops manual	M	1
	Statisticians	Indicators	User guide	M	1
	Scientific advisors	Indicators	User guide	M	1
	Economists	Indicators	User guide	M	1
	Industrialists	Indicators	User guide	M	1

Plan Development

The plan-development phase completes a viability assessment, establishes development guidelines and procedures, and defines goals for each programming cycle across all releases. With this, you are ready to build the solution.

Complete Viability Assessment

The viability of the final release recommendation is assessed. The probability is determined that the build phase will meet the functional requirements, the implementation architecture meets the nonfunctional requirements, and the deployment is successful. This assessment also considers whether the development and implementation skills are available, the client acceptance of the technical elements, the available funding, and future release cycles.

For Churchill's architects, the success of the technical prototype reduced the overall project risk. This final checkpoint determined whether the project would move to the next stage by examining capabilities for the build.

Establish Guidelines and Define Goals for the Build Programming Cycles

The detailed design is leveraged to define the build specifications. These determine the program modules and describe the internal logic, flow, and structures for each module, as well as the unit test plans. The overall complexity relates to the business logic based on business events, taken from the use-case scenarios.

For Churchill's architects, this process started by looking at the events based on the use-case scenarios, as shown in Table 4.6. Each event was carefully considered to determine the source of intelligence, the organization targeted to react to it, and the logic by the way of "if/then conditions" for action and response to the event. At this point, thought had to be given to the test cases required for testing this logic

Table 4.6: Examples of Portals Reacting to Events Using Functional Logic

Use Case	Event Description	Information Source	Portal Sensing and Responding to Events	Action and Response Required
2.2.1	Imminent raid on airfields	Radar, observers, Ultra	Bentley Prior, Storey's Gate, Whitehall	Deploy fighters
2.2.2	Imminent raid on industrial targets	Radar, observers, Ultra	Bentley Prior, Storey's Gate, Whitehall	Deploy fighters and anti-aircraft
2.2.3	Imminent raid on towns or cities	Ultra, radar, observers	Bentley Prior, Storey's Gate, Whitehall	Deploy fighters or anti-aircraft
4.4.2	Low fuel reserves	Supply chain/ Whitehall	Storey's Gate, Whitehall	Increase convoy fuel shipments
4.4.3	Low ammunition reserves	Supply chain/ Whitehall	Storey's Gate, Whitehall	Re-deploy resources
4.3.1	Low food stocks	Supply chain/ Whitehall	Storey's Gate, Whitehall	Negotiate with allies

In the overall iterative process, there are several programming cycles within each build, and several builds within each release, as shown in Figure 4.14. The next step is to determine at what point these are created by establishing goals for each programming cycle, as shown in Table 4.7.

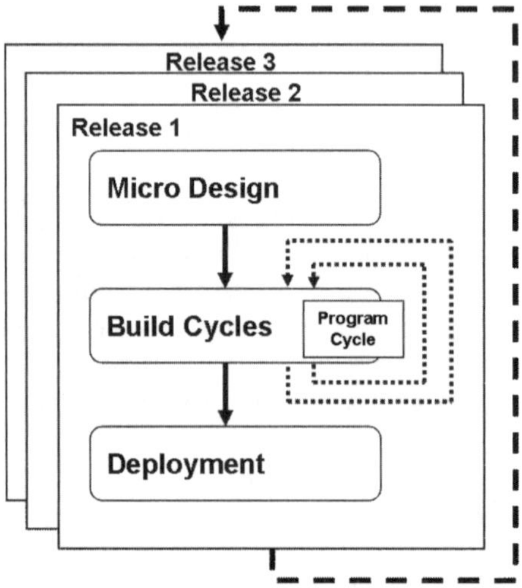

Figure 4.14: Within each release, there are several build cycles. These, in turn, contain several programming cycles.

Table 4.7: Goals for Each Build and Programming Cycle

Organization	Build Cycle	Prog. Cycle	Goals for Module Completion
Bentley Prior	1	1	Respond to radar information and deploy fighters (UCS 2.2.1)
	1	2	Respond to observers and deploy fighters and anti-aircraft (UCS 2.2.2)
	1	3	Respond to Ultra and deploy fighters and anti-aircraft (UCS 2.2.2)
	2	1	Respond to radar information and deploy fighters or anti-aircraft (UCS 2.2.3)
	2	2	Respond to Ultra/MI6 and deploy fighters/anti-aircraft (UCS 2.2.3)
Storey's Gate	3	1	Low on fighter engine parts (UCS 4.4.4)

Table 4.7: Goals for Each Build and Programming Cycle, *continued*

Organization	Build Cycle	Prog. Cycle	Goals for Module Completion
	2	2	Respond to Ultra warning of imminent raid (UCS 2.2.3)
Bletchley	1	1	Indication that Ultra is compromised (UCS 5.5.1)
Whitehall	3	1	Low fighter-engine parts stocks (UCS 4.4.4)
	3	2	Low fuel stocks (UCS 4.4.2)

CONCLUSION

The following sections summarize the major points of this chapter and how they relate to your business today. For more information on these concepts, search the Internet for these keywords and phrases: *information architecture*, *lead and lag indicators*, *static testing*, *technical prototyping*, *master test plans*, *data mapping*, *interactive model*, *user interfaces*, *usability*, and *federated portal*.

Major Points, Considerations, and Lessons Learned

Churchill's architects, with an architecture model in place, focused on the component model, interactive models, and user interfaces to:

- Complete the functions and functionality of the solution
- Develop a content-management system and simplify the overall content complexity
- Provide insight into the user experience requirements
- Identify training and support requirements
- Identify indicators for populating the executive dashboard

Best Practices for Your Organization

- One of the keys for a successful federated portal implementation is to define content value, ownership, and accountability, and institute content-management procedures. The benefits include the following:
  - Accountability and change management of owned content

    - More effective content distribution and promotion
    - Better reuse and interoperability of content and infrastructure
    - Better interface with internal and external partners
    - Reduction of costs due to duplication of content, applications, or infrastructure

- Ensure that content providers understand the granularity of information and the numerous ways it can be accessed.
- Select content that drives portal usage and speeds up user adoption.
- Refine the content model to match functional requirements, not organizational hierarchies.
- Use information architecture to validate content, taxonomy, and function, and to structure content in a manner that will be relevant to the users.
- Ensure that user-interface guidelines are in place, design is consistent across the federated portals, and users interact with similar "look and feel" to reduce relearning.
- Determine the degrees of federation required with a federated portal.
- Keep usability simple. For example, are there real requirements to "wow" users with impressive graphics, splash screens, or animations?
- Focus on the functions, components, and experience that the users want and need, not those that the designers want them to use.
- Focus on workflow, the transactions and activities that users need to perform, and develop the tools to simplify these.
- Reduce the risk of technical complexities through technical prototyping.
- Ensure that features and functions (business requirements) are not too tightly coupled to the user interface, so they can be rapidly changed to improve the user experience.

Questions You Can Ask Today

At this stage in the project, you should organize your thoughts into the following categories and ask the questions listed:

Detail the design:

- Have you completed and refined operational, component, and contents models and a recommended information architecture?

- Do you have a completed technical prototype with recommendations from all relevant participants?
- Do you have a definition of the user experience with completed user scenarios, interfaces, and models?

Plan training and development:

- Have you built a definition of training and support requirements and detailed plans for development and releases?
- Have you completed static testing and developed a master test plan?

CHAPTER 5

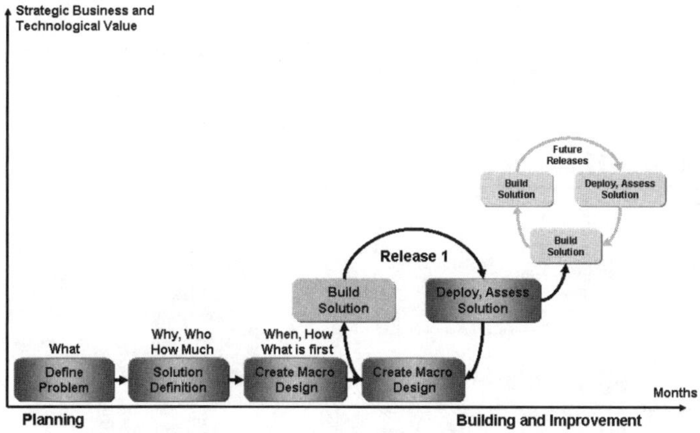

Build Solution

Personally I'm always ready to learn, although I do not always like being taught.

Sir Winston Churchill

CHAPTER OBJECTIVES

In this chapter, you learn how to build user interfaces, develop configuration data, perform the programming cycle, and complete the testing. This will enable you to assess the risk of going live and allow you to make a go/no-go decision about whether to proceed with deployment. An incremental build is important, as it allows the builder to meet specific and disparate objectives. Each build cycle addresses different programming and user experiences. As the effort iterates, more of the portal is developed and in a short time, a broad but focused solution is completed.

When you are done with this chapter, you will be able to build the portal. With this, you will be able to move on to chapter 6, in which you start to deploy the portal.

WHAT STEPS DO I NEED TO FOLLOW?

You go through the five steps shown in Figure 5.1 to complete the build:

1. Initiate solution build.

2. Prepare solution release.
3. Build solution release.
4. Test solution release.
5. Plan support and deployment.

To get you warmed up to the subject, let's walk through these five steps with Churchill's portal as a backdrop.

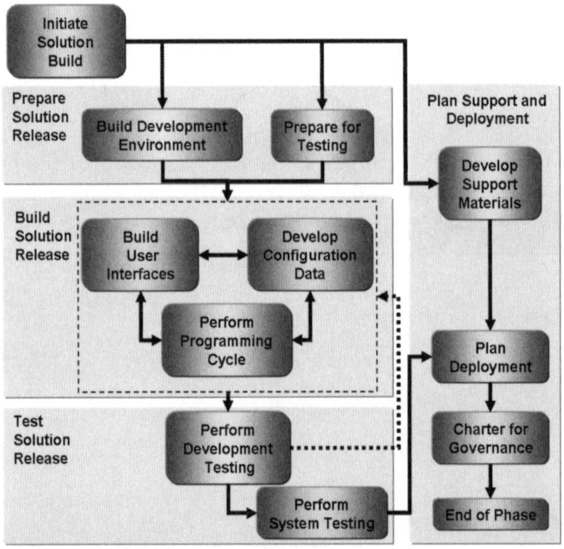

Figure 5.1: The build solution focuses on preparing, building, and testing a release.

Initiate Solution Build

In the Solution Definition, the "Release Plan" highlights the number of solution releases. The micro design breaks the release down into several build cycles and each contains several programming and user experiences resulting in the nesting of development "loops." The build prepares for deployment of a specific release of the portal by incrementally developing and testing it, until the objectives of the build cycle are achieved. The approach follows the philosophy of small build cycles and rapid deployments.

Prepare Solution Release

In preparing the solution release, you build the development environment and refine the required test plans. Preparation is essential if the testing is to be objective and meet the goals of the project. This phase should include planning the levels of testing required and ensuring that the right kinds of tests are selected. The bottom line is "if you fail to plan, then plan to fail."

Build Development Environment

You need to ensure that a suitable environment, necessary to support development, is in place. This includes everything from facilities to equipment. Based on the decisions in the macro design, you might need to acquire and install the products and tools for development, testing, documentation, deployment, and education.

For Churchill's architects, a development environment was not critical for the first release, as it was a new environment going into production for the first time. However, for ongoing and future releases, the development environment had to be different from the production environment, so the nonfunctional requirements like security and performance would not be compromised.

Prepare for Testing

In preparing for testing, you refine and complete the detailed test plans, build the test environment, check individual test plans and cases, select the testing team, and define the success criteria for going live.

Refine Test Plans

The first step is to complete the detailed test plans developed earlier in the book (in Table 3.10). The test plans specify what tests will run, in what order, and with what infrastructure, environment, and data. It also determines the test teams created for unit, integration, and system tests, as shown in Table 5.1. All the tests start small, with unit testing, and scale up.

For Churchill's architects, one of the most significant objectives of the test plans was to test the scrambling of fighters, as highlighted by the static testing experience shown in Table 4.4.

Table 5.1: Types of Testing Available

Development Testing		System Testing
Unit	Integration	System
Functional (component functions, logic, and code)	Functional (inter-component functions, interfaces), usability	Functional (inter-portal) Nonfunctionals: stress, performance, regression, capacity, recovery, configuration, security

The created test plans define how the test environment and data are set up, and how the tests are run and logged. It also prepares the test team and determines when and how the test environment is torn down.

The *unit test plan*, created by the development team, periodically checks work-in-progress. It outlines tests to verify individual functional components and modules of codes that have changed. The *integration test plan* ensures the functional component integration is tested, irrespective of whether the functional components interface with external applications. The *system test plan* ensures that the functionality of the portal is tested, including interfaces to external portals, applications, and sources of content. Both functional and non-functional tests are performed.

Churchill's architects needed to complete a comprehensive strategy for testing the effectiveness of each portal as part of the federation. They also had to consider the impact of each portal on the principal objectives of scrambling fighters to meet the raids and testing the early warning system. The approach started small, by testing its reaction to single-fighter raids. It then scaled up to test reactions to multiple raids and those by large bomber formations.

Build Test Environment

In building the test environment, you prepare, build, and assemble a test environment from plans, and ensure that the test tools are installed and appropriately integrated, as shown in Table 5.2.

Table 5.2: Test Environment Build Table

Factors to consider	Definition
Scope of the environment	The size of the simulated environment, based on the type of tests
Simulated components	The simulated applications and software and extracted portions of live files and data, with confidential fields encrypted
Tools, transaction engines	Simulated transactions or user populations

With the portal outlined, the right software components need to be identified from the object libraries and assembled into the test environment. This requires defining a baseline for levels, versions, and locations of components. A release-management process, through a configuration tool, assures that the correct versions of the components are removed from the library and tracked with audit trails. They are compiled, installed, and packaged for promotion into the test environment. Computer simulations and models are used to reduce testing time, complexity, and cost.

Churchill's architects created several simulated test environments. For example, at Bentley Prior, the environment was set up for testing the early-warning system and fighter scrambles. This required using individual radar stations and observer posts as part of the test environment. Friendly aircraft from the northern groups simulated enemy raids by flying over the southern coast to test the effectiveness of the early-warning system. The testers were not aware that the aircraft were friendly.

Check Individual Test Plans

Each of the individual test plans is checked for completeness, as shown in Table 5.3. Test plans contain test cases that define the functions and features at a sufficiently low level of detail to verify specific conditions.

Table 5.3: Checking Individual Test Plans

Test Plan Questions	Unit	Integration	System
Does it provide for all required functions?	✓	✓	✓
Are all assumptions and dependencies clearly identified?	✓	✓	
Is the testing strategy valid and feasible?	✓	✓	
Are the testing entrance and exit criteria specified?	✓	✓	
Are there enough test cases to verify all the functions?	✓		
Are there enough technical/business test cases?		✓	✓
Are the test case efforts identified to facilitate testing preparation and execution monitoring?	✓		

Churchill's architects created test plans at the unit level to test the responsiveness of individual radar stations, at the integration level to test the responsiveness of combined radar stations within Bentley Prior's early warning system, and at the system level to test integration with other federated portals.

Check Individual Test Cases

Test cases consist of input data and anticipated results for each test condition, which are then compared to actual results. Specific to a test script, a test case includes detailed instructions for setting up and executing the test and then evaluating the results. A test case is outlined for each testing objective, specifying what is being tested, how, with what data, with what expected outcome, and with what results. For each test plan, the test case is reviewed to answer the questions in Table 5.4.

Table 5.4: Checking Individual Test Cases

Test Case Questions	Unit	Integration	System
Is the test case's purpose complete?	✓		✓
Are all dependencies identified?		✓	
Are set-up requirements explicit and clear?	✓		✓
Are normal/abnormal completions identified?	✓		✓
Are the operator instructions explicit and clear?		✓	
Are conditions in place to test intended variations?	✓		✓
Are results, messages, and return codes verified?	✓	✓	✓
Can the test case be automated?	✓		
Has each test allocated a business severity and testing priority?		✓	

For Churchill's architects, this was the equivalent of setting up test cases at a unit level to verify the test conditions of the individual radar stations (unit logic) and to determine whether the responsiveness met the anticipated results. The test cases at integration level tested the responsiveness of several combined radar stations as part of the overall radar chain.

Select the Testing Team

Who should do the testing? An independent group, not directly involved in the project to date, should do the testing to ensure objectivity and due diligence. The group needs a clear mandate with the authority to make go/no-go decisions. This requires strong executive support. Sponsors might be involved as observers, to increase their understanding and buy-in.

Churchill's architects went outside of the all-important southern organizations and groups, who were the primary beneficiaries of the first releases. They selected personnel from the northern groups as independent members and observers for the testing team, primarily to maintain objectivity.

Define Success Criteria for Going Live

The project requires success criteria for going live. The success criteria are used later to identify risk factors and refine service levels. Some examples of these criteria might include the following:

- Deploy the portal without disrupting existing services and provide a continuum of operation for a fixed, designated period.
- Meet the expected levels of services through collected and measured feedback.

Churchill's architects had some very clear goals from which they could define the critical success criteria for going live. They had to meet certain service levels, as defined in chapter 2. In order of priority, these included meeting the overall fighter scramble time by squadron and location; staying within the Ultra decoding and dissemination window; and delivering supply-chain indicators for the executive dashboard within a decision window.

BUILD SOLUTION RELEASES

The steps discussed in this section are iterative. They build the user interfaces, develop configuration data, and perform a programming cycle. This is the core of the chapter and is fundamental to the project's overall success.

Build User Interfaces

All design specifications for the user interfaces are formatted and optimized for the portal and then tested. Any development decisions are documented for use in the next build iteration.

For Churchill's architects, several different models had to be completed, as discussed below.

Bentley Prior User Interface

The map model was deployed across all Fighter Command operations centers. Since the decision-making processes were hierarchical, the map model had to be consistent. The tote board model displaying squadron readiness was unique to group headquarters. The decisions associated with the development of the tote board model would have related to its scope, how many sectors and squadrons would be displayed by it, and how it would evolve.

Bletchley Park User Interface

The traffic analysis model was unique to Bletchley Park. It required the identification of traffic patterns and then mapping colors against these patterns. The development decisions associated with the model would have related to the geographic extent and number of wireless stations transmitting Enigma signals.

Storey's Gate User Interface

The map room's indicator model was critical to Storey's Gate, and an executive dashboard was critical for Churchill. It required the identification of key indicators from Bentley Prior, as shown in Table 4.1, by the Whitehall ministries and Bletchley Park. Initially, most of these indicators would have come directly from the original source in the supply chain, presented in reports. As the importance of these indicators was recognized, however, the data was collected into a storage model to decrease the lag time. Today, a data mart would be used for this, underpinned by a logical data model.

The design decisions associated with this model would have related to the number of indicators delivered in each build and release, and the lag time for these, which was critical for real-time modeling in a battle situation.

Whitehall User Interface

The ministry of aircraft production's indicator model was a superset of supply-chain indicators for the industrial production of fighters. Storey's Gate extracted a subset of these indicators for the map room.

The design decisions associated with this model would have related to the minimum number of indicators required to manage the supply chain successfully. Also, the design had to address how the ministry decision-makers using the model would interface with Bentley Prior for fighter loss numbers.

Develop Configuration Data

The content attributes and taxonomies are reviewed to facilitate the development of portal code. The portal code is developed so that it is able to access content. The content also must be accessible by the portal code.

Understand the Content Attributes and Taxonomies

A portal provides the ability to create, define, populate, and manage a *taxonomy*, or directory. The taxonomy is the basis of the navigation scheme. It provides different views for user needs.

Churchill's federated portal had to leverage data from multiple sources in different formats, like paper, image, electronic, and voice, as shown in Table 5.5. Churchill's architects had to examine each organization closely to determine the content attributes and taxonomies and how each federated portal was going to access this content, and the initial mapping of content to the data stores.

Table 5.5: Information Flow Among the Organizations

Destination Source	Bentley Prior	Bletchley Park	Whitehall	Storey's Gate
Bentley Prior	Management decision-making	Requests for intelligence	Downed fighter locations, CRO	Fighter/pilot loss reports
Bletchley Park	Order of battle report	Management decision-making	Enemy supply chain, resources	Ultra decrypts, reports
Whitehall	Fighter production report	Orders, requests	Management decision-making	Supply-chain indicators
Storey's Gate	Orders, requests	Orders, requests	Orders, requests	Executive decision-making

Develop the Portal Code

Ensuring that the portal code is able to access content requires an understanding of how the content is handled by the portal. The content flow must be understood from its aggregation, to how it is processed and stored, to its dissemination to users. For Churchill's architects, this involved breaking down the content flow for each of the four federated portals, as listed below.

Bentley Prior Content Flow

By far the most complex operation, Bentley Prior aggregated and integrated dissimilar pieces of information: radar positioning data, observer corps estimates and coordinates, pilot observations, Ultra decryptions, Y station plots, and information from Whitehall. The data was aggregated in real-time by communication through the *filter room*, as shown in Figure 5.2.

The filter room was an information clearinghouse, a telephone exchange with switchboards that collated, cross-checked, and simplified the intelligence. It translated and processed the information through its own plotting table, mapping positions and determining whether the sighting was hostile or friendly. The processing was not reliant on data storage, but on interpreting it directly into real-time models.

The filtered information was disseminated to the Bentley Prior operations center. Much work had to be done to interpret the aggregated information before the final plot could be seen on the map table. This information was then cascaded down to group 11 and its sector operations centers. Not all information came direct from its original source. Within the sector operations centers, information on enemy aircraft in flight was phoned through by radar dispatch, integrated with information and reports from observer corps and pilots, and laid out on a map table. At group headquarters and sector stations, the decision was made on how to best react to the raid—whether to use intercept fighters or anti-aircraft fire, or both. This information was then disseminated and cascaded to pilots and anti-aircraft. Within subsequent future releases, barrage balloon command, bomber command, air ministry would all be added.

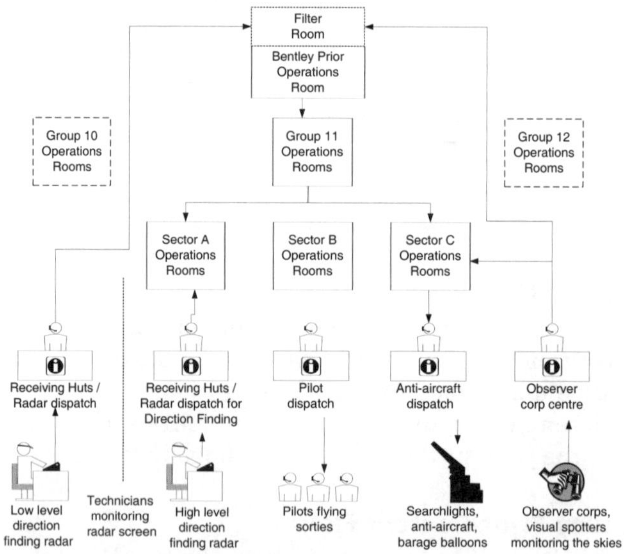

Figure 5.2: Integrated information from radar, observers, and pilots was plotted on the map model and used for decision-making.

Bletchley Park Content Flow

The Y stations intercepted Enigma messages and transmitted these to Bletchley Park, either by courier or over secure lines. There, the data was aggregated in real-time through a control room, where the controllers controlled the flow of cribs to hut 6, as shown in Figure 5.3.

Hut 6 contained the cryptologists, the bombes, and the staff that ran the operation. The decoding and general breaking of codes was done in the crib room, which worked particularly closely with the registration room. Collecting cribs was important for decrypting, and a library was established.

The raw, decrypted messages from hut 6 were disseminated to the adjacent hut 3, which further processed these and added value. Hut 3 performed language emendation and translation, evaluated the intelligence contents and determined its reliability, sorted it into categories, and selected the recipients for its dissemination. The decrypted messages were filed in the index room of hut 3. Feedback from the hut 3 intelligence section was based on previously decoded messages and the growing body of knowledge. The intelligence section determined which messages were to be given top priority and assigned resources to these. After checking the advisers' work, the release was evaluated for precedence and accuracy and passed to the Special Liaison Units (SLU) for dissemination. Any action taken by a recipient based on an Enigma decrypt had to be strictly controlled.

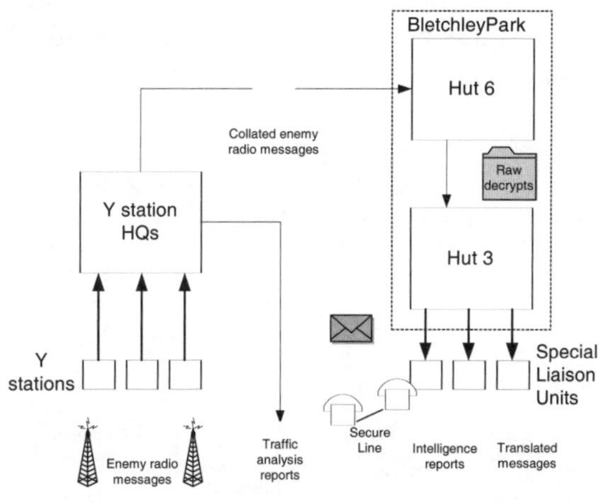

Figure 5.3: Information on decrypts flowed from Y stations through Bletchley Park and distribution through SLUs.

Whitehall Content Flow

The ministry of aircraft production aggregated and integrated information from the supply chain, which included the factories and shop floors, the transportation network, military RAF depots, distribution centers, and networks.

Production data was collected through data counting and statistical techniques, like sampling inspections and defect estimates. The data was passed back in batch mode to the ministries through paper reports, as shown in Figure 5.4. Detailed records would have been stored in a mechanized filing system, useful for rapid access and based on the logical data model, as shown in Figure in 3.3. Today, the data would be extracted, transformed, and loaded into a data mart/warehouse, the modern-day equivalent.

The ministry of aircraft production was particularly important to the supply chain. There, Beaverbrook short-circuited red tape and established a direct link with group 11 Air Marshall Keith Park. He would call Park daily to determine the number of fighters required.

Beaverbrook needed reliable inventory information, not just from the supply chain, but also from the Civilian Repair Organization (CRO). Beaverbrook opted to run a minimum inventory so he could roll out as many complete aircraft as possible. He safeguarded production from raids by the distribution of manufacturing not only to factories but also to small garages all over the country. The operational CRO required information from Bentley Prior so it could rapidly locate downed aircraft for repair. This information would affect how quickly aircraft could be put back into the air. Within the CRO, special "low loaders" quickly collected damaged aircraft. Those damaged beyond repair were stripped of all usable parts and placed in spare-parts storage. Even

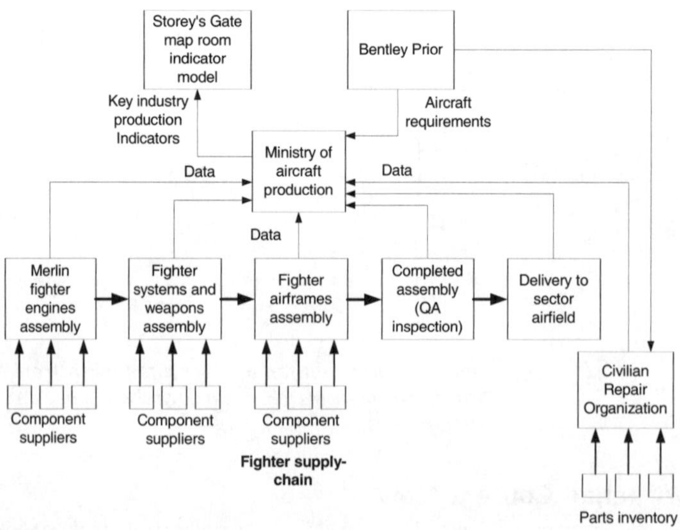

Figure 5.4: The flow of data from key elements of the supply chain into the ministry was synthesized into indicators.

enemy aircraft were dismantled and smelted for new aircraft. As a result, Beaverbrook was able to maximize production.

Storey's Gate Content Flow

As the ultimate top command center (or super portal), aggregated information was synthesized and carefully prepared for Churchill and the War Cabinet. For the most part, it was passed from the ministries in batch mode through paper reports. This was further supported by Churchill's indicators. The indicator model (the executive dashboard) operated in near real-time to provide information on the overall picture of business events, like changes in battle fronts and the performance of key elements of the supply chain. As a result, Churchill had a big-picture view of what the other federated portals could see.

Perform Programming Cycle

In the programming cycle, the enterprise's core logic and procedures are developed and tested, the physical data model is designed, and the next programming cycle is prepared. This step represents the inner loop of an incremental development process that can repeat many times for each build, running serially or in parallel, or both. The functions and features of a specific release, business events, and use-case scenarios drive the length and number of instances of a programming cycle, the number of modules to be developed, and the size of the programming team.

Develop Logic and Procedures

Individual program modules are developed for the functional components in accordance with design specifications and quality assured through a process of visual inspection, where the code is compared to the logical flows from the detail design.

For Churchill's architects, this step was required for setting up the individual organizations; that is, moving from the drawing board to the functioning unit. The architects had to incorporate in each organization the unique, core business logic and the if/then conditions to allow processing in real-time. To do this, each organization was treated as a black box with inputs and outputs, as shown in Figure 5.5.

Test Logic and Procedures

Individual program modules are tested for functionality in a development environment to determine that they do what they are supposed to do. Typically, the programmer does this to catch obvious errors before more comprehensive testing.

For Churchill's architects, the first programming cycle of the first build was for Bentley Prior. It related to the business event "imminent raid on airfields" based on the planned development shown in Table 4.7. This step tested the black-box logic for functionality, and the inputs and outputs for expected results. The goal was for each operations center to respond to radar, model the information, go through a decision-making process, and then deploy fighters to an intercept point, at a specified height and in predefined numbers.

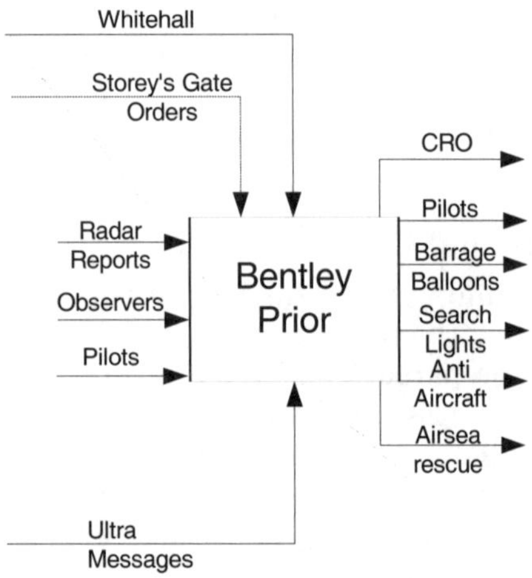

Figure 5.5: The first programming cycle for the build was with the Fighter Command operations centers.

Design Physical Data Model and Implement the Data Mart

At this point, the physical data model is designed. It converts the logical data model from Figure 3.3 to a physical data-storage construct made up of tables and files. This results in the implementation of the data mart. Finally, the previously sourced data is cleansed, loaded in the data mart, and readied for testing.

For Churchill's architects, this required the physical construction of a filing system using punch-card technologies. These were configured to reflect the physical record structure of the logical data model and used by Whitehall.

Prepare for the Next Programming Cycle

As you go through the programming cycle, each developer refines the performance and evaluation goals, builds and unit-tests the code, updates for the next implementation design models, and reviews the results to refine the goals for the next programming cycle. The output of the build procedures is an executable copy of the program, required files, and links. It is essential to record details on how the system is generated and any required passwords, and to document all key decisions taken for use in the next releases.

For Churchill's architects, the second programming cycle of the first build was also for Bentley Prior and the business event "imminent raid on airfields." However, in this cycle, the goal was for each operations center to respond to a different source of input, specifically, warnings from the observer corps, who could provide much more detailed reports on aircraft type and numbers. Also, the output was to deploy anti-aircraft fire. This required the dissemination of information through a different command. Both these required slightly modified logic.

Test Solution Release

The development and system testing is performed as defined in the test plans. Both are hardcore, dynamic testing activities and are absolutely critical to the overall iterative approach.

Perform Development Testing

Defining the approach to development testing includes unit and integration testing, according to Table 5.2. Although some testing takes place in development, the testing in this phase is more formalized.

Define Approach to Testing

The build assembles the physical components incrementally into the test environment, according to the test plan and the levels of progressive testing required. Testing is conducted at increasing levels of detail, where components are unit-tested first, then assembled and integrated, and then tested again. This scales up to the next level of integration, as application subsystems are integrated and tested, and then the applications are integrated and tested themselves. The test environment is continually adjusted through incremental builds. The testing tracks the test plan and follows the test scripts and cases.

The test team monitors the results through the progressive levels of testing to determine what parts have been successfully tested, how many variances were detected, and their overall impact. The output of the testing is a set of results, a pass or a fail. The test plans define pass or fail criteria for the selected tests. If any tests fail, the library is notified so the components are removed or marked accordingly. Based on the severity of the failure, the section either passes the problem for a re-review or for re-tests.

Churchill's architects had to ensure that components were individually tested and then integrated for a scaled-up integration test. Doing this successfully required understanding how the overall business objectives were achieved through the combination of components. For example, the event-management component was extremely important to the event-tracking system, as was information aggregation and publishing to modeling information on the map table. Collaboration was essential to decision-making, but so were all the former components that needed to be integrated.

Unit Testing

With development complete, the results of the programming cycle are individually tested, sometimes by the programmers. Specifically, the customized functional components are examined and unit-tested by initially testing the program code, the internal logic and design functions, the test paths and conditions, the test exception conditions and error-handling, and the interfaces between modules under test. This step also tests the portal code through test cases, for situations where actual and predicted results may differ.

Before the portal is tested as a whole, each unit needs to be verified as defect-free. This testing verifies the execution of functional components, and not the interface with external applications. For Churchill's architects, this involved testing the component logic within each of the four federated portals:

- At Bentley Prior, Dowding's architects had an extensive and complex network to test. Unit testing was critical to ensure each operations center, radar station, or observer post functioned according to design.
- At Bletchley Park, most of the unit testing centered on hut 6 and the breaking of Enigma code signals from a single source, or one set of related messages. This verified whether the correct processes were in place. The emphasis was on the speed of code-breaking, and the process was continually refined to reflect this.
- At Whitehall, the unit testing centered on business processing of individual ministries, notably the ministry of aircraft production. It verified whether the right information and indicators were collected. It also tested the storage and retrieval mechanisms of the punch-card filing system and record structure.
- At Storey's Gate, the unit testing focused on specific functional components. It tested the flow of information and indicators into the portal, and ensured that these were modeled properly by the map room's indicator model.

Integration (and Usability) Testing

Integration testing ensures that the various programs and functional components within the portal communicate with each other. The integration test plan details the testing methods, testing tasks, and responsibilities. The test acceptance criteria verify this and document the results. Interfaces to other applications and content sources are tested at a later point.

Integration testing validates the proper execution of several components or subsystems together. It tests hardware, communications, networks, data stores, data processing (applications), processes, and organization. It tests the portal as a whole, including nonsoftware components such as documentation, to ensure the system meets the stated functional requirements and performs within the target operational environment.

Usability testing provides feedback about whether the portal is meeting its usability goals for ease of use, interaction, navigation, or display. The testing verifies with users, through scenarios and observations, that the interfaces provide adequate levels of support. In creating the test cases, it is important to identify the 20 percent of use-case scenarios that will be executed 80 percent of the time.

For Churchill's architects, this was testing the black-box logic of each of the four organizational federated portals. This required measuring the inputs and outputs and then comparing them to expectations and SLAs:

- At Bentley Prior, the integration testing ensured each of the operations centers integrated according to design, for example, headquarters to group, group to sector, and sector to fighter. Fighter and sector stations were connected only by a telephone line. The former were important, as sector controllers could strategically place squadrons closer to the attacking enemy. It also tested the integration of stations to their commands, for radar and observer posts. Finally, it tested the integration between fighter operations, radar, and observers. Usability testing was particularly important in the operations centers and the map model users.
- At Bletchley Park, the integration testing centered on the integration of the Y stations, hut 3, and hut 6. The focus was not just on breaking Enigma code, but on pooling this information with previous messages and the enormous bank of knowledge created. The output framed the messages in a larger context of what was happening on the enemy front, to help ensure that this intelligence was used effectively.
- At Whitehall, the integration testing centered on the business processing of several ministries, notably aircraft production and, in

supporting roles, supplies and transportation. Testing reviewed the information sourced from the supply chain to give an overall view, including the information from the punch-card filing system and record structure.

- Storey's Gate was the overall command center for the whole operation. Although the other federated portals operated autonomously, Storey's Gate was the master of masters. The integration testing here centered on the decision-making processes and how all the major functional components combined to support this and the map room indicator model.

Reviewing the programming cycle experiences is essential for future planning. Examining the test results against the detailed goals uncovers prerequisites and adjusts the goals for future cycles. For example, for Bentley Prior, initially it was thought that the long-range readings from the radar stations should only be transmitted to the group and sector operations centers because the fighter stations would not require them. When this proved otherwise, refinements of integration and usability goals were rapidly made.

Perform System Testing

System testing is performed according to Table 5.1 to verify the proper execution of all the portal components, including the interfaces with other portals. Both functional and nonfunctional tests are performed to verify that the portal is operationally sound in a productionlike environment.

The functional and nonfunctional tests execute according to documented procedures, specifications, and test cases, and verify successful execution of all new, changed, or affected paths. The test team maintains a log of the tests executed, fixes problems, and retests in unit and integration tests. The team also promotes fixes according to configuration-management procedures, runs regression tests in the test environment, documents findings and results, and initiates an action plan for unresolved problems.

The testing team raises issues, enforces standards, makes architectural decisions, and revises architecture models, as appropriate. For example, issues might arise about the developer's difficulties in interpreting architectural templates policies, or discrepancies might be found between system test results and integration test results. Based on these results, the team and users determine whether to exit the current build cycle or add additional programming cycles.

System testing is completed when the team completes the tests outlined in Table 5.6 and collects both quantitative and qualitative data.

Table 5.6: Types of Nonfunctional Testing

Testing	Definition
Stress	Verifies that the portal handles peak volumes in short periods placed against various components
Performance	Verifies that the specific performance objectives of the portal, such as response times, are met and that any potential bottlenecks are identified and corrected
Capacity	Verifies that the specific capacity objectives of the portal, such as planned growth, are met
Recovery	Verifies the portal and manual procedures are in place to allow the portal to be restarted with full data integrity following a hardware, software, or communications failure
Configuration	Verifies the portal operates properly in the target hardware, software, and communications environment
Security	Verifies the portal protects access to facilities, and that data meets the security requirements

The Integration Challenge

For Churchill's architects, some of the integration between the four portals was particularly challenging because of the interface and security implications shown in Table 5.7. For example, caution had to be taken in handling Ultra, so that it was not disseminated through an insecure interface into an organizational hierarchy prone to security breaches.

Table 5.7: Integrating the Applications

	Bentley Prior	Bletchley Park	Whitehall	Storey's Gate
Bentley Prior	Telephone hierarchy	None	Direct	Direct
Bletchley Park	SLU	N/A	Via Storey's Gate	SLU
Whitehall	Telephone, teleprinters	None	N/A	Two-way
Storey's Gate	Telephone, teleprinters	Telephone, teleprinters	Telephone, teleprinters	N/A

At Bletchley Park, Special Liaison Units (SLUs) were created by the RAF under the auspices of Captain Fred Winterbotham for the sole task of security and distribution. Information from a top-secret source would be distributed to the director of intelligence of the service ministries, as shown in Figure 5.6.

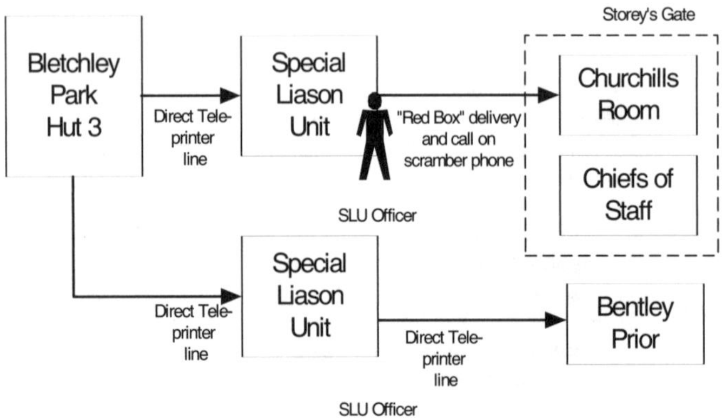

Figure 5.6: The dissemination of information was performed by various SLUs and distributed through different channels, such as teleprinters, bag couriers, and secure links.

The list of the recipients of Enigma information was strictly limited to a grand total of nine: the military chiefs of staff and of intelligence; the chief of Fighter Command; the chief of the Home Guard; and the prime minister. SLUs were located at Bletchley Park and then later overseas in Gibraltar, Malta, Cyprus, and Egypt, to be closer to the front lines.

System Testing the Federated Portal

For Churchill's architects, system testing was where the portal was viewed holistically for the first time, as shown in Figure 5.7, and some critical testing could begin. System testing was critical to Bentley Prior, particularly testing its overall sense and response. For weeks, the entire early-warning network system, interlinking all the various components, was tested incessantly, with British aircraft simulating enemy formations. Critical nonfunctional requirements like stress, performance, and capacity were tested as various conditions were simulated and adjusted. As this testing evolved, the RAF was able to perfect a formula for intercepting the raids. In effect, fighters needed at least 15 minutes of early warning to scramble and get into a position at 20,000 feet to be effective. The pilots had a few minutes' margin of safety in racing into their positions.

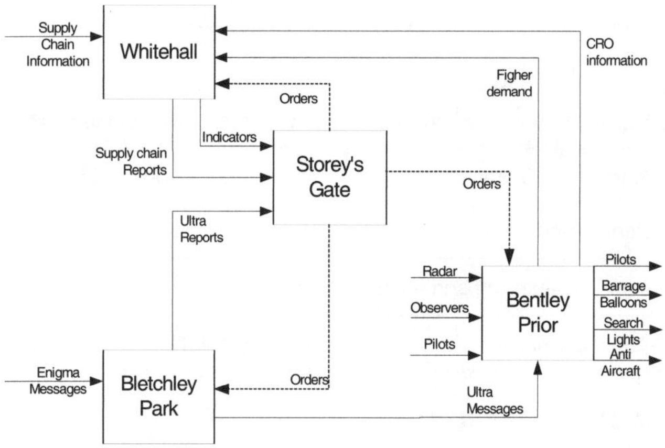

Figure 5.7: This black-box view of the organizations represents the inputs and outputs of all the organizations.

Another example of system testing was the cross-checking of messages at Bletchley Park. For important messages, this could be taken a step further, by reacting to a particular event in a certain way and then monitoring the enemy response by reading the Ultra signals. Critical nonfunctional requirements like configuration and security were tested as various conditions were simulated and adjusted. These feedback loops were essential later on for Churchill, as he could better understand the mind of his enemy.

These are very good examples of how a complex system is refined to perform at its optimum through iterative testing. It also highlights the value of testing, as this was a life and death situation for the pilots.

Review Portal Results

You must review and assess the results of the tests for any unexpected issues that might have arisen. For example, the results might have passed all the criteria, but all expectations might not have been met. Unexpected performance degradation might be an issue.

For Churchill's architects, the output of this review is Table 5.8, which outlines the types of issues uncovered. The impact of any identified issues should be assessed through a try-and-see approach, based on intuition and some guesswork. At this point, the alternatives for going live are determined.

Table 5.8: Issues Table

Issues	Definition
Operations center interconnections	Unreliable; calls need to be rerouted.
SLU integration to Storey's Gate	There are time delays because of security procedures.
Portal startup requiring configuration	Startup abruptly stops and needs manual intervention.
Links requiring balancing and tuning	Bottlenecks on 20% of the lines cause resource conflicts.
Integration bug discovered	An integration bug might have a serous impact on SLAs.

Assess Deployment Risk

The risk is reassessed to evaluate whether any test issues prevent deployment. An unsatisfactory output invokes a review of the alternatives and a step back to testing or a complete back-out of the process. A satisfactory output continues to the next step. This process is critical, as it might be the last opportunity to stop a risky implementation. It is particularly important because the emphasis is on the business over the technical, and issues are ranked according to their impact on the business. From this process, you need to answer the following questions:

- Could the portal adversely affect the existing service-level agreements (SLAs)?
- Could the portal have a negative effect on current business operations, groups, processes, or customers?

Once risks have been identified, key project stakeholders need to assess their individual and collective impacts to determine where they are significant. These are reviewed to provide recommendations and to decide whether alternatives need to be assessed.

With the risks identified, Churchill's architects assessed the individual and collective impacts to determine where they were significant. For example, could the existing fighter production be disrupted, or could the existing military command structures be affected by the addition of Storey's Gate? These were reviewed with key stakeholders (Churchill, Beaverbrook, and Dowding) with recommendations and whether alternatives needed to be assessed.

Plan Support and Deployment

Planning for deployment develops support materials and functions. It is the start of the transition process of delivering the solution to the organization and getting people ready for it. This is a critical success factor that plays an important part in user acceptability.

Develop Support Materials

Support materials are developed according to the training and support requirements identified during the micro design in chapter 3. These materials are collected throughout the project, so this step merely assembles them.

Assess Support Material Requirements

Any turnover from development to operations requires the transfer of knowledge for the successful continued operation and maintenance of a portal. Through on-the-job training, the portal support team goes through observations, education, and media provided by the developers, so this team should be well-positioned to maintain the portal. A portal maintenance turnover package is tested to ensure that all required materials turned over are effective.

For Churchill's architects, the challenge was finding the right level to pitch the materials at. The staff came from different backgrounds of technical knowledge, including military, civil service, academic, and civilian. Therefore, different documents had to be created, as shown in Table 5.9. For example, the user guide provided the how-to, or procedural, information, in the form of detailed tasks. Background information (the "why") was in a separate book, explaining the objectives and how these will be met by the portal. The manager's overview provided a more complete view of the overall functionality. The tutorial provided a walkthrough of access and security.

Table 5.9: Developing Support Materials for Staff

Categories	Bentley Prior	Bletchley Park	Whitehall	Storey's Gate
User guide (operations manual)	Map and tote models	Bombes	Production indicators	Map room indicator model
Background information	Purpose and service levels	Purpose and service levels	Purpose and service levels	Purpose and key decisions
Manager's overview	Operations centers	Hut 3 and hut 6	Individual ministries	War Cabinet
Tutorial	Access and security	Ultra security	Access and security	Access and security

Develop Support Functions

Support functions are created at three levels, so the organization can meet the portal's SLAs and answer questions related to the performance improvement, content management, and lead-indicator lag time.

First-level Support

Frontline support functions involve those staff members who monitor, operate, and control the production environment. Frontline support is traditionally attributed to the operations staff, such as a help desk or call center. Collectively, these staff members are responsible for the following portal-management functions:

- *Operations management* determines that all the programs needed to support the portal are started and run. It ensures help desk services are available and includes on-line, batch, and network management.
- *Change management* determines the planning and testing of changes as required. Whether bug-fixes, patches, or modifications, the changes are managed so as not to affect the portal service in anyway.
- *Problem management* detects and determines problems within the portal. It then leads to their resolution and recovery in an optimum time. This also includes proactively preventing problems.
- *Availability management* determines the planning, testing, and implementation of procedures required to alert the organization about an impending outage and recover portal services back to normal.
- *Service-level management* manages all the above functions so the portal meets the SLAs laid out with the users.

First-level support functions for Churchill's federated portals were oriented to keep the portals operational at all times according to service levels. The priority of first-level support was on getting things right from the start, working proactively to ensure a smooth-running operation. This was mission-critical for Bentley Prior, Storey's Gate, and Bletchley Park, where problems had to be solved very quickly and effectively. Testing helped orient the test team to the support functions and level of support required when things did not go right.

Second-level Support

This level supports the front line, providing backup support and more specialized functions like a technical support group responsible for these management functions:

- *Performance management* measures how well your portal is performing and meeting user expectations for service-response time and performance levels. Real-time monitoring tools help identify bottlenecks, and performance alerts determine environmental degradation. These are essential in taking appropriate actions to prevent downtime.

- *Capacity management* determines the throughput capacity of the portal, based on likely utilization, and establishes the current and maximum levels. A cost/benefit analysis of additional capacity investments should be determined.
- *Security management* determines violations of security against the portal that could interfere with the overall service delivery. This is becoming an increasingly complex function with the risks associated with the Internet, such as hacking, viruses, and deliberate sabotage. Online security alerts are important in detecting potential problems.

For Churchill's federated portals, second-level support functions were oriented to proactively ensure that the portal's operation was uninhibited by growth in communities, content, and functionality. Supervisors ensured that enough staff were available. For example, hut 6 code-breakers required high levels of administration to meet performance targets, as did Whitehall. Bletchley Park and Storey's Gate needed very effective security management.

Third-level Support

Third-level support is responsible for application management, which requires a more detailed knowledge of applications within the portal. Supporting applications through a portal is vastly more complicated than traditional application-support because of application interdependencies. The 24/7 operations window further inhibits quick problem-source identification. Support needs to be organized along end-to-end flows of transactions, across applications and portal products.

Third-level support functions for Churchill's federated portals required an understanding of the portal interdependencies for information. For example, how Storey's Gate shared indicators with Whitehall had to be understood in context with the use of the indicator model. The experience of system testing the inputs and outputs between the organizations needed to be carried into support through the staff and documentation.

Plan Deployment

Deployment of the plan is performed after the completion of all the build cycles. It is done once for the release. It prepares for the deployment of the release by refining the deployment plans, first developed in macro design, based on the experience gained in the build cycles. For Churchill's architects, this produced a more complete release model, as shown in Table 5.10.

Table 5.10: Release Model

Portal	Release 1
Bentley Prior	Integration of group 11 operations centers to radar, pilots, and observers
Bletchley Park	Integration to Storey's Gate and Bentley Prior, complete manual procedures
Whitehall	Integration to Storey's Gate through indicator model
Storey's Gate	Integration to Bletchley Park, Whitehall supply chain (indicator model)

Create a Charter for Portal Governance

Creating a charter for portal governance further refines the governance framework from chapter 1. This is particularly relevant to a federated portal, as a number of fundamental questions need to be answered prior to the next release, for example:

- What qualification is required to enter the federation?
- How are new portal opportunities reviewed?
- What funding is needed?
- How can confidence be built around security and privacy?

A governance framework needs a charter to address the above questions. It requires the following:

- A *mission* that defines the purpose and approach to nurturing and managing the federated portal and its growth within the organization
- An *organization* such as a committee to define the structure, reporting relationships, and connections between the portal staff and their counterparts in other areas of the organization
- *Roles and responsibilities* that define the required work for the portal groups and the individuals who will perform them
- *Processes* that define the activity flow for the necessary actions in response to events, and the creation of portal outcomes
- *Measures* that define the accountability mechanisms for the portal at the enterprise, operating, process, group, team, and individual levels

- *Policies* that define the portal decisions with associated boundaries, standards, and latitude, including portal/Web policy and usage
- A *content model* that defines consistency in content and its portrayal on Web sites, so that decentralized execution of content management can be performed in a coordinated, well-planned manner

For Churchill's architects, it was obvious that the federated portal would expand quickly, in terms of new communities and content—after all, it was a war-time situation. The governance framework was very much in the hands of the War Cabinet and Churchill, who had almost dictatorial control of resources and projects. Nevertheless, there is little doubt that they had to go through many of the considerations presented in the charter.

Conclusion

The following sections summarize the major points of this chapter and how they relate to your business today. For more information on these concepts, search the Internet for these keywords and phrases: *integration planning and testing*, *user interfaces*, *software build and test*, *functional / nonfunctional*, *integration and regression testing*, *support materials and functions*, and *governance*.

Major Points, Considerations, and Lessons Learned

- For Churchill's architects, this chapter was critical, given the complexity of the portal environment. Testing would bring important issues to light.

Best Practices for Your Organization

- Document all development decisions for use in the next build iteration.
- Build in small cycles, integrate, and test.
- "If you fail to plan, then plan to fail." Include planning for the level of testing required, and be sure to select the right kind of tests.
- Select from a broad array of available nonfunctional tests that test the availability of a solution.
- Assign the operations staff ownership of testing, to maintain objectivity.
- Review the results and assess the business and technical risks through the test process.
- Define alternatives to launch (e.g., withdrawal), including back-out plans.
- Use computer simulations and models to reduce testing time, complexity, and cost.

- Ensure that an independent test group performs the testing.
- Ensure the testing is not just based on application or function, but also incorporates nonfunctional testing.
- Develop support materials and functions.
- Create and deploy a portal governance framework.

Questions You Can Ask Today

At this stage in the project, you should organize your thoughts into the following categories and ask the questions listed:

Prepare a solution release:

- Do you have a completed development and test environment, with test plans refined to test-case level?

Build a solution release:

- Have teams completed user interfaces, the programming cycle, and configuration data for the first release?

Test solution release:

- Has performance and system testing of all predefined test criteria been completed?

Plan support and deployment:

- Do you have complete support materials, with an outline of the deployment plan?

CHAPTER 6

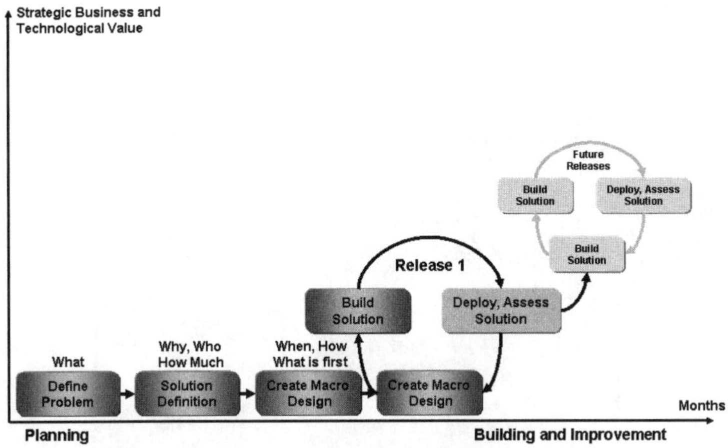

Deploy, Assess Solution

It is a mistake to try to look too far ahead. The chain of destiny can only be grasped one link at a time.

Sir Winston Churchill

CHAPTER OBJECTIVES

In this chapter, you learn how to complete the final testing. You prepare and configure the deployment environment, support organization, and processes to deliver and assess the solution. The activity takes the output of chapter 5 and deploys the portal release into production through a carefully controlled pilot. You identify and assess significant risks and relevant issues that might affect deployment, and if required, invoke earlier plans.

When you are done with this chapter, you will be able to deploy and run the portal in production and complete your project for that particular release.

WHAT STEPS DO I NEED TO FOLLOW?

You go through the following three steps to complete deployment, as shown in Figure 6.1:

1. Initiate deployment.

2. Deploy portal.
3. End project release.

To get you warmed up to the subject, let's walk through these three steps with Churchill as a backdrop.

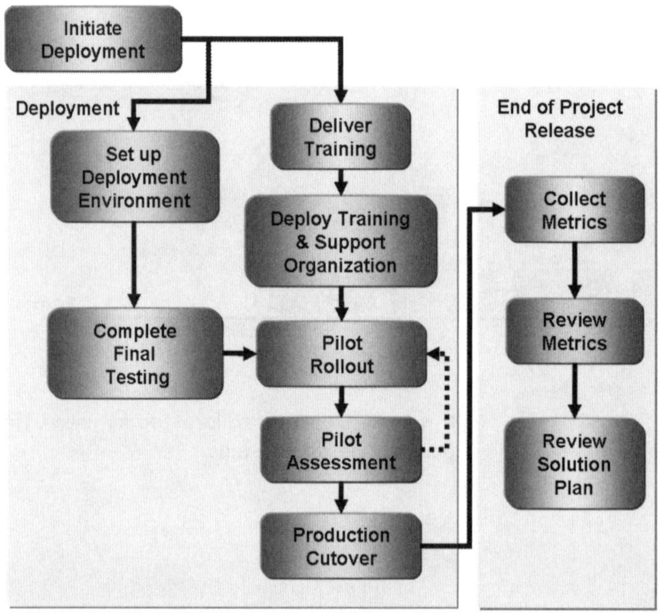

Figure 6.1: Deploy the portal release.

Initiate Deployment

The macro design phase developed a plan for deploying a pilot that would determine user groups within each community and who would use the pilot first. At the end of each release, the pilot is deployed to the users once it has gone through final testing.

Deployment

The overall deployment phases involve setting up the deployment environment and completing final testing. The complexity of a portal, in terms of the number of products, requires a carefully controlled deployment through a pilot into a well-controlled environment. This testing is critical because it is the last opportunity to prevent a flawed deployment. Testing has to be objective, honest, and balanced. The testers should be as independent as possible. Incentives might be needed to ensure objectivity.

Set Up Deployment Environment

The portal is loaded incrementally as the hardware and software are set up in the production environment, processes, organization, and tools. A configuration tool is set up so that the integrity of the library is maintained. A release-management process is also set up, with version control, to assure that the correct components are used from the library.

Incremental Loading of Portal

Loading of the portal is performed only on a satisfactory outcome of testing. The portal release requires careful and controlled deployment from the test environment into the live production environment. It is checked for approved versions of components, like the levels of software. The baseline for levels, versions, and locations of components are updated as part of the configuration tool.

For Churchill's architects, the testing environment transformed the production environment as the solution was built from scratch for the first release. The operations staff, involved in the testing, was prepared for promoting the portal release into production.

Loading the portal also invokes the release-management process, which involves building a database, transferring data, and setting up applications and tools. It ensures that the content and information is made available to the portal. The main deliverable from the section is an incremental build in the live production environment.

For Churchill's architects, incremental loading of the release focused on the integration of Bentley Prior to the group 11 operations centers and to radar, pilots, and observers. Content and information from supply-chain indicators were made available to Whitehall and, as a result, to Storey's Gate. At Bletchley Park, all manual procedures were completed and incrementally loaded.

Complete Final Testing

Completing final testing puts each of the increments through acceptance and operability testing according to the test plan. For example, applications and databases are individually tested one at a time. If tests fail against preset measures in the test plan, or if there are any doubts, then the back-out plan is invoked. It is essential that this holds true, and that the testers are confident they can stop the implementation. This phase also refines service-level objectives and agreements.

Acceptance Testing

Acceptance testing verifies that the functionality is correct and operationally sound and obtains sponsor approval to begin usage. It determines whether the developed portal reflects the requirements, ensures that any problems have been fixed, and determines that the production environment is stable. It also demonstrates that the operability requirements are met and acceptable for operations staff. The tests are run according to the test plan, which details the testing methods, tasks, responsibilities, and acceptance criteria. Tests are run with the participation of the sponsors and the users of a pilot community. It is important to carefully balance the level of completion and perfection with the effort required. A good rule of thumb is "launch and learn."

For Churchill's architects, acceptance testing required satisfying a number of executive sponsors/players, notably Churchill and Dowding, who were principal users of the first releases. The testing was particularly important for these users, who were looking for how well they were equipped for decision-making through the information provided and the functionality in place.

Operability Testing

Operability testing, completed by operations staff during the off-peak business hours, verifies that the portal meets the operability requirements and is acceptable for production operations. Tests are run to test technical aspects of the portal and its management functions.

Once the tests are complete, the results are documented and reviewed. If any problems are found, necessary corrections to the portal are made. Following that, executive sign-off is obtained.

For Churchill's architects, these were the final test and refinements prior to deployment. For example, with Bentley Prior, the Women's Auxiliary Air Force (WAAFs) completed the operability tests using the operations center's map table.

Refine Service-level Objectives (SLOs)

All the portal service levels should be measured and reported in user-perceived terms. There is no sense agreeing to any service level if it cannot be achieved, consistently met, or understood by the user. SLOs outline the criteria by which the service is measured. They typically include service times, response times for both the application and vendor responses to problems, exclusions, and penalties to be paid when the objectives are not met. Examples of SLOs include the following:

- *Times of service*—Availability is specified for each service and/or application.
- *Critical service times*—These times occur in a specific hour, day, week, month, or year.
- *Response time*—Guaranteed levels are usually expressed in terms of average and maximum response times allowed, for example, "mean time to action is two minutes."

For Churchill's architects, the starting point for refining SLOs for the first release was related to activities in all four portals, as shown in Table 6.1.

Table 6.1: Service-level Objectives

Portal	Definition	Times of Service	Critical Times of Service	Response Time
Storey's Gate	Decision-making	7 A.M.–7 A.M.	7 A.M.–7 A.M.	1 hour
Bentley Prior	Operation centers	7 A.M.–7 A.M.	7 A.M.–7 A.M.	1-3 minutes
	Fighter scrambled in air	7 A.M.–8 P.M.	8 A.M.–6 P.M.	3 minutes
	Ground crews (refuel/refit)	7 A.M.–8 P.M.	8 A.M.–6 P.M.	15 minutes
	Anti-aircraft	7 P.M.–7 A.M.	10 P.M.–3 A.M.	3 minutes
	Searchlight units	7 P.M.–7 A.M.	10 P.M.–3 A.M.	3 minutes
Bletchley Park	Code breaking, hut 3	7 A.M.–7 A.M.	7 A.M.–7 A.M.	6 hours
	Intelligence from hut 6	7 A.M.–7 A.M.	7 A.M.–7 A.M.	1 hour
	Dissemination with SLUs	7 A.M.–7 A.M.	7 A.M.–7 A.M.	15 minutes
Whitehall	Ministry indicators	8 A.M.–8 P.M	8 A.M.–8 P.M.	1 hour
	Civilian repair organization	8 A.M.–8 P.M.	8 A.M.–8 P.M.	2 hours

Bentley Prior's primary goal was to meet an imminent enemy raid on target with either fighters or anti-aircraft (as discussed in chapter 2's use-case scenarios 2.2.1, 2.2.2, 2.2.3). Fighters had to be deployed to the right place, at the right time, airborne at 20,000 feet in formation to face the imminent raid.

Timing was critical. Any delays meant pilots would lose crucial height advantage, so they had to be available on standby at any point in daylight hours.

Refine Service-level Agreements (SLAs)

Typically, the portal governance committee determines the SLAs from SLOs, and the service quality manager refines the SLA processes from the use-case goals. This requires establishing well-defined and measurable goals for service quality delivery.

For Churchill's architects, achieving their SLOs meant fighters had to be scrambled and positioned in three minutes. This was based on the short channel-crossing time for enemy aircraft flying at 300 MPH (or five miles per minute) across the 40 miles to the English coast in eight minutes, sector airfields in 12 minutes, and London in 20 minutes.

In a business process, many service providers might be part of a process chain, all adding value to the overall service. It is imperative to identify these service providers so that the enterprise view of the service is fragmented into them, their interdependencies are established, and their individual roles and responsibilities are defined.

Churchill's architects needed to examine the service-delivery chain of processes to determine what was required in each process to achieve the overall goal of a three-minute fighter scramble. For example, fighters depended on a sector operations center passing an imminent raid warning in under a minute. Likewise, group operations centers had to pass their warnings in under a minute. Hence, the chain in Figure 6.2 emerged.

For each process, the SLA metrics and targets need to be simple, manageable, and constantly refined through each release. As a result, the organization learns what works, which results in more meaningful SLAs. Predicting how the SLAs will evolve is difficult.

Dowding's architects spent many weeks testing and refining the fighter-scramble SLAs, reducing precious seconds across the whole service-delivery chain. By tracking this, Dowding's architects could readily measure the battle success rate of early airborne fighters and correlate it to scramble times. Also, this overall early-warning system preserved precious fuel stocks by maximizing fighter time on the ground and by targeting them accurately at enemy planes.

In addition, supporting mechanisms and ongoing management processes for SLAs are created. Reporting and analysis tools need to be available for SLA management, and SLA results need to be acted on by service providers.

Finally, SLAs need to be analyzed for how they support decision-making. SLAs should measure usage rather than utility, where usage is about volumes. These measurements can support decisions on business goals or determine whether usage goals are being met.

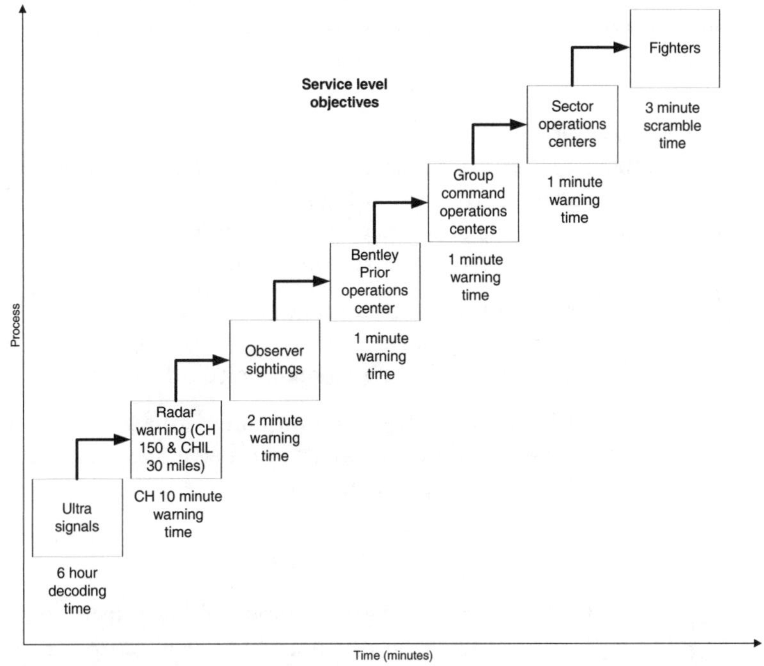

Figure 6.2: The dependency chain for SLOs provides a starting framework for establishing measurable goals, in this case for scrambling fighters.

For Churchill's architects, SLAs were also applied to areas like the supply chain, where information delivery, indicators, and reports were really important for decision-making at Whitehall. Here, the SLAs had to be continually overhauled and improved.

Deploy Training and Organization Support

Deploying training and organization support prepares both the business and technical sides of the staff through the training and documentation developed in the build cycle.

Deploy Training

Deploying training begins in parallel to setting up the deployment environment. It prepares the staff needed to support and maintain the portal. Using tools like the users' guide and the operations manual, it implements the training and support requirements.

For Churchill's architects, this required segregating the technical and business support requirements and delivering training. As the federated portal provided new functionality without an existing system equivalent, training was on-the-job, learn-as-you-go.

Deploy Support Organization

The support for the organization staff on the business side is deployed through the support documentation materials developed in the build cycle. This phase sets up the technical support and maintenance of the federated portal by extending the existing organization at three levels:

- First-level application management includes operations staff, possibly fronted by a help desk or call center, providing a single contact point for all problems. They are responsible to all users.
- Second-level application management includes the management functions of performance, capacity, and security, and the service levels needed to meet the portal's SLAs.
- Third-level application management requires detailed knowledge of the applications and analytical support.

Today, a portal automates the functions that required an army of administrators in 1940. Churchill's architects had to set up support for the federated portals both for the technical and business sides. Since the distinction between the two is sometimes blurred, the following sections will provide a better understanding of how the federated portals were used and supported.

Storey's Gate Support Organization

From Storey's Gate, Churchill and the War Cabinet ran the war. Eventually, they acquired a support staff of 2,000, split evenly by gender, working 24 hours a day. The first-level support included the engineers and technicians, security personnel (guards), and Women's Royal Naval Service (WRENS) administrators who handled all paperwork, acted as map-room plotters, and updated the indicator model.

The second-level support included the WREN officers who managed the performance of WREN administrators, and the security officers who managed the security guards. The third-level support included the senior aides who analyzed and interpreted sub-portal information for the decision-makers, working from the models.

On the business side, the duty officers, representing the three branches of the Armed Services, commanded the map room, collaborated and coordinated the arms, and then communicated and interfaced with their respective organizations' cascading information, directly linked to the room. The business side also included Churchill and the War Cabinet.

Bentley Prior Support Organization

Bentley Prior's portal required staff to support a wide array of very complex operations, initially across group 11. The first-level support included the communication engineers who managed equipment and switches; the radar technicians who analyzed the radar images and determined the number of planes, distance, and altitude; and the observers who confirmed the radar information with aircraft positions. All this information was passed to the map table at Bentley Prior's operations center, where WAAF administrators plotted the evolving air battle, shown in Figure 6.3.

The second-level support included the dispatchers who passed instructions to the WAAF plotters through telephone headsets. Both were highly trained. The WAAF officers managed the performance of the plotters, and security officers managed the security staff.

The third-level support included the group 11 controllers and sector controllers who interpreted the integrated information and collaborated with the liaison officers from the Royal Artillery and RAF. The former passed information to anti-aircraft batteries indicating where to fire and whether friendly aircraft were in their area. Within the group 11 operations center, the tote-board model indicated squadron and fighter availability and readiness. This was passed to a sector controller who gave pilots locations to fly to, operational height, directions on how to group, and enemy formations. When the enemy was spotted, command was passed to the squadron leaders. The controller also informed people like aircraft refuellers, armorers, mechanics, medical authorities, and many other positions in the airfield.

On the business side, the operations center staff officers consulted and provided input to the air battle and followed its every move. A few senior officers were privileged to Bletchley Park information, passed securely, identifying targets of an enemy raid and the number of aircraft.

Bletchley Park Support Organization

Bletchley Park's complex operation required staff in three main areas: codebreaking (hut 6), intelligence (hut 3), and the dissemination of secure information (SLUs).

Figure 6.3: The RAF group 11 operations center at Uxbridge was dominated by the map table.

The first-level support included the engineers and technicians, security personnel (guards), and the WREN/WAAF administrators who handled all paperwork across the organization. The engineers and technicians managed the telecommunication switches and the computing equipment like the bombes, which were part of the prototype.

The second-level support included the security officers who managed the security staff. It also included the hut 6 staff; the code breakers who used the bombes to break the daily-changing Enigma keys; the registry room staff who logged, sorted, and distributed all the messages; and the crib room staff who monitored messages for address, title, or irregularity in procedures for give-aways to message content.

The third-level support included the hut 3 staff members who received the raw decrypts from hut 6. The hut 3 production line had a "watch room," shown in Figure 6.4, where watchkeepers were responsible for removing errors and translating decrypts, supported by backroom experts and a glossary of terms for technical subjects. The watchkeeper concealed Enigma by providing an alternative source and passed the decrypt to Number 1, who checked it and passed it onto Army and RAF technical advisers, who evaluated it for new intelligence and significance. It was cross-checked with the library index and against previous messages. Finally, the decrypt was passed for release by the duty officer liaising with the SLUs.

On the business side, the staff in the field SLUs attached to Bletchley Park disseminated information on a need-to-know basis. The recipient was given the information by the SLU officer. For security reasons, all the recorded information was destroyed. Information destined for Churchill underwent further scrutiny and interpretations.

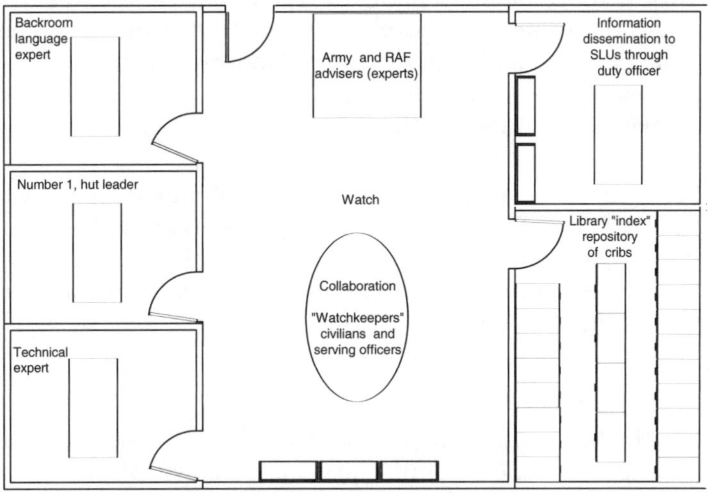

Figure 6.4: Hut 3 operation and organization support shows the basic layout of this important facility.

Whitehall Support Organization

New ministries were created and set up with staff, including ministries of aircraft production, supplies, food, and information. These were jointly responsible for managing the supply chain. Here, administrators, civil servants, junior ministers, and ministers collected information for indicators and performed analysis on these indicators.

The first-level support involved people like factory production managers, who collected shop-floor production information for the indicators. Civil servants analyzed these indicators and were also responsible for creating reports. The second-level support came through junior ministers, who helped manage the civil servants and interpreted the aggregated indicator information.

The third-level support was provided through ministers, who aggregated the indicator information for the business side (Churchill and his cabinet). Third-level support also included Churchill's statistical unit, which had a staff of economists and statisticians. By June 1940, this unit also advised ministerial committees on economic and related subjects and digested statistics prepared by departments.

Pilot Rollout

During pilot rollout, users of the pilot community are allowed parallel access to their existing systems and to the portal for comparative evaluations. Before cutover, it is important to track user readiness, receptivity, and response to the portal, and to identify any issues, concerns, risks, and areas for improvement. This includes understanding executive behavior, estimating support, and getting the user-adoption strategy right. This requires one-on-one coaching to build personal skills and comfort. Monthly alignment discussions help highlight portal relevance and value. Executives then work with managers and support the communication.

For Churchill's architects, the priority of pilot deployment related to Storey's Gate, Bentley Prior, Bletchley Park, and Whitehall. However, making Bentley Prior operational was critical, and this was the first priority of the pilot. Executive adoption was also critical, especially for high-profile users like Churchill, the War Cabinet, and Dowding.

Storey's Gate

For the first release, deployment would have been made available to the principal users: Churchill, the Cabinet, chiefs-of-staff, ministers, and senior aides.

Bentley Prior

For the first release, deployment would have been made to group 11, closest to the French coast. Subsequent releases would have been available to groups 10 and 12, and then been fanned out across the UK, based on most pressing need. The principal users were Fighter Command's commander Dowding, and group commanders Air Vice-Marshals Park (Group 11) and Leigh-Mallory (Group 12), and controllers at the sector level.

Bletchley Park

For the first release, deployment would have been made available to the principal users: Churchill, the chiefs of staff, the chiefs of intelligence, the chief of Fighter Command, and the chief of the Home Guard.

Whitehall

For the first release, deployment would have been made to available to the principal users, who included ministers like Beaverbrook, as well as junior ministers.

Pilot Assessment

Pilot assessment is optional for the executive sponsor, but is beneficial to the portal project team. Through this process, users in the pilot deployment community give feedback to the portal developers to determine whether the portal is, in fact, going to provide the required services. There is nothing worse than cutting over to production and then discovering there has been a misalignment with user expectations. This is also a microcosm of the more detailed reviews in the solution plans at the end of the project-release phase.

Churchill's architects faced a life-critical situation with the success of the pilot. The solution had to work the first time, especially for Bentley Prior. Hence, incessant testing was needed to this point to ensure success. For Fighter Command pilots and Bentley Prior staff, there had to be absolutely no doubt of success.

Production Cutover

In production cutover, the pilot community is live and monitors the release holistically. All precautions have been taken to minimize the risk and to improve the overall success.

For Churchill's architects, the production cutover was not as precise as defined above. Because of pressing business needs, the federated portals became operational as soon as available, with no other system alternatives in place.

Monitor the Created Whole

Each incremental load is monitored holistically for environmental anomalies or glitches. This certifies the readiness of the portal for live operation to begin. In monitoring, look for any discrepancies over a predefined length, since a busy period that has a major impact on the portal might appear only at the end of the month. If no discrepancies exist, the deployment activities can be seen as complete, and the deployment is declared officially live. The withdrawal option is available at any point. Monitoring should continue as part of the standard day-to-day functions of operations staff or first-level support.

For Churchill's architects, the task was challenging because of the extent and scope of deployment, with all four portals within the federation going live.

End-of-Project Release

At the end of the project, you verify the success or failure of the portal release by collecting and reviewing metrics. Based on the findings, including critical success factors, you adjust the solution release plan.

Collect the Metrics

Collecting metrics builds up an overall insight into the conditions and behavior of the portal. The challenge is in knowing which metrics to collect and using this information to assess and improve future releases. Typically, two forms of metrics are collected: hard (or quantitative) and soft (or qualitative). These metrics can be internal or external to an organization.

Collecting Hard Metrics

Hard metrics are system-generated. They can be part of the output of an application or service, and are collected through manual or automated processes. Examples include reports, error messages, transactions, and statistics. These metrics tend to be explicit, time-stamped, and accurate, but they usually require aggregation and interpretation. Reports for these metrics include the following:

- *Operational logs*—In the production environment, these highlight all the portal-related activities. They are a very important source of information, as they are time-stamped.
- *Service problem reports*—These reports are generated by the help desk in supporting internal groups and the call center in supporting customers. They identify problems, their types, frequency, and impact on the user and productivity.
- *Environmental metric reports*—These include business and operational metrics automatically collected from the portal. Business metrics are transactional and are the life-blood of an organization, where the flow increases and decreases depending on the varying service demands. Transaction metrics collected over time are invaluable in building up very accurate trends. Web analyzer tools collect metrics related to the activity of portal visitors. They provide insight into user behavior as interests are identified. Operational metrics include error and warning messages generated by applications, or computer components in an abnormal state. These indicate the health of the portal.

For Churchill's architects, collecting hard metrics was relatively straightforward because of the various models that had been set up. Clear targets, through SLOs and SLAs, had been defined for the success of the portal. For example, Bentley Prior metrics were related to fighter scramble times. Bentley Prior also depended on other portals: Bletchley Park to provide information on incoming raids and Whitehall for supply-chain metrics like production figures for fighters. In addition, Churchill's statistical unit, with a staff of economists and statisticians, prepared progress reports on how departments were fulfilling ministerial decisions.

Collecting Soft Metrics

Soft metrics include input from users, customers, and suppliers. These are solicited through interviews, meetings, workshops, focus groups, and surveys. They tend to be subjective, difficult to collect, and prone to error, but they can be very insightful to performance. Soft metrics include the following:

- *User feedback*—Feedback from users, typically employees, is invaluable and essential for assessment. Users can generally be found in the support organization, among employees, as customers, and as intermediaries. Users should include the managers involved in the pilot. The feedback should determine the level of satisfaction, the portal impact, how the portal meets expectations, and how it compares to competitive services. For Churchill's architects, a priority was given to collecting feedback from executives like Churchill, Dowding, and Beaverbrook. Feedback was also solicited from critical roles in the overall operation. For example, RAF officers and controllers in the Bentley Prior operations centers were significant decision-makers.
- *Customer feedback*—Customers are an obvious source of feedback for service experience. Their feedback is collected through focus groups, third parties, phone interviews, e-surveys, or questionnaires. It is important to target customers, recognize their segments, and understand the value of the segment to the organization. It is also important to recognize that individual aspirations make the feedback highly subjective. For Churchill's architects, customer feedback involved gathering information on the population and its overall morale, collected through the social survey department, which was part of Whitehall. This was critical, as the population was subjected to intense aerial bombing for the first time in Britain's history.
- *Supplier feedback*—Useful feedback is also solicited from distributors or suppliers in the organization's supply chain, who usually work closely with certain internal departments, like procurement. For Churchill's architects, this included collecting information on the supply chain from suppliers and distributors, through the ministry of supplies at Whitehall.

For Churchill's architects, collecting soft metrics was more challenging than collecting hard metrics. For example, for Bentley Prior, soft metrics included verbal reports from observers and pilots on the number of enemy aircraft destroyed. Often, pilots claimed the same aircraft "kill," so much time was spent collecting and corroborating the input.

Review the Metrics

The collected metrics are reviewed a few weeks after the production cutover of the portal release. This review determines the performance of services delivered through the portal by examining success criteria, service-level reports, and important end-user measures.

Review Success Criteria for Going Live

Chapter 5 defined the following success criteria for going live:

- Deploy the portal without disrupting existing business services and provide a continuum of operation for a fixed, designated period.
- Meet the expected levels of business services through collected and measured feedback.

These criteria are reviewed to determine whether they were met by examining how well the SLOs were met, taken from the service-level reports.

For Churchill's architects, with no existing services, disruption was not an issue. However, a continuum of operation for a fixed, designated period was critical for all the federated portals—hence, the need to meet nonfunctional requirements like availability and redundancy within the production environment.

Service-Level Reports

Service-level reports are associated with SLOs and SLAs. They provide an insight into how the services were performing prior to the cutover, list any anomalies after, and indicate whether SLOs and SLAs were met. A service-level report compares planned versus actual workload characteristics and service for a reporting period. This makes it easier to determine if missed service levels were due to excess work or inadequate performance on any part of the portal.

For Churchill's architects, this report was critical for Bentley Prior. The system testing provided the metrics for the likely planned workload characteristics. The report compared this against actual outputs. For this portal, the massive volumes of aggregated information could have a severe effect on the performance, and therefore would require balancing.

Important End-User Measures

The measures of service that are most important to end-users are typically response time and availability of service, as these directly affect service.

For Churchill's architects, the fighter scramble (response) time was defined in minutes. If the system was designed and implemented to provide a three-minute average response time, the SLA defined the response time as that for 95 percent of scrambles, with no fighters responding in more than four minutes. This allowed for varying factors affecting the scramble time. The fighters had to be available in daylight hours—typically, 14 hours a day.

Review Solution Plan

The solution plan developed during the macro design is reviewed by the project manager and the executive sponsors based on the experience from the development effort. Together, they prepare for the next release and ensure that the overall plan can deliver a portal that will meet the organization's requirements within the available time and budget. An estimate of the work effort for the next release is also given.

Churchill's architects reviewed the delivered portal functions versus those planned, and then assessed whether the content matched the community needs. This required asking questions related to satisfaction about the quality and value of content needs, so that content with little value could be removed. They also reviewed the adequacy of the federation strategy.

User Adoption

All possible barriers to user adoption or acceptance should be identified. Most organizations start with usability, but other methods of driving usage and adoption include organizational mandates and incentives. For example, adoption can be done by mandating usage, limiting other publishing channels, personalizing content, increasing user training, offering incentives, and integrating common applications.

For Churchill's architects, this was critical. Not only did the top executives need to use the federated portal, but they also needed to help promote it so its importance filtered down to other users. Churchill's supreme position allowed him to remove barriers to user adoption and mandate the usage.

Adequacy of Next Release

In assessing the success of the portal, you determine what the next releases should be based on. Specifically, you need to know how well the use-case scenarios were met. In reality, portal evaluation never actually stops; it continues to the nth release.

For Churchill's architects, time was pressing, so the sequence of releases had to be rapidly deployed in months. Release 1 was carefully reviewed to determine what had been done well and how this could be further exploited with releases 2 and 3, in terms of the next use-case scenarios and integration requirements. The planned goals were reexamined, as shown in Table 6.2.

Table 6.2: Release Model

Strategy for Releases

	Completed Release 1	Next Release 2	Release 3
Storey's Gate	Integration to Bletchley Park, Whitehall supply chain (indicator model map room)	Integration to Bentley Prior and cabinet rooms (collaboration) for use cases 3.1.1, 3.1.2, and 3.1.3	Transatlantic phone
Bentley Prior	Integration of group 11 operations centers to radar, pilots, observers, and Bletchley Park	Integration to Storey's Gate, anti-aircraft, CRO, supply chain, and Fighter Command groups 10 and 12	Integration to Bomber Command, and to Fighter Command groups 9,13, and 14
Bletchley Park	Integration to Storey's Gate and Bentley Prior, complete manual procedures	Automate manual procedures; integration to Bomber Command	Scale up the automation
Whitehall	Integration to Storey's Gate through indicator model, CRO	Complete indicator model; integration of ministries air production and supplies	Integration of ministry of food

Churchill's architects adjusted the release goals and activities according to what had been learned:

- Bentley Prior was a proven success, so integration with the supply chain and particularly the CRO was given a high priority. This was a short-term high priority, and new SLOs would have to be defined.
- Storey's Gate provided Churchill with Ultra information. He quickly grasped its enormous potential and significance as a weapon. Bletchley Park required a lot of automation, to keep up with the increase in Enigma traffic and the demand for Ultra information. This was a mid-term high priority.
- The information for the map room's indicator model at Storey's Gate proved to be more difficult to obtain than initially thought.

Improvements had to be made to the information processes in the Whitehall portal.

- The integration of the ministry of food into the Whitehall portal was deemed a lower priority, which could wait until releases 4 and 5.

Churchill's architects changed the priorities according to what made sense.

CONCLUSION

The following sections summarize the major points of this chapter and how they relate to your business today. For more information on these concepts, search the Internet for these keywords and phrases: *software testing methods, release management, test teams, deployment, cutover, service level agreements,* and *objectives*.

Major Points, Considerations, and Lessons Learned

- Churchill's architects had to pay particular attention to the support organization and ensure it was well-prepared for the portal. The organization had to continually measure and improve the portal performance and improve its SLOs in response to new Luftwaffe tactics.
- Churchill's architects used this phase to carefully assess the initial performance of Bentley Prior and determine if they were on the right track to meet preset objectives.

Best Practices for Your Organization

- Use a release-management process with version control to assure that the correct components are used from the library.
- Set up independent test teams that have strong incentives to test objectively.
- Ensure that users are involved in testing in the deployment environment, to ensure impartiality.
- Establish the ability to stop a portal deployment if the testing fails or is badly flawed.
- Avoid a testing process that lacks the political support in the organization at a senior level and the "teeth" to be effective.
- Ensure SLOs and SLAs are set up according to plan and followed with due diligence.
- Identify all barriers to user adoption and remove them.

- Measure the types of content that users find valuable. Remove information after one release if it is not found valuable.
- Go back to the release plan with an open mind to determine if it is correct and whether all the releases are correctly prioritized.
- Be prepared to develop to the *n*th phase. Portal evolution never really stops.
- Develop and deploy applications one at a time, but don't wait until everything is developed before deploying.

Questions You Can Ask Today

At this stage in the project, you should organize your thoughts into the following categories and ask the questions listed:

Deployment:

- Have you completed the deployment (production) environment?
- Has your team completed final testing acceptance and operability testing with a summary of results?
- Are you ready to make recommendations on whether to cut over the portal to production?

End of project release:

- Do you have a selection of feedback metrics to determine how well the portal is performing and delivering business services, with a summary of results from cutover into production?

CHAPTER 7

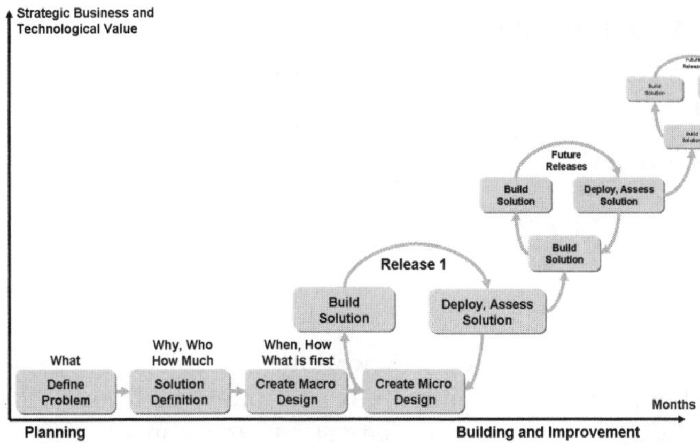

A Few Months into the Solution

We shall not fail or falter; we shall not weaken or tire . . . . Give us the tools and we will finish the job.

Sir Winston Churchill

CHAPTER OBJECTIVES

This chapter jumps forward in time, to a point when the project has completed several releases of the on demand solution. One of the most difficult questions to answer is whether the solution achieved what it was originally designed for. Did it meet the on demand requirements, and did it help the organization reach its goals?

A project review, normally completed after the solution has been in production for several months, determines the effectiveness of the solution by examining how it assisted in an on demand situation and helped the organization react to events in this period. This approach identifies the factors that contributed to the overall success, which otherwise might not have surfaced.

This chapter differs from the previous six, as it first determines the overall success of the portal project across multiple releases and then determines what is needed to wrap it up. It also examines the operational use of Churchill's federated portal by looking at the historical sequence of events following its deployment in June 1940. This highlights how powerful the federated portal was in sensing and responding to the situation and its overall impact for Churchill. Completing this analysis provides your organization with lessons on how to create best practices for future portal projects.

What Steps Do I Need to Follow?

As shown in Figure 7.1, you go through these four steps to determine the success of the project:

1. Initiate project review.
2. Discovery.
3. Analysis.
4. Future actions.

To get you warmed up to the subject, let's walk through these four steps with Churchill's federated portal as a backdrop. It is unlikely that you will experience a project on the scale of Churchill's portal, but to be successful, it is important to undergo reviews for all your projects, even small ones.

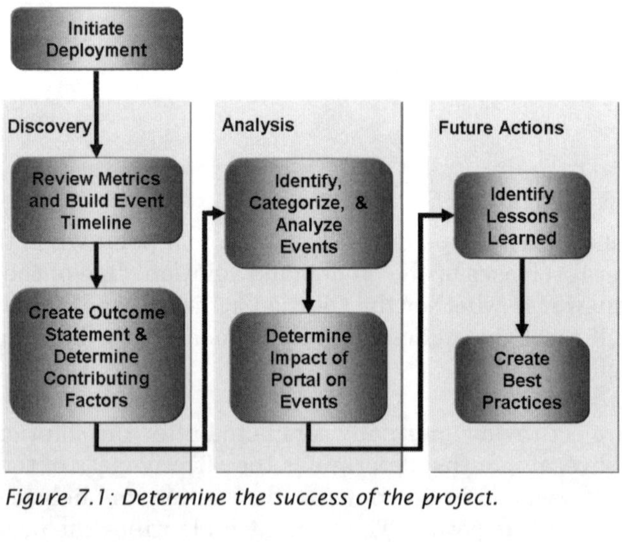

Figure 7.1: Determine the success of the project.

Initiate Project Review

Typically, it is difficult to accurately measure the success of a portal project in financial terms because some of the benefits are intangible. A project review helps confirm the business case and determine its success. Portal projects, specifically for employees, can be difficult to justify, as the benefits are perceived to be soft: time savings, improved white-collar productivity, or improved decision-making.

Discovery

The "discovery" step collects the metrics and builds the event timeline of the portal operation. It provides the information required for analysis to begin. It asks questions related to the outcome, what happened, and what should have happened.

Review the Metrics and Build the Event Timeline

You collect all the facts through data, metrics, and feedback, as discussed in chapter 6. This needs to be done quickly, so as not to lose the data, which is used to create the event timeline of how the organization reacted to an on-demand situation.

Following the Battle of Britain, Churchill and his staff reviewed the victory. They drew testimonies from participants, staff members, users of the portal, specialists, and technical experts to determine the factors that influenced the outcome. This information was then used to further evolve Churchill's federated portal.

Table 7.1 examines the operational use of Churchill's federated portal by looking at the sequence of daily events from June through October 1940, after deployment. Reviewing this information, you can see how the portal helped Churchill and his decision-makers.

Table 7.1: Event Timeline, June to October 1940

Events ID	Portal Response to Events for June	Significance of Portal Response
E1.1	Fighter command learns of 509 fighters lost in Norway and France.	An adequate defense needs 52 squadrons, but only 28 are available. Production is stepped up.
E1.2	Ultra messages decoded by Bletchley Park indicate invasion preparation.	Troop movements and the assembly of barges are revealed. These become bombing targets.
E1.3	Churchill learns of the pilot shortage and sends a memo to the Air Ministry.	Churchill asks why more of the hundreds of interested and experienced pilots are not being trained.

Table 7.1: Event Timeline, June to October 1940, *continued*

Events ID	Portal Response to Events for June	Significance of Portal Response
E1.4	Churchill learns the true cost of the Dunkirk evacuation.	The British army has only 200 heavy/medium tanks, and 300 light tanks. Production is stepped up.
E1.6	The War Cabinet learns of increasing military-production shortfall.	The production of hundreds of household goods is banned in Britain.
E1.30a	The War Cabinet learns of the occupation of the Channel Islands.	The invasion could not get closer. The dire situation sinks in.
E1.30b	Fighter production rate is below target rates.	Beaverbrook removes obstacles and increases fighter production from 292 to 446 per month.
Events ID	**Portal Response to Events for July**	**Significance of Portal Response**
E2.1	A "traveling" map room becomes operational for Churchill.	Churchill follows enemy movements and changing fronts in real time, while in transit.
E2.2	Churchill learns what troops and guns are available in each area.	Churchill grills his field commanders on their state of readiness, and increases pressure.
E2.3	Churchill monitors the Royal Navy stand-off with the French fleet at Oran.	The Royal Navy puts the French fleet out of action to deny access for the Axis powers.
E2.10	Bentley Prior learns of first large-scale bombing raid on British cities.	Hitler orders plans to establish air superiority, and the Battle of Britain officially commences.
E2.14	Low morale spurs Churchill to broadcast a rousing speech.	Not since Elizabeth I had anyone spoken of the English like this. The nation's morale is elevated.
E2.15a	Ultra messages decoded by Bletchley Park reveal Operation Sea Lion.	The air battle pits 1,700 bombers and 1,100 fighters against 675 British fighters.
E2.15b	Bletchley Park passes 200 decoded messages to Bentley Prior every day.	Dowding receives hourly detailed knowledge of advanced plans and last-moment changes.

Table 7.1: Event Timeline, June to October 1940, *continued*

Events ID	Portal Response to Events for July	Significance of Portal Response
E2.15c	Dowding is under pressure to adopt new tactics and respond en masse.	Dowding resists pressure and relies on his early-warning system. Churchill fully supports him.
E2.16a	Ultra messages decoded by Bletchley Park reveal the invasion's strength.	Twenty enemy divisions have assembled in the French seaports.
E2.19a	Churchill learns of Hitler's peace offers.	Churchill rejects the terms, but buys precious time to further prepare for battle.
E2.31	Beaverbrook learns of essential spare parts and aircraft storage.	Beaverbrook wrestles control from the Air Ministry to maintain aggressive fighter production.
Events ID	**Portal Response to Events for August**	**Significance of Portal Response**
E3.9a	Bletchley Park passes repeated warning messages to Bentley Prior.	Messages indicate "Eagle day" for a forthcoming massive attack. Dowding prepares.
E3.9b	Dowding learns that Göring is looking for an all-out assault on the RAF.	Intelligence indicates the enemy believes the RAF can be defeated in four days.
E3.10	Bentley Prior learns of a shortfall in pilot replacement numbers.	The operation training period for qualified pilots is cut from six months to two weeks.
E3.12	Bentley Prior learns of attacks on its airfields and coastal radar stations.	The attack in the southeast is met. Surprisingly, it does not continue on subsequent days.
E3.13	Storey's Gate learns of enemy night raids on two fighter factories.	The attack indicates night bombers carry a sophisticated guidance system.
E3.14	Churchill receives a message from Roosevelt offering a trade.	The trade of destroyers/planes for American military bases on British soil is accepted.
E3.15	Apprised by Ultra, radar, and observer corps, Dowding is ready for battle.	Bentley Prior carefully preserves its resources and avoids stretching these to the utmost.

Table 7.1: Event Timeline, June to October 1940, *continued*

Events ID	Portal Response to Events for August	Significance of Portal Response
E3.16a	Bentley Prior recognizes attacks are only against its airfields and fighters.	Targets spared include the vital radar stations.
E3.16b	Bentley Prior learns of heavy fighter losses.	Defensive strategy is adjusted accordingly. The faster Spitfire fighters are sent in first.
E3.18	Dowding learns that Bentley Prior is under tremendous pressure.	A fourth day of raids continues to devastate sector stations around London.
E3.19a	Bentley Prior gets a short respite, as the Luftwaffe pauses.	Luftwaffe losses are 236 against 213 RAF (in ten days). RAF losses are unsustainable.
E3.19b	Bentley Prior learns from Whitehall of fighter production-rate shortfall.	Beaverbrook appeals to the CRO to increase their shifts, to get aircraft back in the air.
E3.20	Churchill broadcasts his speech in recognition of pilots from Storey's Gate.	"Never in the field of human conflict was so much owed by so many to so few."
E3.22a	Storey's Gate learns of the worsening situation in the Middle East.	Churchill takes a massive gamble and dispatches a convoy with 150 tanks.
E3.22b	The War Cabinet learns financial reserves will be exhausted in four months.	Beaverbrook urges continued purchase of American materials to tie the U. S. closer to Britain's cause.
E3.24a	Dowding learns of further attacks on the RAF.	Main sector airfields are very badly damaged.
E3.24b	Whitehall informs Storey's Gate of further raids on aircraft factories.	Spitfire and Hurricane production is affected.
E3.24c	Churchill learns of an attack on the City of London.	Enemy bombers accidentally drop bombs on London suburbs.
E3.25	The War Cabinet orders a reprisal raid on Berlin.	Although the British raid is small, the German population is shocked. Hitler and Göring are dismayed.
E3.26	Bentley Prior Group 11 airfields are under continuous attack.	Dowding directs Group 12 to protect Group 11 airfields.

Table 7.1: Event Timeline, June to October 1940, *continued*

Events ID	Portal Response to Events for August	Significance of Portal Response
E3.29a	Bentley Prior learns of huge fighter concentrations in a fleet of 600.	Approximately 80% of the total Axis fighter force is concentrated on the Pas-de-Calais.
E3.29b	Bentley Prior realizes new fighter tactics are limiting fighter detection.	Fighters cross the channel at a very low altitude to avoid radar detection and then rapidly climb.
E3.30a	Bentley Prior is aware of a huge fighter attack.	Dowding orders RAF fighters to disengage where possible against such odds.
E3.30b	Bletchley Park decodes a message stating that Hitler will determine the invasion date.	September 10th is set as the deadline, with a target of September 20th.
E3.30c	Bentley Prior is aware that the RAF is at its breaking point.	RAF pilots fly 1,000 sorties in a single day; some pilots fly four sorties without rest.

Events ID	Portal Response to Events for September	Significance of Portal Response
E4.1	The War Cabinet learns of attacks on the populations and big cities.	Hitler mistakenly believes his fighters have mastery of the skies.
E4.5	Bentley Prior realizes the switch in enemy tactics to London is ongoing.	The news is significant, as it allows Dowding to rebuild Group 11 squadrons.
E4.6	The War Cabinet learns RAF losses were creeping up to Luftwaffe levels	RAF loses 466 fighters and receives 269 new ones; 103 pilots are killed and 128 wounded.
E4.7a	Bletchley Park fails to warn Dowding of a massive 900-aircraft attack.	Too few pilots are in position to adequately defend London, which sustains major damage.
E4.7b	Storey's Gate issues an alert: "invasion imminent and probable in 12 hours."	Churchill orders the Bomber Command to attack the channel ports crammed with 1,000 barges.
E4.8	Churchill broadcasts his defiance to bombing in a speech from Storey's Gate.	"...A people who will not flinch from the struggle—hard and protracted though it will be."

Table 7.1: Event Timeline, June to October 1940, *continued*

Events ID	Portal Response to Events for September	Significance of Portal Response
E4.9	Dowding learns of huge incoming raids.	Dowding switches tactics and operates squadron pairs. Outnumbered, enemy fighters break off.
E4.10	Bletchley Park learns Hitler has postponed invasion until September 21st.	Göring assures Hitler that the RAF will be defeated.
E4.15a	Bentley Prior learns of a massive attack of 328 bombers and 769 fighters.	All RAF fighters are thrown into battle. Luftwaffe pilots are shocked to see the RAF's fighter strength.
E4.15b	Bentley Prior learns of a second raid, apprised by Ultra.	Refueled RAF fighters once again route the Luftwaffe and break the offensive.
E4.17	Bletchley Park decrypts orders to dismantle equipment at airfields.	This was Hitler's order to abandon Operation Sea Lion and end the Battle of Britain.
E4.17b	Churchill broadcasts to the people of Czechoslovakia from Storey's Gate.	"Be of good cheer, the time of your deliverance will come." Churchill is a rallying voice.

Outcome

By October 31st, the Battle of Britain was officially won. The blitz of London continued into the winter of 1940, and was extended to other cities. The goal was to bomb England into submission. However, the Luftwaffe losses were staggering: 2,700 aircraft destroyed and 600 damaged. British losses were about 900 pilots.

Winston Churchill believed that another invasion attempt was possible in March or April 1941. However, it was not until June 1941, when Hitler turned his attention to the Soviet Union, that an invasion of Britain was scrapped.

Create Outcome Statement and Determine Contributing Factors

Create an outcome statement and define the factors contributing to it. Using the Churchill analogy, the first question might be, "What impact did Churchill's federated portal have on the overall battle?" The answer is, "It helped secure a victory and prevented an imminent invasion." This is the outcome statement. To decide whether the statement is correct, you need to determine the contributing factors.

You can define the contributing factors for the articulated outcome statement using input from Table 7.1. For example, Churchill's federated portal was able to provide critical information to decision-makers that could help them do the following:

- Better understand enemy intentions.
- Carefully select investments, in terms of the choice of military equipment.
- Focus very slender resources.
- Avoid an all-out battle of attrition.
- Engage in a fight only when the odds were favorable.
- Quickly rebuild depleted squadrons with fighters.
- Minimize pilot casualties.
- Give confidence to its leaders in the heat of battle.

These are still general statements that refer to overall conditions. They need to be further refined and combined to create the following unique contributing factors:

- The RAF was not defeated. It was still intact to repel the Luftwaffe at the end of the invasion window in October.
- The supply chain could adequately support the RAF, which could sustain a prolonged air battle in the mid-term.
- Churchill was still defiant, full of confidence, with the full backing of the nation, and in full control of his forces. He could implement his overriding and longer-term strategies to defeat the Axis.

These statements are further refined in the following sections.

Contributing Factor 1: The RAF was still able to fend off all Luftwaffe raids

Churchill's federated portal averted the RAF defeat by providing vital, integrated, timely information to Fighter Command for decision-making. Here's how:

- Bletchley Park provided early warnings of imminent raids, including the direction and strength of the attacks.

- Through Bletchley Park, RAF commanders at Bentley Prior received messages before their Luftwaffe counterparts did.
- Radar visualized a raid up to 150 miles away, as the planes took off in Europe.
- Observer corps tracked the incoming raids and confirmed radar information.
- Operations centers scrambled fighters to be in the best possible position.
- Anti-aircraft and balloon barrages were synchronized with fighter operations, and so the impact of these barrages was maximized.
- Through careful countermeasures, Bletchley Park remained uncompromised.
- The number of available pilots was rapidly accelerated through shortened training and the introduction of pilots from other countries.
- RAF pilots who were shot down were recovered and back in the air in a matter of hours.
- Information on fighter production rates (from the supply chain) influenced Dowding and led to his refusal to get drawn into a war of attrition.
- Bentley Prior convinced Luftwaffe pilots that the RAF was much stronger than it was. In reality, the RAF was 24 hours from defeat if attacks had been sustained.

Contributing Factor 2: The supply chain could adequately support the RAF

Churchill's federated portal provided Whitehall with information so the supply chain could be adequately managed to best support the RAF. As a result, Bentley Prior could sustain a prolonged battle in the mid-term. Here's how:

- Beaverbrook transformed production by focusing resources and distributing manufacturing to smaller factories and workshops. As a result, the fighter production rate was better synchronized to losses. It also caught up and outpaced Axis fighter output.
- Beaverbrook, through his relationships in North America, was able to solicit the production of fighter engines from industrial giants.
- The operational CRO was able to rapidly salvage aircraft. This ability to get cannibalized parts back into production had a major effect on getting aircraft back into the air.

- Critical resources and supplies, like ammunition and fuel, were given priority to be produced and transported as needed.
- Enemy aircraft were salvaged for scrap metal.
- Information on fighter loss rates (from Bentley Prior) influenced Beaverbrook and helped determine fighter production rates in the supply chain.

Contributing Factor 3: Churchill, still defiant, enables his strategies

The federated portal provided Churchill and the War Cabinet with critical information for decision-making. This allowed Churchill to concentrate on the overall war aims and the longer-term strategy. Although Churchill let his commanders get on with the battle, he played a very significant hand in supporting them with the actions he undertook. Here's how:

- Churchill was completely in touch with the battle on a daily basis. He would visit key Fighter Command operations centers, like Northholt. He made morale-rallying speeches based on events he saw.
- He strongly backed and stood by his lieutenants through the thick of battle. He gave them confidence to continue in their cause.
- He encouraged occupied countries to establish free governments in Britain. He became a focal point for human rights and a spokesman for all free peoples.[1]
- He convinced President Roosevelt (through actions at Oran and the French fleet) that the war could be continued. His personal relationship with Roosevelt was Britain's lifeline.
- As the battle progressed, he was able to swing U. S. public opinion to his side through London-based foreign correspondents.
- He approved a raid on Berlin that provoked Hitler into switch to bombing civilians targets, turning Hitler's attention away from vital airfields.
- He moved one of only two armored divisions to Egypt at a critical point in the battle.

ANALYSIS

A detailed analysis determines the impact of the portal on the victory. The purpose of this analysis is to determine what happened and why. How did the portal help the organization react to events?

[1] For example, Churchill supported the Free French and Charles De Gaulle as "the man of destiny."

Identify, Categorize, and Analyze the Events

Use the contributing factors to identify and categorize the reaction of the portal to an event:

- *Were best reacted to*—Definitely contributed to the victory
- *Were somewhat reacted to*—Possibly contributed to the victory
- *Unsure*—Could have had both a negative and a positive impact
- *Detrimental*—Likely prevented or limited the victory

The process selects the events that the portal best acted on. It determines the events that the portal identified and helped the organization react to. The best-reacted-to events are as follows:

- For CF1, the RAF was still able to fend off all raids (events E1.2, E2.15b, E3.15, E3.30a, and E4.15b).
- For CF2, the supply chain could adequately support the RAF (events E1.6, E1.30b, E2.31, and E3.19b).
- For CF3, Churchill, still defiant, enables his strategies (events E1.3, E2.3, E2.14, E2.15c, E2.19a, and E3.22a).

Determine the Impact of the Portal on Events

You are now in a position to start determining the significance of the portal and its impact on events. In this exercise, you look at how the portal affected the event, and its significance. Let's stay with the three contributing factors.

Contributing Factor 1: The RAF was still able to fend off all raids

The events relating to CF1 are listed in Table 7.2. They are predominantly external, occurring outside the organization.

Table 7.2: Events Related to Contributing Factor 1

Event ID	Actions Taken in Response to Portal Information	Significance of Actions
E1.2	Reveals order of battle.	Better prepares Bentley Prior to respond.
E2.15b	Reveals imminent raids.	Bentley Prior reacts with counter-measures.
E3.15	Reveals seven concurrent attacks.	Bentley Prior reacts with counter-measures.

Table 7.2: Events Related to Contributing Factor 1, *continued*

Event ID	Actions Taken in Response to Portal Information	Significance of Actions
E3.30a	Bentley Prior assesses 600-fighter raid. Dowding orders fighters to disengage.	Luftwaffe misinterprets action as the defeat of the RAF. Goring sets date for deciding invasion.
E4.15b	Bentley Prior amasses 300+ fighters to counterattack a massive raid.	Luftwaffe pilots panic, thinking RAF is defeated, and the raid is broken up.

Without a doubt, Churchill's federated portal vastly improved the Fighter Command's position. Let's take a look at why:

- By decoding Enigma message traffic, Bletchley Park was able to build up an accurate order of battle for the Luftwaffe. Not all messages were decrypted, but those messages that were gave Dowding a clear view of what Fighter Command was up against and when the raids would occur.
- A steady stream of over 200 Ultra messages gave Dowding, hour by hour, detailed knowledge of Luftwaffe advance plans for a raid, as well as last-minute changes. This gave him a more than an equal chance to make the most efficient use of his very limited resources and to avoid over-commitment and risk of defeat.
- Although Ultra intelligence forewarned of impending attacks, coastal radar (underestimated by the Luftwaffe) was able to accurately pinpoint flights of incoming enemy planes, as observers tracked them in real time.
- Dowding ordered RAF fighters to disengage where possible against massive fighter attacks. Reports back to Luftwaffe leaders of fighters shying away were passed to Hitler with the claim of "unlimited fighter superiority." Hitler and Göring believed the RAF was on its last reserve and was defeated.
- Luftwaffe pilots were told that fighter command was on its last legs, so they were shocked to be met by 300 RAF fighters on September 15th.
- On October 12th, Hitler issued a statement stating that invasion plans were postponed for 1940. Unofficially, the Battle of Britain was over. Hitler had run out of time, and the Fighter Command could not be breached.
- Without the portal, fighter squadrons would have had to fly patrols to find and pinpoint attack formations. This would have required squadrons continuously in the air expending fuel, but more important, there were only a limited number of sorties that the RAF pilots could mount.

Contributing Factor 2: The supply chain could adequately support the RAF

The events relating to CF2 are listed in Table 7.3. They are predominantly internal, based on a condition or a decision.

Table 7.3: Events Related to Contributing Factor 2

Event ID	Actions Taken in Response to Portal Information	Significance of Actions
E1.6	Production is switched over from household goods.	Huge public support boosts government morale.
E1.30b	Beaverbrook removes all production obstacles.	By end-of-month, fighter production doubles and starts to catch up to enemy production.
E2.31	Beaverbrook removes obstacles for CRO.	CRO recovery increases, and so does fighter deployment into squadrons.
E3.19b	Beaverbrook appeals to CRO for more hours.	CRO staff agrees. Downed fighter are recovered and deployed into squadrons faster.

Without a doubt, Churchill's federated portal improved supply-chain management. Let's take a look at why:

- Whitehall production indicators helped Beaverbrook closely monitor Bentley Prior fighter losses and match production to these losses.
- Beaverbrook elevated the efficiency of fighter recovery through the CRO to the point where output was the equivalent of a fighter factory. The Luftwaffe failed to take into consideration the CRO contribution and the number of fighters put back into service—a gross mistake.
- Churchill strongly backed Beaverbrook and Dowding in public, which cut through the politics and allowed them to pursue key strategies to the overall objectives.
- Without the federated portal, fighter production would not have been so closely tied to loss rates. With a greater lag time, the number of fighter squadrons would have been stretched to breaking point.

Contributing Factor 3: Churchill, still defiant, enables his strategies

The events relating to CF3 are listed in Table 7.4. They are predominantly internal.

Table 7.4: Events Related to Contributing Factor 3

Event ID	Actions Taken in Response to Portal Information	Significance of Actions
E1.3	Churchill removes obstacles for pilot recruitment.	The Air Ministry widens its net for recruitment.
E2.3	Churchill orders an attack on the French fleet.	The attack sends a strong message to Hitler and convinces Roosevelt that Britain will fight on.
E2.14	Churchill delivers a rousing speech.	The speech raises public morale to continue the fight.
E2.15c	Churchill backs Dowding's strategy.	The strategy continues to successfully evolve at the expense of the Air Ministry.
E2.19a	Churchill refuses Hitler's peace terms.	Churchill's consideration of terms buys some time. His refusal influences Roosevelt to support the fight indefinitely.
E3.22a	Churchill takes a massive gamble.	The redeployment strengthens Britain's position in Egypt but weakens home defense.

Without a doubt, Churchill's federated portal enabled Churchill and the War Cabinet to implement his strategies. Let's take a look at why:

- The Royal Navy put the French fleet out of action by force. The attack on Britain's ally brought Churchill much personal sadness and anguish, but he later learned that the action convinced President Roosevelt that Britain and the Commonwealth could and would fight on. It also sent a message to Hitler that Churchill was looking to continue the fight. Hitler was still looking for a peaceful settlement.
- Churchill readily accepted Roosevelt's offer of destroyers and aircraft in return for naval and air bases. He fervently believed he could draw the United States into the war and ultimately win.
- In 1940, Churchill regularly broadcast to the people of occupied Europe. They looked to Churchill as their only beacon of hope.
- Churchill recognized the contributions of the young pilots of Fighter Command and praised them to the nation. This reinforced the role of Fighter Command, to the annoyance of the Air Ministry, which was favoring Bomber Command as the force to win the war.

- By August, Churchill was in a difficult position, as Egypt was under great threat of invasion. He took a momentous decision to send one of only two armored divisions to defend Egypt, at great risk to the defense of England. This demonstrated his holistic view of the war and of engaging the enemy in the longer term. It also demonstrated his sheer confidence.
- Without the federated portal, Churchill would not have had the big-picture intelligence to be able to make critical decisions that affected his long-term strategy.

Future Actions

Determining the best approach for future actions ensures the goals are met again for future releases and other portal initiatives. This process determines how the success of the current project can be repeated. For this, you need to identify lessons learned, review the initial cost/benefit analysis, create best practices, and implement these best practices.

Identify Lessons Learned

From the Churchill analogy, the key lessons include the following:

- Ultra information from Bletchley Park was significant. However, only a fraction of its potential was leveraged in terms of what could be collected and what was available to decision-makers, because of security concerns.
- In using Ultra information, great caution had to be taken not to arouse enemy suspicion. Through the war, the Axis high command never wavered from its belief in the security of Enigma. They confidently deployed it throughout their war machine.
- The Luftwaffe attack on five radar stations was not sustained; otherwise, the portal would have been severely "blinded." This was a weak point in the Bentley Prior portal that had to be addressed.
- Bentley Prior allowed a minimized fighter force to offset a more powerful opponent. In fact, it did the job of what would have taken double the number of fighters.
- The CRO proved significant in its operation. Its recovery and repair rate was the equivalent of the output of another fighter factory. The enemy tracked RAF losses, but failed to consider the impact of the CRO on the overall production of fighters.
- Whitehall supply-chain indicators were significant to Churchill, Dowding, and Beaverbrook. They were able to closely align fighter production to fighter losses and meet the on demand requirements.

- The fighter scramble times had been refined by testing the whole service-delivery chain for many weeks.

Review the Cost/Benefit Analysis

The cost/benefit analysis of chapter 3 is reviewed to determine the success of the initial analysis. The review assesses whether the benefits are as predicted for each of the categories of cost savings: increase in productivity, increase in business velocity, and increase in intellectual capital. It collects available metrics to recalculate the formulas. It questions how substantial the direct and indirect benefits are, and how these are perceived by the users and communities. It looks for any surprises in unexpected benefits across all portals.

For Churchill, the benefits of the federated portal went beyond the fiscal—it was a case of survival. Nevertheless, the key benefits across all the federated portals lay with decision-making and collaboration, the ability to sense and respond, and visibility into business operation like the supply chain. One of the most significant cost savings lay in the ability to wage the battle with approximately half the expected number of fighters and pilots. This single benefit offset the costs of the federated portal, as it meant savings in capital costs, operations, staff, and training.

Create Best Practices

From the lessons and the cost/benefits analysis discussed in the previous sections, the following best practices are created and leveraged in future releases:

- Further expand and leverage critical portals, like Bletchley Park, to gain the maximum from the significant information available. For example, shortly after the Battle of Britain, Bletchley Park received a large investment in resources through newer technologies (bombes) and people. As a result, Bletchley Park grew from several hundred to several thousand staff in a year.
- Once the value and significance of specific information is recognized, like the Ultra messages, ensure this information is secured, protected, and not compromised through the incorrect use of procedures. Radar information not only had to be protected, but contingency planning involving multiple stations was needed, giving alternative paths to the information.
- Ensure that once the value of specific information, like the Whitehall indicators, is recognized, it is fully exploited and other similar indicators are quickly identified.

- Recognize that decision-making occurs at different levels in the organization, and hybrid models are required for information dissemination, as with the federated portals.
- Ensure the portal solution undergoes continuous refinement and testing to improve performance and to meet SLAs, as was done with Bentley Prior.

The above best practices are then implemented to meet the following goals:

- Ensure that processes are available that can monitor the value of information based on the impact of decisions made.
- Ensure that all portals have feedback mechanisms so information requests evolve, becoming better refined to improve decision-making.

CONCLUSION

The following sections summarize the major points of this chapter and how they relate to your business today. For more information on these concepts, search the Internet for these keywords and phrases: *project reviews*, *metrics analysis*, and *root cause analysis*.

Major Points, Considerations, and Churchill's Federated Portal Lessons

- The Battle of Britain fully tested Churchill's federated portal in the heat of an all-out battle. It showed what a significant tool it was, enabling the RAF fighters to fight proactively, in a very focused way, to defeat a larger and more powerful air force.
- Churchill showed unbelievable leadership skills in nurturing and evolving the federated portal at the outset. He selected leaders beneath his command who could deliver and supported them through the low points of battle so that their strategies were eventually fulfilled.

Best Practices for Your Organization

- Proceed with a review after any major portal deployment, but also consider it as a standard operating procedure for all projects, specifically after a period in production.
- Ensure that critical metrics are automatically collected and other metrics are collected quickly.
- Create an event timeline, as this is the starting point for a review.
- Closely examine and use Web metrics.

Questions You Can Ask Today

At this stage of the project, you should organize your thoughts into the following categories and ask the questions listed:

Discovery:

- Have you conducted a complete review of the project, supported by the procedures in place for conducting the review and compiling metrics?

Analysis:

- Did you perform an analysis of the business to determine the event timeline?

Future actions:

- Have you identified the lessons that your organization has learned?
- Have you reviewed and are you comfortable with the results of the cost/benefit analysis?

CHAPTER 8

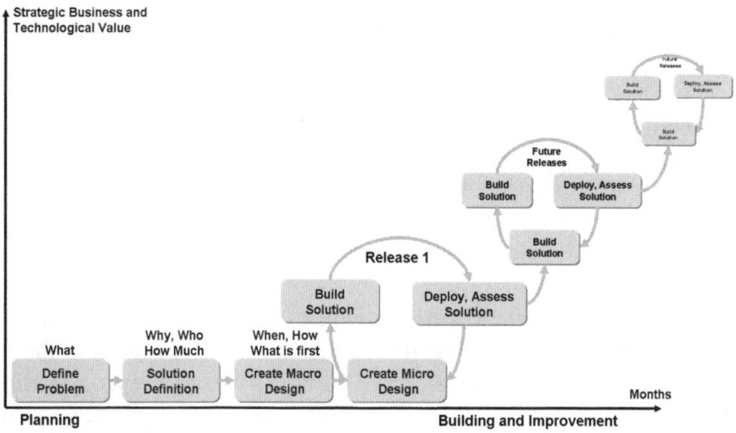

Recapping the Journey

The British nation is unique in this respect. They are the only people who like to be told how bad things are, who like to be told the worst.

Sir Winston Churchill

CHAPTER OBJECTIVES

This book advocates that you, as a business manager, should be a full participant in the proposed project, since you might be responsible for it, its funding, and its deliverables. Your goal is to ensure that your portal project meets the short-term goals of the required functional and on demand objectives, is acceptable to the organization and customers, and meets the longer-term strategic objectives of the organization.

Now that your project is complete, this chapter reviews the book's key points, starting with your portal and then extending to Churchill's federated portal. It concludes with a recap of the four major issues addressed by this book.

RECAP OF YOUR PORTAL PROJECT

Many organizations recognize that their customers' needs are changing. They make significant changes to respond to these needs, knowing that if they don't, nimbler competitors will force them into a commodity space in the marketplace.

An on demand solution helps an organization better respond to changing and potentially detrimental situations by increasing its ability to sense things using pattern recognition. For example, changes in customer preference signals, or competitive threats or moves. It then responds accordingly, either with predetermined actions or collaborative decision-making. Finally, it monitors the impact of the response, to see whether the response effectively counteracts the detriment.

Today, portal technologies provide these on demand capabilities. Although they require an investment, they can significantly improve an organization's responsive behavior and white-collar productivity. This might be difficult to prove upfront, however; hence, the need for an approach that incorporates a business case.

In the early phases of your portal project, you are faced with many choices and decisions. You need to know what technology is available, but this should not be driving your project yet. To put a shape to what you are trying to do, you need a clear vision, goals, and a direction. You then employ strategies to get you there.

You need to carefully look at the organizational groups in the front line. What could people do with better information, if it was available in the right timeframe and format? How could this information change decision-making, or the tasks that groups directly perform? From this analysis, you identify your communities and target audiences, as well as the content, functions, and nonfunctions required. You can start to prioritize these and explore the benefits. You then determine a conceptual design and the preliminary costs. Next, you complete a business justification. This is laid out as an iterative cycle that grows by release. Each community is taken care of, one step at a time.

You need to ensure that your project stays true to its vision and direction through each stage of the lifecycle. It is not feasible for you to micro-manage the project, so you have to ensure that everyone involved understands the project vision clearly and is empowered to analyze information, determine risks, and present critical issues at steering-committee meetings. Strategies like starting with a pilot or small project and then rapidly scaling each project lifecycle minimize the impact of poor decisions. Undoubtedly, strong leadership, like Churchill's, is essential to the project.

The following is a summary of the most significant global best practices:

- Ensure the business drives the portal strategy and project, and that a clear vision is in place.

- Ensure that portal governance is in place before proceeding with the project.
- Create comprehensive business models to better understand the business.
- Provide the strong leadership and clear strategy that portal projects need to grow.
- Avoid excessive analysis. Focus on the portal's purpose, how it will be used, and whether the flexibility offered by portal technology is appropriate.
- Recognize that organizational changes caused by a portal can be significant.
- Pay attention to user experience and create use-case scenarios.
- Identify new and existing communities and their needs, and carefully match those needs to content that provides value.
- Choose content and applications for end-users and communities that will drive portal usage and user adoption.
- Plan the adoption campaigns for the organization to improve acceptance and remove barriers to usage.
- Focus the cost/benefits analysis on both tangible and intangible factors.
- Ensure that your business requirements, user interface, and technical infrastructure are not tightly integrated, so that they can be rapidly changed.
- Understand that portals are living organisms, which must grow with the business.
- Determine the degree of federation required with a federated portal.
- Start with a pilot, and then scale up rapidly. Use prototypes to test concepts and technologies, and therefore reduce the overall risk.
- Ensure that technology is scalable and open for rapid growth.
- Ensure comprehensive testing is planned for and completed without compromises. Use independent teams and suitable environments, and maintain objectivity.
- Ensure that adequate feedback loops are in place for continuous improvements. Ensure that business processes affected by the portal are monitored and changed as required.
- Ensure SLOs and SLAs are set up according to plan.
- Measure the portal in production, and ensure critical metrics are collected quickly. Measure the content to ensure users find it useful.

Recap of Churchill's Federated Portal

The following pages review the portal: why it was built, how it was built, and what it delivered.

Why the Portal Was Built

Churchill was not only facing an imminent threat of invasion, but also the fact that most of his government's senior members were resigned to defeat. With very few options, he had to do something to bolster the defenses, if he, his government, and his country were going to survive.

Churchill was able to quickly grasp the power of real-time intelligence and the possibilities of what it could provide. He and his advisors determined what the War Cabinet and Fighter Command could do with early-warning information. This, with other capabilities, gave him some options to continue the fight and make up for the shortcomings of his military capability, especially fighter strength.

How the Portal Was Built

In the early phases, Churchill was faced with numerous choices and decisions. He was able to clarify the short-term goal of preventing an invasion. As important, he recognized the need for longer-term goals: scaling up the war economy, rallying popular support, and continuing the war.

Churchill and his government were very much driven by the possibility of defeat to move the federated portal into service. The testing was rapid, as it was quickly deployed into production. By September, Churchill's federated portal had expanded and grown into a massive solution, with thousands of users.

What the Portal Achieved

Churchill's architects had all the pieces of technology to create an elegant solution that could greatly leverage information and have a multiplier effect on Fighter Command. What was truly impressive was how the disparate pieces of information were integrated into a federated portal to provide a system of rapid sense-and-respond against attack. Churchill's federated portal achieved significant results for its communities and helped them meet their objectives, for example:

- Bentley Prior was able to sense enemy raids and respond by placing fighters at 20,000 feet, ready and waiting for combat. This proved incredibly demoralizing for the Luftwaffe pilots. Through timely intelligence, Dowding was also able to read Luftwaffe tactics and avoid the all-out battle of attrition that Göring was looking for.

- Bletchley Park evolved from mere code-breaking to accurately forecasting enemy moves. It also built up and maintained a vast repository of knowledge, where every detail about the enemy and its order of battle was collected, down to its units and individual commanders.
- Whitehall supply-chain indicators were significant. They allowed Beaverbrook to closely align fighter production to fighter losses, to meet the on demand requirements of Fighter Command on a daily basis. This was bolstered by a resourceful recycling and recovery system.
- Storey's Gate, the center of Churchill's operation, monitored indicators and gathered intelligence from across the portals to use in decision-making. Here, Churchill and the War Cabinet collaborated to define strategies. They selected and managed multiple projects, resources, risks, and costs, in response to enemy moves.

Churchill's federated portal was a true adaptive business system, although this is not at first apparent, as history has presented the elements as separate, disparate organizations and technologies. In reality, they were closely integrated and federated, and could sense and respond to situations. Throughout the whole period of the Battle of Britain, both Churchill and Dowding had advanced warning of the Luftwaffe battle orders and imminent raids. Dowding controlled the air battles overhead, and Beaverbrook made sure he had the fighters to wage those battles. In the end, staving off the invasion was a very close race.

Why the Portal Was So Successful

Churchill understood the power of the federated portal and leveraged it extensively. He created a traveling map room that was always close by, because he had become so dependent on it. The day the Battle of Britain turned, on September 15th, he was in Group 11's operations center watching the battle unfold in real time on the map table.

The external effects of the federated portal were significant. As the air battle continued overhead, the world's media focused on how the battle was turning through indicators like plane losses. Both sides took these indicators very seriously and passed numbers daily to the media. As the battled escalated, these numbers became a critical way of measuring progress not only for Churchill, but also for Dowding, who was focused on maintaining morale in the RAF, and for Beaverbrook, who was determined to prove his supply-chain and production systems were working in step with Churchill and Dowding.

Churchill's confidence soared through the use of his federated portal. He exuded this confidence in the rallying speeches he delivered to his nation. The federated portal let him flourish and focus on the overriding strategies of fighting for human rights and freeing nations. He also concentrated on wooing Roosevelt, and this became the turning point for the whole war.

Churchill's Role in the Project

One of Churchill's great personal strengths was that he listened to his experts, the scientist and technologists. He was able to recognize the brilliant mavericks like Beaverbrook, Dowding, and Winterbotham, and bring them to the forefront. When they presented their ideas and solutions to him, he had the foresight to allow them to get on with them. He backed them when needed, helping remove all obstacles in their paths.

As a long-standing and skillful politician, Churchill knew the mechanics and politics of government. As a war-time prime minister, he had a lot of power. He could navigate around the "mandarins" and civil servants of the ministries, knowing which strings to pull. Churchill was also a military man, having served in the army and navy. He understood the military organization, mind, and culture. Through the federated portal, Churchill was able to unite these organizations, which coexisted in bitter rivalry, harnessing their energies in the same direction to fight for the same cause.

Based on all this information, it is easy to understand why Churchill was such a great leader. It would have been all too easy to go with the majority of the establishment, sue for peace, and set up a "Vichy England." Instead, Churchill resolutely went against massive pressure and put up a fight that eventually led his nation to victory.

Discussion of the Four Major Issues Addressed in this Book

The preface indicated that this book would address four high-level issues in the portal industry. Let's take a look at these issues (expressed as questions), their solutions, and the resulting benefits:

- *How can I successfully react to events by making use of the most critical information available and discerning useful intelligence?*

The first challenge is sensing and recognizing business events. This can only be done by understanding the types of events that affect an organization. The second challenge is determining the response by understanding the kind of decisions that need to be made, in a specific timeframe. To address the former requires listing, classifying, and prioritizing the events that can have a significant impact on a business. A portal can be programmed to sense and pick up on the characteristics of an event and alert a decision-maker within a related community for a required response. To address the latter requires breaking down the decision-making process and determining what information and content is needed or available in a specific timeframe. Chapter 2 identifies business events, processes, communities, and carefully matches information to them. The biggest problem is in discerning useful intelligence from the glut of information.

- *How can I successfully implement and leverage emerging technologies that synthesize business information and intelligence for decision-making?*

Organization acceptability or adoption is one of the biggest challenges facing portal projects. Communities need to be identified, and their needs carefully understood. They also need to appreciate what a portal can do, the overall vision and benefits, so they buy in. This requires understanding the enterprise and federation benefits. Business units that fail to buy into the project are likely to proceed with their own project, possibly with similar technologies, which might fail to integrate at an enterprise level. Understanding these challenges and identifying the technologies already in place is important, as the overall approach allows for integration and shared usage. This is highlighted in chapter 3.

- *How can I ensure my portal project is not just about technology, but that it is also about business and communities?*

To ensure that portal projects are not just focused on technology that IT organizations instigate, lead, and control, focus on payback and develop a business-case framework. For many portal projects, this is a challenge, as the benefits are often intangible, like improved employee productivity or decision-making. To address this, build a business case in stages, as evolved through chapters 2 and 3. Determine the benefits first, both tangible and intangible, and then the costs once the solution is better understood. You must also understand the decision-making processes and identify the indicators required, as shown in chapter 4.

- *How can I ensure my business processes and organizational structure are realigned for the portal project?*

Process and organization investments and efforts need to be equally matched to technology investments. Therefore, all the users affected by the portal must understand the significance of the changes a portal can bring to an organization. Through this understanding, users can start to identify how the processes and organization need to be modified and realigned to accommodate and take best advantage of the portal's benefits. This is partially realized through the testing in chapters 5 and 6, but it is difficult to predict in an on demand solution. Typically, processes and organization are gradually modified through the releases because of the large scope of work required.

SUMMARY

In summary, I leave you with a simple philosophy: A portal project's success is based on planning, launching, learning, and evolving each release. As for the case study, very few organizations will have to face the scale of problems that Churchill did.

EPILOGUE

A final word on Churchill's federated portal: Most authors and historians agree that the victory had a significant effect on the war. It changed the conduct of war, as it showed the Allies how a sense-and-respond system could be leveraged. As a result, intelligence became the top priority over everything, including other military resources.

The following sections detail what ultimately happened to the three key parts of Churchill's federated portal and to the main players in the drama.

Bletchley Park

Bletchley Park was the birthplace of the intelligence and communications revolution, the cradle of the Knowledge Age. It was a community that dramatically pushed emerging technology to its limits and created the first working, programmable electronic computer, Colossus, in 1943. It provided a glimpse into the future we see today.

Bletchley Park was completely dismantled and eradicated after the war to preserve the Ultra secret, which was not revealed until 1974.

Bentley Prior

Bentley Prior became the archetype for command-and-control centers around the world, still used today. Its use of the filter room and real-time models through the map table and tote board were breakthroughs. Images of the operations center are probably best remembered through the WAAFs moving counters around the map table using croupier sticks.

Storey's Gate

Today, the Storey's Gate complex is completely intact and operates as a museum. It was completely closed down and mothballed on the last day of the war. Nothing was removed or changed, so the map room still has the indicators for industrial production and the orders of battle for the last days of the war.

Churchill's Career

In 1945, the war ended, and the Labour party was swept into power on the euphoria of optimism and expected social change. Churchill's career never again reached its wartime peak, although he became a peacetime prime minister in 1951, at the age of 76. In 1965, he died and had a state funeral reserved for the greatest Britons.

Beaverbrook's Career

Not many people in Beaverbrook's ministries enjoyed being treated like his newspaper staff, and of course he could not understand why, reflecting his character. As minister, he persistently complained of the difficulties that he faced. He fired off many letters of resignation, until finally, one was accepted. In September 1943, he was back as Lord Privy Seal, for Churchill could not live without his counsel[1], despite all their differences.

Dowding's Career

In October 1940, there was a postmortem of the Battle of Britain. Dowding was under pressure for not using the big wing tactics developed by Group 12, which proved successful in the later stages of the battle. However, Leigh-Mallory, commander of Group 12, was not apprised of Ultra information, and Dowding was unable to defend his case without betraying Ultra to a junior officer, Douglas Baeder, sent by Leigh-Mallory. As a result, Dowding could not justify his position and was sacked. Ironically, the man who had won the Battle of Britain was replaced by Leigh-Mallory. Dowding's career was not the last one sacrificed to keep Ultra secret. Dowding was due for retirement on July 14th, but delayed his retirement until the end of October.

[1] Source: http://www.beaverbrookfoundation.org/bbrook.htm

APPENDIX A

Important Background to 1940

The following sections look at the background to Churchill's case study in more detail. If you are less than familiar with the era and the events, you might find this review to be helpful.

Background to Storey's Gate

The bombing of undefended cities occurred during the First World War and the Spanish Civil War, causing many civilian casualties. This fear troubled successive British governments in the 1920s and 1930s. In 1940, London was the most populous city in the world, with 8 million inhabitants. It was also the capital of an industrialized economy at the center of the world's largest overseas empire.

The development of air power and bomber technology made the threat of strikes on London very real. By 1938, the question of how the prime minister, his Cabinet, and the central core of the military command could be protected in the event of a war became urgent. To address the concern that the public might think their leaders were deserting them, the planners looked at a secure "war room" in central London.

The site chosen was nothing grander than the basement chambers of the Office of Works building, ten feet below ground. Work began in June 1938. It offered the strongest structure of any in Whitehall, and was conveniently situated between Parliament and the prime minister's office-residence at Number 10 Downing Street. This became the heart of the portal.

Because of its location in central London, many of the staff had to live in the complex during air raids. Conditions were primitive. All water was pumped in by hand, and fresh air was circulated with vast ventilators, with filters in the event of gas attacks. The site covered a six-acre underground maze, with more than a mile of corridors.

Today, Storey's Gate is part of the Imperial War Museum. It can be found on King Charles Street, London, very close to Downing Street.

Background to Bletchley Park

Military Intelligence (Enigma)

Commercial encryption devices were patented in London in 1920. However, they were exploited by German banks and railways, and then by the German military as Enigma through the 1930s. Long before the war began, the airwaves were full of coded messages. Blitzkrieg depended on surprise, demanding speedy communication, and radio was crucial to the attack plans.

The German high command trained thousands of wireless operators in preparation for war. Their job was to interpret Morse code in any conditions. The German military adopted a seemingly invincible code-making machine.

Countering Enigma with Ultra

In the 1930s, a number of European governments invested resources in breaking the Enigma code. Notably, Polish students of mathematics began working on the ciphers. From January 1934 until December 1938, they were able to read almost all Enigma encrypted messages. In July 1939, with war imminent, they gave the British and French three copies of the reconstructed Enigma machine and all the available methods of decrypting messages. The British Government Code and Cipher School (GC&CS), part of the Foreign Office, looked for a site where its work could carry on unhindered by enemy air attacks. The first GC&CS staff arrived at Bletchley Park in August 1939. Early intercepts were made, but not enough detail was available to break the code.

The Polish Enigma machines enabled the British and French code-breakers to make critical progress in working out the order in which the keys were attached to the electrical circuits, an impossible task before. A fundamental design flaw meant that no letter could ever be encrypted as itself. This gave the code-breakers a toehold. Errors in messages sent by tired and stressed operators also gave clues. Armed with this knowledge, the code-breakers were able to exploit Enigma. In January 1940, mathematician Alan Turing was sent to France to meet with the exiled Polish cryptanalysts. He saw their electromechanical code-breaking machines and brought back with him a replica Enigma machine. By May 1940, Bletchley Park was positioned to start breaking codes by hand. However, the operation was still fledgling. To be effective, it had to mature into what resembled a production line, automated through electromechanical machines.

Background to Whitehall

Air Power, 1936-1940

As Germany rearmed in the mid-1930s, priority was put on expanding the Luftwaffe. To instill fear, Nazi propagandists put great emphasis on the capabilities of the Luftwaffe to level cities. As a reaction, the British government invested in fighter programs in 1937 with the Hurricane, and in 1938, the Spitfire.

The unbeatable image of the Luftwaffe was enhanced by its performance in Poland in September 1939 and ongoing military campaigns. In May 1940, the Luftwaffe was estimated to have 1,100 fighters and 1,700 bombers. The RAF had less than 500 operational fighters. On a daily basis, British fighter production was 15 and the number of new pilots trained was six. However, the Spitfire was slightly superior technically. Also, with most of the fighting over southern England, RAF pilots shot down could be back in the air within a few hours, while Luftwaffe pilots would go into captivity.

Ministry for Aircraft Production

"Before the war, 'shadow factories' had been created in readiness to build aircraft when hostilities began. But by the summer of 1940, when Beaverbrook took up his post, the vital Spitfire shadow factory at Castle Bromwich, Birmingham, had yet to produce a single aircraft. Beaverbrook telephoned Vickers-Supermarine, manufacturers of the Spitfire, and told them to take over Castle Bromwich and to forget about the Air Ministry's orders to tool up for bomber production[1]."

Beaverbrook galvanized the industry. He instituted a seven-day work week and "work without stopping." Beaverbrook helped to fulfill Churchill's short-term strategy of accelerated production of fighters at the expense of bombers. He slowed down development of all projects so that production could be concentrated on five types vital to the Battle of Britain—the Hurricane and Spitfire, and the Wellington, Whitley, and Blenheim bombers[2].

---

[1] Source: Len Deighton, Battle of Britain, Jonathon Cape 1980

[2] Source: http://www.eagle.ca/~harry/aircraft/typhoon/ty_hist.htm

Beaverbrook used his powers on both sides of the Atlantic to assist aircraft production in Britain. He approached automotive tycoon Henry Ford to assist in building Rolls-Royce Merlin engines under license. Ford refused, stating it was not the policy of the United States to become involved in the war in Europe. Beaverbrook became even more determined and approached the Packard Organization. After lengthy discussions and the promise of enough money to enlarge the factory, a deal was signed.

Aircraft manufactured in Canada and the U. S. were shipped across the Atlantic by the Merchant Navy. The process was slow and sometimes dangerous because of u-boat activity. Beaverbrook approached the Air Ministry and proposed that the aircraft should be built to flying condition, then ferried to be finally fitted out. The Air Ministry objected, stating that it was impractical and absurd. Beaverbrook went ahead with the decision without the War Cabinet's approval, and the Atlantic ferry system came into being. By March 1941, 160 aircraft had been ferried across the Atlantic, with only one aircraft lost—a remarkable feat.

Beaverbrook was concerned about the materials for the construction of aircraft. He thought up the idea of getting public participation by having people donating all their old aluminum saucepans, pots, and pans. It would impress upon the people that they were "doing their bit" and boost morale. The "Saucepans to Spitfires" program was a public-relations exercise that became an inspiration to all, with overwhelming response from British housewives.

Beaverbrook's irascible zeal soon proved its worth. Fighter and bomber production was immeasurably increased. "This was his hour," Churchill later declared. "His personal force and genius, combined with so much persuasion and contrivance, swept aside many obstacles. Everything in the supply line was drawn forward to the battle."

Background to Bentley Prior

An old Gothic house became the office of Air Marshal Sir Hugh Dowding on his appointment as head of Fighter Command in 1936. Over time, this became the operations center of Fighter Command.

Today, Bentley Prior is still in use as part of the RAF, which very occasionally opens up the historic mansion to the public. It can be found in Stanmore, Middlesex.

An operations room that can be readily visited today is RAF Uxbridge, which is a museum. The former Group 11 headquarters of Fighter Command was responsible for London and the southeast coast, where much of the battle was centered.

END TO THE BATTLE OF BRITAIN

The Blitz brought an end to the Battle of Britain. During the conflict, the RAF lost 792 planes and the Luftwaffe lost 1,389. There were 2,353 men from Great Britain and 574 from overseas who were members of the air crews that took part in the Battle of Britain. An estimated 544 were killed, and a further 791 lost their lives in the course of their duties before the war came to an end.

OVERALL STATISTICS

Fighter Production

The number of new aircraft produced under Lord Beaverbrook steadily increased reaching a peak in July 1940 as shown in Table A.1. Beaverbrook did manage to provide enough planes to keep Fighter Command's "head above water." In July, British workers turned out 496 new fighters, at least 100 more than the German workers were turning out for the Luftwaffe.

Table A.1: Monthly Fighter Production Output, 1940[3]

Month	Planned	Achieved	Overall Available
February	171	141	
March	203	177	
April	231	256	
May	261	325	
June	292	446	600
July	329	496	644
August	282	476	708
September			746
October			734

[3] Source: "Battle over Britain", Francis K. Mason, McWhirter Twins, 1969; and http://www.geocities.com/Broadway/Alley/5443/fcweek.htm

Pilot Availability

As shown in Table A.2, Fighter Command had 1,259 fighter pilots in early July and was 197 pilots below the authorized strength of 28 pilots per squadron. However, the number of pilots available grew during the battle, as pilots from Poland, Czechoslovakia, France, Belgium, Canada, other British dominions, and the U. S. were made operational.

Table A.2: Number of Fighter Pilots in Fighter Command, June–November 1940[4]

Date	# of Pilots Authorized	Actual # of Pilots	Deficiency or Surplus
June 15	1,456	1,094	–362
June 30	1,482	1,200	–282
July 6	1,456	1,259	–197
July 13	1,456	1,341	–115
July 20	1,456	1,365	–91
July 27	1,456	1,377	–79
August 3	1,588	1,434	–154
August 10	1,588	1,396	–192
August 17	1,588	1,379	–209
August 24	1,588	1,377	–211
August 31	1,588	1,422	–166
September 7	1,588	1,381	–207
September 14	1,662	1,492	–170
September 21	1,662	1,509	–153
September 28	1,662	1,581	–81
October 5	1,714	1,703	–11

[4] Source: Wood, Derek, with Derek Dempster. *The Narrow Margin.* Washington D.C.: The Smith-sonian Press. 1990

Table A.2: Number of Fighter Pilots in Fighter Command, June–November 1940–*continued*			
Date	**# of Pilots Authorized**	**Actual # of Pilots**	**Deficiency or Surplus**
October 12	1,714	1,752	+38
October 19	1,700	1,737	+37
October 26	1,727	1,735	+8
November 2	1,727	1,796	+69

The War Economy

The proportion of GNP devoted to the war was about 50 percent in Britain, and at the end of the war, it was even higher in Germany. Between 1938 and 1944, the value of consumer goods and services purchased in Britain fell by 22 percent. The average pre-war diet in Britain derived about 37 percent of energy from livestock products. At the end of the war, it was 30 percent[5].

The United Kingdom, which appeared to have the most insuperable strategic problems in feeding its population, was able to overcome them so triumphantly that the success of its agricultural policy during the war became the yardstick by which other countries' efforts were measured. Over most of the world, agricultural economies were unable to cope with the difficulties caused by interruptions of supply and changes in markets.

Manufacturing of Goods

Table A.3 outlines the Ministry of Supply indices of munitions production. They all show consistent and dramatic increases in aircraft, tanks, artillery, and bombs. Capital investment seems to have been heavily biased toward extending the capacity of plants to produce finished armaments.

Table A.3: Output of Certain Goods in Britain, 1939–1944

Goods	Measurement Units	1939	1940	1941	1942	1943	1944
Steel	000 tons	13,221	12,975	12,312	12,764	13,031	12,142
Electricity	M, kw hrs	27,733	29,976	33,577	36,903	38,217	39,649

[5] Source: "War, Economy and Society 1939–1945," Alan S. Milward, Penguin Books Ltd. 1977.

Table A.3: Output of Certain Goods in Britain, 1939–1944, *continued*

Goods	Measurement Units	1939	1940	1941	1942	1943	1944
Coal	000 tons	231,338	224,299	206,344	209,944	198,920	192,746
Aluminum	000 tons	24.96	18.95	22.67	46.78	55.66	35.47
Iron ore	000 tons	14,486	17,702	18,974	19,906	18,494	15,472
Cotton yarn	m. lbs	1,092	1,191	821	733	712	665
Total aircraft	Number	7,940	15,094	20,094	23,672	26,263	26,461
Special bombers	Number	758	1,967	3,275	5,439	7,352	7,903
Tanks/ artillery	Number	969	1,399	4,841	8,611	7,476	N/A
Bombs	Short ton	Na	51,093	147,848	211,048	233,807	309,366

The annual output of machine tools in Britain was 37,000 before the war. In 1942, it was 95,788[6].

Food Production

The introduction of food rationing came into force in January 1940. Most foods were rationed by their weight or by points. Food and other vital items were progressively rationed as follows:

- May: fish and milk
- June: margarine and cooking fat
- July: clothes and petrol

The 3,500 people employed by the Ministry of Supply in April 1940 grew to around 39,000 by 1943. By 1945, it employed some 50,000 officials, such was its importance.

[6] Source: "War, Economy and Society 1939–1945," Alan S. Milward, Penguin Books Ltd. 1977.

APPENDIX B

Layers of the Functional Component Model

The information in this appendix gives further details on the layers of the functional component model. The information will be helpful as you work through the first half of the book.

Table B.1: The Portal Components by Category

Categories	Component	Description
Presentation	Device Support	The services adapt the content and user interface of Web applications to match the requesting device based on device type and processing rules.
	Telephony Services	Computer Telephony Integration and Interactive Voice Response provide a telephony-based front end to an application.
	User Interface Services	These services are characterized by multiple windows and icons designed for ease of use and consistency, with an interface to a browser, GUI, or PDA.
	Language Translation	This manages the user session's language preference.

Table B.1: The Portal Components by Category, *continued*

Categories	Component	Description
	Web Presentation services	These define component details for the provision of an HTTP Web server, load balancing, supporting requests from clients, and managing, collating, and serving HTML pages with static and dynamic content.
Portal Access Integration	Interaction manager	This controls the interaction with a portal by invoking portal applications, or portlets, and assembling user interfaces from static information and application data. It invokes authentication and personalization services.
	Customization	The services enable users to tailor the look and feel and to determine the content and services they wish to see.
	Personalization	This provides the right content or user interface based on role, with associated privileges/needs. For example, based on a static profile or from usage patterns, the following personalization can be applied: 1. Profiles allow users to specify the site's look and the filters for news, stocks, etc. 2. Rules-based personalization applies generated rules to suggest additional products or to customize the look and feel. 3. Matching commonalities among sets of customers and using that knowledge identifies likely next-product choices. 4. Neural networks employ technology to actually learn about the customer and leverage that knowledge.
	Subscription	This manages changed information on a specific topic on a regular basis.
	Context management	This manages the user session state on a portal. It shares this information across multiple applications on the portal.

Table B.1: The Portal Components by Category, *continued*

Categories	Component	Description
Application	Transaction Services	These ensure all transactions against a database leave it consistent or return it to its initial state, both for procedural and object-oriented functions.
	Web Application Services	Services provided by Web applications, although tightly integrated with the Web, can be integrated into other technology and channel protocols.
	State Management	Connection/session management supports a seamless, persistent connection across several disconnected events/transactions, on a long timescale.
	Event Management	This provides a means to notify a user of a predefined event by supplying content or a link to it.
Information Aggregation/Publishing	Search	This locates information that fits a user's needs, according to search criteria, with the relevant results ranked across all information sources.
	Content Management	This provides functions for the management and publishing of material to be made available over the portal.
	Query/Data Access	This provides a transparent means for applications to access data stored in databases through a common interface.
	Metadata/Indexing	A Web crawler traverses the content (documents in other formats, media, and databases) and creates metadata.
	Digital Media	This enables the storage and delivery of multimedia content to users, and the ability to stream digital media content to a user desktop on demand.
Collaboration	Portal Workflow	This provides the tool support for automated execution of documents based on processes, controls their execution, and routes documents to editors.
	Group Productivity	This provides asynchronous many-to-many communication, like team rooms, newsgroups, discussion databases, calendaring, and scheduling.
	Conferencing	This provides synchronous many-to-many communication channels, such as real-time conferencing and same-time chat.

Table B.1: The Portal Components by Category, *continued*

Categories	Component	Description
	Messaging	This provides asynchronous one-to-one communication channels, such as email, pager, and SMS messaging services.
	Expert Location	A user directory is sorted by user interests and skills to facilitate the location of subject-matter experts.
Application Integration	Message Brokering	This targets program-program sequences, with no human interaction. It is distinct from workflow and human processes.
	Document Management	This supports business processes, dependent on the receipt/manipulation of business documents coupled with the business workflow component.
	Business Workflow	This provides an environment for business components to participate in business processes. It implements a business process model that describes the process steps to be performed to achieve a specific business goal.
	Message Services	The services pass information between programs in a distributed network by storing and retrieving messages from queues.
	Database Access Services	This provides a transparent means for applications to access data stored in databases through a common interface.
	Legacy Access	This provides through Wrapper technology (a new program interface to a legacy system) screen scrapping and terminal emulation.
Security and Directory	Authentication	User IDs and passwords are used to establish and record the secure and precise identification of users by the applications or servers to access.
	Authorization	This authorizes access.
	Single Reduced Sign-on	This coordinates authentication/authorization across the portal, content, and applications. It uses a policy approach or a Web server plug-in.
	Privacy Management	Users control the use or disclosure of their personal information.

Table B.1: The Portal Components by Category, *continued*

Categories	Component	Description
Security and Directory	Intrusion Management	This detects and manages intrusions into the portal.
	User Provisioning	This is the administration of user access rights across heterogeneous environments.
	Security Management	This manages the granting and revocation of user identity and privileges.
	Directory Services	This presents a source of all available resources in a distributed network and the means for any authorized user to access these resources.
Environmental (Portal Management)	User Management	This administers the registration and support of users on the portal, and manages the resources they use.
	Web Tracking	Usage data on the portal is captured to provide reporting statistics to the portal owner.
	Systems Management	This indicates the full set of services to manage the systems, applications, databases, and networks associated with the portal.

Table B.2: Mapping Matrix Components to Nodes

	Conceptual	Specification	Physical
Presentation Function	How data is accepted from and displayed to end users	Specify actual type of technology (teleprinter, voice, etc.) and the technology capabilities.	Vendor product selection
Processing Function	Specification of the processing-oriented deployment unit on this node	Specify sizes of processes, priority requirements, other process dependencies, and the process control mechanism.	Actual implementation of processes or threads of execution

Table B.2: Mapping Matrix Components to Nodes, *continued*

	Conceptual	Specification	Physical
Data	Specification of the data-oriented deployment unit on this node, and scope of recovery	Specify size and volumes of data, frequency of use, and currency requirements.	Data replicated in backup office
Infrastructure	Connections and other requirements needed by this node in business terms (such as fast access)	Specify any required middleware for security and messaging.	IBM Component Broker for AIX
Presentation services	Color screen, menus or icons, drag-and-drop	Provide the exact specification of a standard detail, e.g., CUA with icons, and drag-and-drop.	Windows, programmed to the specifications
Processing Services	Type of processing required for functional and nonfunctional requirements.	Specify the components required to support the business function.	Encina translation manager
Data Services	Concurrency requirements, data access mode criticality of data loss, remote data access, etc.	Provide the actual specification of the functions required from the data layer, i.e., stored procedure, number of connections, users, etc.	Parallel DB2, multi-node for AIX and HP-UX OS, 128 User License data replicated to offices
Hardware	Space limitations, number of users to support, performance characteristics, and environmental issues	Specify the hardware devices, as represented by nodes.	RS/6000 and IBM PCs
Operating System	Services that control the hardware. Real time? Number of users, process model? Thread model? Priority control over tasks?	Provide the exact specifications of real time, number of threads supported, parallel hardware support, etc.	AIX on Server for single processor RS/6000 128 user

Table B.2: Mapping Matrix Components to Nodes, *continued*

	Conceptual	Specification	Physical
Connections	The requirements for wireless and phone line access	Specify protocols (Morse), cable types, and topology.	Ethernet, TCP/IP protocol without FTP capability outside firewall
Management	Local support capability for servers, workstations, backup and recovery, software installation, and recovery	Specify systems-management software and services, the actual protocol required (SNMP, CMIP), software distribution method, and frequency.	Software distribution on a RS/6000 model
Components	The distribution of application and technical components on the nodes	Components are provisionally placed on "nodes," the system pieces adequate to support the component interactions on different nodes, and their stored data.	

Table B.3: Node Descriptions

Type	Description
General	Catch-all for nonfunctional requirements that do not fit in any other categories
Users Presentation	News pads, audiotape, reports, etc., and clerical users, managerial users, etc.
Performance and Capacity	Average/peak transaction rate, data volume and frequency of access, number of users at each time interval (night shift), etc.
Availability	Availability window during 24/7 operation and components that affect availability: ■ Components in place, potential single-points-of-failure ■ Redundant/backup components measured for application availability

Table B.3: Node Descriptions, *continued*

Type	Description
Cost/Benefit	Cost of a specific element and its benefit to the operation
Security	Application integration, single sign-on, hardware/software encryption, network secure printing, external access security requirements, physical security of systems, information
Risk	Mission-critical information (critical decisions)
Flexibility	Platform neutrality, process change
Node Management	Remote management, sensitive data, recovery time, problem management, software distribution, configuration management, etc.

APPENDIX C

What to Expect from Your Project

This appendix contains a checklist in Table C.1 that you can use to track the progress of your project. Specifically, Table C.1 describes the deliverables by phase for your project, where the lead for a deliverable is indicated by the • symbol, and those involved are indicated by the ▸ symbol.

Note that as the project progresses, the following team members will provide their input:

- *Project manager*—Responsible for the implementation and coordination of all the activities, as well as for completing the project on-time, on-budget, and to the client's satisfaction. Aware of portals and their impact on the business. Directs all program-related activities and coordinates issues. Also responsible to the steering committee for the status of tasks and deliverables. Coordinates all related off-site activities necessary to complete the project.
- *e-business consultant*—Responsible for the business requirements and justification of the project, establishing the value of on demand, defining what is or is not in scope, and determining the requirements for the portal. Takes the lead on solution definition and acts as a guide to the solution architect in macro and micro design.
- *Solution architect*—Responsible for the technical solution's integrity, design of functionality and nonfunctionality, and systems architecture. Also responsible for providing a consistent design philosophy for the

development phases. Supports solution definition, takes the lead in macro design, and acts as a guide for micro design.

- *Integration/development coordinator*—Responsible for all project construction and development; oversees integration teams, programming, documentation, and module testing. Works closely with the solution architect to ensure the development meets the architectural vision, functional requirements, conceptual design goals, and detailed design. Also works closely with the operations analyst to ensure that the implementation is free of technical complications. Leads micro design and build solution.
- *Operations analyst*—A representative of operations services, responsible for ensuring operations requirements are met and for coordinating subprojects oriented toward supporting the implementation and acceptance of the project. Directs the teams for implementation preparation, documentation, implementation, production testing, and acceptance testing. Leads deploy, assess solution.
- *Technical analysts*—Responsible for supporting requirements definition, design, test plans, programming, testing, and documentation.
- *Information architect*—Responsible for reviewing the content and information to create an information architecture, wireframes, layouts, and navigation schematics.
- *Usability consultant*— Responsible for creating a user-friendly navigation for high interaction and seamless online transactions. Determines the usability requirements and recommends functionality to make the portal intuitive and easy to use.
- *Organizational and process consultants*—Required when the project needs organizational and process changes and alignments typically in redesign.
- *Service representative*—Works with the operations analysts in defining service-level requirements. Collects and reviews metrics late in the project to confirm its outcome.
- *Business user*—Works with the business consultant early in the project on all aspects of the business, and the operations analysts through to solution acceptance.

Table C.1: Project Deliverables

		Business		Executive		Project Team						Special Teams		
	Project Task	Service Reps	Business End Users	Business Sponsor	IT Sponsor	Project Manager	e-business Consultant	Solution Architect	Integration Coordinator	Operations Analyst	Information Architect	Technical Analysts	Usability Consultant	Org./Process Consultants
Project Management														
	Project Definition	◗	◗	◗	◗	●	◗	◗						◗
1	Organizational Readiness Assessment	◗	◗	◗	◗	●	◗							◗
2	Preliminary Project Scope	◗		◗	◗	●		◗						
3	Preliminary Business Case/Justification		◗	◗	◗	◗	●							
4	Risk Assessment Document	◗		◗	◗	●	◗	◗						
	Project Planning and Management	◗	◗	◗	◗	●								
1	Project Identity	◗	◗	◗	◗	●								
2	Project Resource Plan			◗	◗	●								
3	Draft Project Plan					●								
4	Project Change Management			◗	◗	●								
5	Project Communication Plan			◗	●									
6	Program to Measure Success			◗	◗	●								
7	Process to Manage Scope					●								
8	Project Definition Report					●								

Table C.1: Project Deliverables, *continued*

		Business		Executive		Project Team						Special Teams		
	Project Task	Service Reps	Business End Users	Business Sponsor	IT Sponsor	Project Manager	e-business Consultant	Solution Architect	Integration Coordinator	Operations Analyst	Information Architect	Technical Analysts	Usability Consultant	Org./Process Consultants
Define the Problem														
	Initiate Problem Definition		◗	◗	◗	●	●	◗						
	Articulate the Business Problem		◗	◗	◗		●	◗						
	Changes Affecting Your Organization		◗	◗	◗		●	◗						
	Current Capabilities	◗	◗	◗	◗		●	◗						
	Desired Capabilities	◗	◗	◗	◗		●	◗						
	Define Alternative Solutions to the Problem		◗	◗	◗		●	◗						
	Evaluate Governance Framework		◗	◗	◗		●	◗						
	Confirm End (Review Project)		◗	◗	◗	●	◗							
Solution Definition														
	Initiate Solution Definition	◗	◗	◗			●	◗						
	Formulate Strategy	◗	◗	◗			●	◗						
	Review Business Environment	◗	◗	◗			●	◗						
1	Define Business Terms		◗				●	◗						
2	Collect Document Inventory		◗				●	◗						
3	Describe Business Context		◗				●	◗						
4	List Business Events		◗				●	◗						
5	Describe The Business Organization		◗				●	◗						
6	Confirm Current Business (Interaction) Model		◗	◗			●	◗						

Table C.1: Project Deliverables, *continued*

		Business		Executive		Project Team						Special Teams		
	Project Task	Service Reps	Business End Users	Business Sponsor	IT Sponsor	Project Manager	e-business Consultant	Solution Architect	Integration Coordinator	Operations Analyst	Information Architect	Technical Analysts	Usability Consultant	Org./Process Consultants
7	Validate Business Issues and Goals		◗				●	◗						
8	Validate Project Objectives		◗				●	◗						
	Review Technical Environment				◗			●						
1	Review Current IT Infrastructure				◗			●						
2	Establish System Context				◗			●						
	Develop Business Strategy		◗	◗			●	◗						
1	Review Leading Portal Practices		◗				●	◗						
2	Evaluate Competitive Position		◗				●	◗						
3	Document Strategic Direction	◗	◗	◗			●	◗						
	Define Requirement	◗	◗	◗	◗	◗	●	◗		◗	◗		◗	◗
	Define Community Requirements		◗				●	◗						
1	Discern Target Audience		◗				●	◗						◗
2	Develop User Profiles (within Communities)		◗				●	◗						
3	Identify Key Use Cases		◗				●	◗						
4	Categorize and Prioritize Requirements		◗	◗			●	◗						
	Define Function Requirements		◗				◗	●						
1	Transfer the Business into Functional Requirements		◗				●	◗						

Table C.1: Project Deliverables, *continued*

		Business		Executive		Project Team						Special Teams		
	Project Task	Service Reps	Business End Users	Business Sponsor	IT Sponsor	Project Manager	e-business Consultant	Solution Architect	Integration Coordinator	Operations Analyst	Information Architect	Technical Analysts	Usability Consultant	Org./Process Consultants
2	Introducing Archetypes		◗				◗	●						
3	Business Model and Application Functions		◗				◗	●						
4	Outline the System Function Model		◗				◗	●						
	Define Content Requirements		◗				●	◗						
1	Content Assessment		◗				●	◗			◗			
2	Outline Logical Data Model		◗		◗		◗	●			◗			
3	Outline a Process/Data Usage Matrix				◗		◗	●			◗			
	Nonfunctional Requirements		◗				◗	●						
1	Runtime Properties	◗	◗				◗	●						
2	Non-Runtime Properties	◗	◗				◗	●						
3	Service Levels	◗	◗		◗		◗	●			◗			
4	Constraints		◗		◗		◗	●						
	Assess Impact		◗				●	◗					◗	◗
	Outline User Experience		◗				●	◗					◗	
	Assess Business Impact		◗	◗			●	◗						
1	Organizational Impact		◗				●	◗						◗
2	Create a Cost/Benefit Analysis		◗				●	◗						
	Define Operational Solution	◗	◗	◗	◗	◗	●	◗	◗	◗				

Table C.1: Project Deliverables, *continued*

		Business		Executive		Project Team						Special Teams		
	Project Task	Service Reps	Business End Users	Business Sponsor	IT Sponsor	Project Manager	e-business Consultant	Solution Architect	Integration Coordinator	Operations Analyst	Information Architect	Technical Analysts	Usability Consultant	Org./Process Consultants
	Outline Solution Strategy	◗	◗	◗	◗	◗	◗	●		◗				
1	Define a testing strategy		◗				◗	●		◗				
2	Define Maintenance and User Support Approach		◗				◗	●		◗				
3	Metrics and Service Level Agreements	◗	◗				◗	●		◗				
4	Refine Impact Analysis		◗				◗	●		◗				
5	Set Up Configuration Management Procedures		◗			◗	●		◗					
6	Sketch Deployment Plan		◗	◗	◗		●	◗		◗				
7	Sketch Release Plan		◗	◗	◗		●	◗		◗				
8	Sketch Static Test Plan		◗				◗	●		◗				
	Confirm End (Review Project)		◗			●	◗	◗	◗					
Create Macro Design														
	Initiate Macro Design		◗				●	◗	◗		◗			◗
	Refine the Business Models		◗				●	◗	◗		◗			◗
	Complete the Business Models		◗				●	◗	◗		◗			◗
1	Refine the Metadata Architecture							●	◗					
2	Refine the Logical Data Model							●	◗					
3	Refine the System Function Model							●	◗					
4	Refine a Process/Data Usage Matrix							●	◗		◗			◗

Table C.1: Project Deliverables, *continued*

		Business		Executive		Project Team						Special Teams		
	Project Task	Service Reps	Business End Users	Business Sponsor	IT Sponsor	Project Manager	e-business Consultant	Solution Architect	Integration Coordinator	Operations Analyst	Information Architect	Technical Analysts	Usability Consultant	Org./Process Consultants
	Conceptual Design						◗	●	◗		◗			
	Select Implementation Architecture						◗	●	◗		◗			
1	Develop Architectural Overview						◗	●	◗					
2	Identify "Stereotypical" Interactions						◗	●	◗					
	Refine User Experience						◗	◗			●			
	Plan Functionality						◗	●	◗					
1	Develop Functional Component Model						◗	●	◗					
	Plan Configuration						◗	●	◗		◗			
1	Configure Community Topologies						◗	●						
2	Develop Content Management System							●			◗			
3	Develop Logical Operational Model							●	◗					
4	Technical walkthroughs							●	◗					
	Conduct Static Tests							●		◗				
	Pilot Selection							●	◗	◗				
	Define Pilot Deployment							●	◗	◗				
	Complete Operational Solution Design						◗	●	◗					
	Develop Physical Operational Model							●	◗					

Table C.1: Project Deliverables, *continued*

		Business		Executive		Project Team						Special Teams		
	Project Task	Service Reps	Business End Users	Business Sponsor	IT Sponsor	Project Manager	e-business Consultant	Solution Architect	Integration Coordinator	Operations Analyst	Information Architect	Technical Analysts	Usability Consultant	Org./Process Consultants
	Design Solution Plan						◗	●	◗					
1	Refine Release Plan						●	◗	◗	◗				
2	Refine Cost/Benefit Analysis						●	◗	◗					
	Define Test Strategy							◗	◗	●				
	Confirm End (Review Project)		◗			●	◗	◗	◗	◗				
Create Micro Design														
	Initiate Micro Design						◗	◗	●		◗		◗	
	Detail Design						◗	◗	●	●	●		●	
	Refine Logical Operational Model							◗	●					
1	Update Logical Operational Model							◗	●					
2	Finalize Nonfunctional Requirements							◗	●					
3	Technical Prototyping							◗	●					
	Evaluate and Select Products and Technologies							◗	●					
	Refine the Functional Component Model							◗	●					
1	Re-examine the Components							◗	●					
2	Complete Detailed Design of Components							◗	●					
3	Integrate Components							◗	●					
4	Complete Business Logic						◗	◗	●					

Table C.1: Project Deliverables, *continued*

		Business		Executive		Project Team						Special Teams		
	Project Task	Service Reps	Business End Users	Business Sponsor	IT Sponsor	Project Manager	e-business Consultant	Solution Architect	Integration Coordinator	Operations Analyst	Information Architect	Technical Analysts	Usability Consultant	Org./Process Consultants
5	Address Federation Questions							●	◗					
6	State Components and Model							◗	●					
	Detail User Experience							◗	◗				●	
1	Complete Release Use-Case scenarios						◗						●	
2	Detail User Interfaces								◗				●	
3	Complete Release Interface Constraints							◗	◗				●	
4	Define Usability Requirements												●	
	Refine Content Model							◗			●			
1	Content Value							◗			●			
2	Content Availability (Identify Sources of Data/Content)							◗			●			
3	Content (Information) Architecture							◗			●			
4	Indicator Model or Dashboard						◗	◗			●			
5	Design Data Mapping							◗			●			
	Refine Physical Operational Model							◗	●					
	Conduct Static Tests							◗	◗	●				
1	Initiate Master Test Plan							◗	◗	●				
	Plan Training and Development							◗	●	●	◗	◗		◗

Table C.1: Project Deliverables, *continued*

		Business		Executive		Project Team						Special Teams		
	Project Task	Service Reps	Business End Users	Business Sponsor	IT Sponsor	Project Manager	e-business Consultant	Solution Architect	Integration Coordinator	Operations Analyst	Information Architect	Technical Analysts	Usability Consultant	Org./Process Consultants
	Define Training and Support							◗		●				◗
	Plan Development							◗	●		◗	◗		
1	Complete Viability Assessment							◗	●		◗	◗		
2	Establish Guidelines and Define Goals for the Build Programming Cycles							◗	●		◗	◗		
	Confirm End (Review Project)		◗			●	◗	◗	◗	◗	◗	◗		
Build Solution														
	Initiate Solution Build							◗	◗	●		◗		
	Prepare Solution Release							◗	◗	●		◗		
	Build Development Environment							◗	◗	●		◗		
	Prepare for Testing									●		◗		
1	Refine test plans								◗	●		◗		
2	Build Test Environment									●		◗		
3	Check Individual Test Plans									●		◗		
4	Check Individual Test Cases									●		◗		
5	Select the Testing Team									●		◗		
6	Define Success Criteria for Going Live								◗	●		◗		
	Build Solution Releases								◗		●	◗	●	
	Build User Interfaces								◗			◗	●	

Table C.1: Project Deliverables, *continued*

		Business		Executive		Project Team						Special Teams		
	Project Task	Service Reps	Business End Users	Business Sponsor	IT Sponsor	Project Manager	e-business Consultant	Solution Architect	Integration Coordinator	Operations Analyst	Information Architect	Technical Analysts	Usability Consultant	Org./Process Consultants
	Develop Configuration Data								◗		●	◗		
1	Understand the Content Attributes and Taxonomies								◗		●	◗		
2	Develop the Portal Code								◗			●		
	Perform Programming Cycle								◗			●		
1	Develop Logic and Procedures								◗			●		
2	Test Logic and Procedures								◗			●		
3	Design Physical Data Model and Implement the Data Mart								◗		●	◗		
4	Prepare for the Next Programming Cycle								◗		◗	●		
	Test Solution Release								◗	●		◗		
	Perform Development Testing							◗	◗	●		◗		
1	Define Approach to Testing								◗	●		◗		
2	Unit Testing								◗	●		◗		
3	Integration (and Usability) Testing								◗	●		◗	◗	
	Perform System Testing							◗	◗	●		◗		
1	The Integration Challenge								◗	●		◗		
2	System Testing the Federated Portal								◗	●		◗		
3	Review Portal Results	◗	◗	◗	◗	◗	◗	◗	◗	●		◗		

Table C.1: Project Deliverables, *continued*

		Business		Executive		Project Team						Special Teams		
	Project Task	Service Reps	Business End Users	Business Sponsor	IT Sponsor	Project Manager	e-business Consultant	Solution Architect	Integration Coordinator	Operations Analyst	Information Architect	Technical Analysts	Usability Consultant	Org./Process Consultants
4	Assess Deployment Risk	◗	◗	◗	◗	◗	◗	◗	◗	●		◗		
	Plan Support and Deployment									●		◗		
	Develop Support Materials						◗	◗	◗	●		◗		
1	Assess Support Material Requirements						◗	◗	◗	●		◗		◗
	Develop Support Functions				◗					●		◗		
1	First-level Support				◗			◗		●		◗		◗
2	Second-level Support				◗			◗		●		◗		◗
3	Third-level Support				◗			◗		●		◗		◗
4	Plan Deployment				◗		◗	◗		●		◗		◗
5	Create a Charter for Portal Governance		◗	◗	◗		●	◗	◗	◗	◗			◗
	Confirm End (Review Project)		◗	◗	◗	●	◗	◗	◗	◗	◗			◗
Deploy, Assess Solution														
	Initiate deployment	◗		◗	◗			◗	◗	●	◗	◗		
	Deployment	◗		◗	◗		◗	◗	◗	●	◗	◗		
	Set Up Deployment Environment							◗	◗	●	◗	◗		
1	Incremental Loading of Portal							◗	◗	●	◗	◗		

Table C.1: Project Deliverables, *continued*

		Business		Executive		Project Team						Special Teams		
	Project Task	Service Reps	Business End Users	Business Sponsor	IT Sponsor	Project Manager	e-business Consultant	Solution Architect	Integration Coordinator	Operations Analyst	Information Architect	Technical Analysts	Usability Consultant	Org./Process Consultants
	Complete Final Testing				◗			◗	◗	●	◗	◗		
1	Acceptance Testing			◗	◗			◗	◗	●	◗	◗		
2	Operability Testing				◗			◗	◗	●	◗	◗		
3	Refine Service Level Objectives (SLOs)	◗			◗		◗	◗		●				
4	Refine Service-Level Agreements (SLAs)	◗			◗		◗	◗		●				
	Deploy Training and Organization Support		◗					◗		●				◗
1	Deploy Training		◗		◗			◗		●				◗
2	Deploy Support Organization		◗		◗			◗		●				◗
	Pilot Rollout		◗		◗			◗		●				◗
	Pilot Assessment		◗	◗	◗			◗		●				◗
	Production Cutover		◗	◗	◗			◗		●				◗
1	Monitor the Created Whole		◗	◗	◗			◗	◗	◗		◗		
	End of Project Release	◗								●		◗		
	Collect the Metrics	◗								●		◗		
1	Collecting Hard Metrics	◗								●		◗		
2	Collecting Soft Metrics	◗								●		◗		
	Review the metrics	◗	◗	◗			◗	◗		●				◗
1	Review Success Criteria for Going Live	◗					◗	◗		●				

Table C.1: Project Deliverables, *continued*

		Business		Executive		Project Team						Special Teams		
	Project Task	Service Reps	Business End Users	Business Sponsor	IT Sponsor	Project Manager	e-business Consultant	Solution Architect	Integration Coordinator	Operations Analyst	Information Architect	Technical Analysts	Usability Consultant	Org./Process Consultants
2	Service Level Reports	◗					◗	◗		●				
3	Important End-User Measures	◗	◗	◗			◗	◗		●				◗
	Review Solution Plans		◗	◗	◗		◗	◗		◗				●
1	User Adoption		◗	◗			◗						●	
2	Adequacy of next release		◗	◗	◗		◗	●		◗				
	Confirm End (Review Project)		◗	◗	◗	●		◗	◗	◗	◗	◗	◗	◗
Project Review														
	Initiate Project Review	◗	◗	◗	◗	●	◗	◗		◗				
1	Discovery					●	◗	◗		◗				
	Review the Metrics and Build the Event Timeline					●	◗	◗		◗				
1	Outcome					●	◗	◗		◗				
	Create Outcome Statement and Determine Contributing Factors					●	◗	◗		◗				
	Analysis					●	◗	◗		◗				
	Identify, Categorize, and Analyze the Events					●	◗	◗		◗				
	Determine the Impact of the Portal on Events					●	◗	◗		◗				
	Future Actions	◗	◗	◗	◗	●	◗	◗	◗	◗	◗	◗	◗	◗

Table C.1: Project Deliverables, *continued*

		Business		Executive		Project Team						Special Teams		
	Project Task	Service Reps	Business End Users	Business Sponsor	IT Sponsor	Project Manager	e-business Consultant	Solution Architect	Integration Coordinator	Operations Analyst	Information Architect	Technical Analysts	Usability Consultant	Org./Process Consultants
	Identify Lessons Learned	◗	◗	◗	◗	●	◗	◗	◗	◗	◗	◗	◗	◗
	Review the Cost/Benefit Analysis	◗	◗	◗	◗	●	◗	◗	◗	◗	◗	◗	◗	◗
	Create Best Practices	◗	◗	◗	◗	●	◗	◗	◗	◗	◗	◗	◗	◗
	Confirm End (Review Project)	◗	◗	◗	◗	●	◗	◗	◗	◗	◗	◗	◗	◗

APPENDIX D

Glossary and Acronyms

Frequently Used Acronyms in the Book

ACL	Access Control List
AO	Automated Operations
AOM	Annual Outage Minute
API	Application Programmatic Interface
B2B	Business to Business Partners
B2C	Business to Consumers
B2E	Business to Employees
B2S	Business to Suppliers
B2X	Business to Stakeholders
BSC	Balanced Score Card
CIP	Continuous Improvement Process
CDSA	Common Data Security Architecture
CORBA	Common Object Request Broker Architecture
CRUD	Create, Read, Update, and Delete (File Records)
CSF	Critical Success Factors

CRO	Civilian Repair Organization
DMZ	Demilitarized Zone
EAI	Enterprise Application Integration
EIS	Executive Information System
EWS	Early Warning System
GC&CS	(British) Government Code and Cipher School
IS	Information Systems
ISP	Internet Service Provider
IT	Information Technology
LAN	Local Area Network
PCRA	Problem/Cause and Recommended Action
PDAs	Personal Digital Assistants
PMBOK	Project Management Book of Knowledge
PMO	Program Management Office
PMI	Program Management Institute
PKI	Public Key Infrastructure
ROI	Return on Investment
RAF	Royal Air Force
RN	Royal Navy
SEI	Software Engineering Institute (Carnegie Mellon University)
SLA	Service Level Agreement
SLO	Service Level Objective
SLU	Special Liaison Unit
SSO	Single Sign On
UCS	Use Case Scenario
UDDI	Universal, Description, Discovery and Integration
WAN	Wide Area Network
WSRP	Web Services for Remote Portals
XML	Extensible Markup Language

IT and Business Terms Used in the Book

Accountability	The demonstration of responsibility through formal reporting of performance to a governing authority.
Adaptive applications	Applications that can adapt to a changing environment.
Agent	An external person or organization that delivers services to the organization's clients, usually for a fee.
Applet	Applications. (See *portlet*.)
Application	A computer program that performs business functions for users. It differs from program development suites, operating system programs, and system management tools.
Application integration	The use of a wide variety of tools and methodologies that allow multiple applications to work together.
Application server	A server usually dedicated to running applications. The term has come to be implicitly associated with the support of component-based technologies like COM+ or EJB/CORBA.
Archetype	A collection of information architectures and models that provide examples of previous portals and combinations of functionality.
Architecture	An abstract view of a system that divides it into components and describes the components and the connections among them.
As-is state	The current state of the business or service-delivery environment.
Assets	The existing technology, finances, controls, and practices an organization uses deliver its required capabilities.
Attributes	Characteristics that cannot be decomposed. Entities are composed of attributes.
Automation	A machine or system (an automated operator) that follows a set of activities in a process, without human intervention.
Availability	A measure of "the service" being there, where high availability implies a higher degree of confidence that the service will be there.
Balance scorecard	A technique that measures an organization through five views: financial, customer, process, learning, and growth.

Benefits	Changes aligned with business needs that, when expressed in quantifiable terms, are advantageous for the organization.
Best practices	Processes or procedures regarded as effective and efficient, defined through experience or formal benchmarking.
Black-box testing	An outside view that looks at what is done rather than how it is done. It includes looking at the outputs and impact on the environment.
Business availability	A high degree of confidence that the business service will be there; that it is always available to its customers.
Business case	A logical, written expression of the business value of a project, intended to secure resource allocation, ensure results, and justify the decision to spend funds.
Business events	A stimulus that prompts the business to act and the points at which interfaces to a solution are needed, how they should be designed, and how the solution should function. (See *events*.)
Business function	A series of work activities done by a person. For example, functions within the sales process include prospecting, qualifying, and proposal-writing.
Business objectives	The expected outcomes of being able to provide a specific capability.
Business operations	The operations or functions followed by the business.
Business process	A series of business functions within defined boundaries, such as a sales process, an invoicing process, or a marketing process.
Business requirements	The specifications for business services, and the preferences and "information styles" defined by a business user or service recipient.
Business services	Electronic business services that are delivered to clients through channels like ATMs, kiosks, the Internet, and the phone.
Business-to-business	An e-business interaction (Internet-enabled transaction) between two organizations.
Business-to-consumer	An e-business interaction (Internet-enabled transaction) between an organization and a consumer, such as Web-enabled banking services.

Business-to-employee	An e-business interaction (Internet-enabled transaction) between an organization and an employee.
Business user	An individual or group within the organization, but outside of IT, that is the recipient of business services to help carry out daily tasks. Also called the *end user*.
Capabilities	The ability of an organization to complete a specific business function.
Change management	The process of introducing changes into the service-delivery environment while maintaining environment integrity and the business-service continuum.
Client	A member of a client group that is the intended direct recipient of a service.
Client device	An access device into a portal for users.
Client group	A population of individuals and companies that are the direct recipients or users of a service.
Client segments	Groups of clients who receive services, as defined by common sets of wants and needs.
Cockpit	An operations control facility or a dashboard for running and monitoring services.
Collaboration	To work with another or others on the delivery of services to a target client group.
Community	A collection of individuals with a common interest who become unified through a portal.
Component	A part of an environment, such as a piece of hardware or software. Components are identified and stored in an inventory model.
Concept	A perception or impression of what needs to be done, in business terms.
Content	All forms of information, from images, documents, and email, to Web pages, audio, and video.
Content management	A coordinated solution that includes integrated systems and processes, providing global access to and management of a common pool of digital assets used to market and/or sell a company's products and/or services.
Continuous improvement	A process aimed at optimizing and improving a technology, process, and organization to meet business objectives, using a feedback system.

Core business	A collection of programs sharing a common affinity or domain for management purposes.
Crawler	A program that visits Web sites and reads their pages and other information in order to create entries for a search engine index. Every major search engine on the Web has such a program, which is also known as a "spider" or a "bot."
Critical Success Factors	The key business goals that must be performed well to achieve business success.
Customer	Any person or business entity that makes a payment to a merchant.
Customization	The modification of a portal page or portlet by a user.
Cut-over	The process of moving a service from one environment to another.
Decision portal	Typically, business-to-employee portals that enhance information quality to facilitate decision-making.
Default page (home)	The portal page that displays to a user at initial portal deployment, before the user completes enrollment. Sometimes used as a synonym for *home page*.
Data mart	A departmental information system specifically designed for storing specific data sets and making these readily accessible for decision-making.
Data mining	The process of accessing large data sets within a data mart or warehouse, and then using statistical analysis techniques for modeling and making sense of this data.
Data warehouse	An enterprise information system specifically designed for storing large quantities of organizational data in data sets, making it readily accessible for analysis and decision-making.
Deliverable	A tangible project output, like a report or a document for the client.
Demilitarized Zone	The area outside of the firewall, but still under the control of an organization. A computer host or small network inserted as a "neutral zone" between a company's private network and the outside public network, to prevent outside users from getting direct access. The term comes from the geographic buffer zone between North and South Korea set up in the early 1950s.

Disaster recovery	The recovery of services to an alternate service-delivery environment off-site.
Dynamic testing	Testing that is carried out by executing the code of an element or solution.
e-business	The Forrester group defines this as online/traditional business activities that use Internet technologies to support communication, collaboration, service, and trade.
e-business service	An electronic business service available to thousands of customers that, when enabled for e-business, is available to anyone with Internet access. It also becomes much more tightly integrated with the other applications and technologies that the organization offers.
e-commerce	The Forrester group defines this as using the Internet to: 1) identify suppliers; 2) select products or services; 3) make purchase commitments; 4) complete financial transactions; and 5) obtain service. Delivery may occur over or outside of the Internet. This encompasses both business-to-business and business-to-consumer activities.
Element	An aggregate of components introduced into the environment (hardware, operating systems, databases, middleware, and applications).
e-markets	Online exchanges that bring together buyers and sellers of business products or services through Internet-based systems.
Enrollment	The process of entering and saving user or user group information in a portal.
Enterprise	One or more organizational entities that collaborate to fulfill a mission established by its governing authority.
Entity	A person, place, thing, concept, or event that is relevant to the business. Entities are composed of attributes, which cannot be decomposed.
Error messages	Electronic warning messages put out by systems.
Event bundles	Related events grouped together, such as events related to someone's life.
Events	Instances that trigger the need for information or knowledge. Events are categorized as *temporal*, a result of the passage of time; *internal*, based on a condition or a decision; or *external*, occurring outside of the organization. See *business events*.

Extended enterprise	The array of suppliers, partners, and other players who have roles in service-delivery.
Extended search	Enables searches across multiple data sources and returns a consolidated list of results.
Extranet	An Internet-based network that serves an organization and selected suppliers, partners, or customers.
Failover	Different levels of transfer of functions, applications, services, and users from a failed to a running node in the environment. This can be manual or automated.
Federated portal	Multiple portals that are either loosely or tightly coupled to allow the sharing of common portal services.
Federated search	Enables searches across multiple search services and returns a consolidated list of results.
Function	An activity or a set of activities.
Functional component	Specific functions that describe the hierarchy of software applications, their tasks, interfaces, relationship, and how they collaborate to deliver the required functionality.
Functional requirement	The specifications and preferences for functions, typically by a business user or service recipient.
Governance	The underlying structure that organizes resources and assets to support the execution of processes that deliver the required value.
Governor	A person or institution to which an enterprise is accountable for its performance.
Hard portal	A portal that is hard-wired to devices.
High availability	A state where all unplanned outages are minimized or masked. Users have access to services and applications during normal operations.
Hosting	The outsourcing of applications or Web sites to a third party.
Implementation diagram	A drawing that shows the configuration of nodes and their components, processes, and objects present (employed) at runtime.
Indicators	Presentations of measurements, bits of information that summarize the characteristics of systems or highlight what is happening in a system.

Instrumentation	The conversion of error text messages to machine-readable messages.
Integration	A variety of techniques that allow multiple applications to work together.
Integrity	The accuracy, quality, validity, and authorized use of data.
Intelligence	The skill that involves reviewing known facts, discerning the relevant from the irrelevant, and concluding by induction or deduction. Also, the end product that is a result of this skill.
Interface	A process or system (automated or manual) that facilitates data exchange.
Internet	A communication mechanism for exchanging information between individuals or organizations.
Interoperability	The ability of different elements to work together.
Intranet	An internal Internet to an organization.
Keys	Primary and alternate keys used for accessing entities in the logical data model.
Leading practice	A superior performance within a function or process independent of industry, leadership, management, or operational methods or approaches, which leads to exceptional performance. It indicates innovation and is used by leading companies.
Logical operational model	Describes the technical architecture of a portal through a series of nodes, which are logical units that deliver a specific type of processing.
Manual	Implies a human following a set of activities in a process.
Metadata	Defines the common language used within an enterprise so that all people, systems, and programs can communicate precisely. Metadata is stored in a repository once the common terms have been agreed.
Meta-search	A search across one or more search engines, that includes a meaningful subset of search functionality through a layer of abstraction generic enough to support a wide variety of search engines.
Methodology	A structured set of guidelines, activities, rules, or steps to assist people in undertaking the development of a solution.

Metrics	Countable entities or distinct, observable events that occur in environments.
Metrics measurement	A logical group of metrics having at least one dimension that can be normalized.
Middleware	Runtime systems software that directly enables application-level interactions among programs in a distributed computing environment. All applications requests require a timeout facility and exception-handling.
Mission-critical environment	A part or whole of a service-delivery environment that is absolutely critical to support the life of a business or the livelihood of an organization.
Model	An intellectual construct descriptive of an entity. It graphically or schematically represents the logical relationship between objects.
Normalization	The process of restructuring a data model by reducing its relations to their simplest forms. This results in normalized data, or data taken to its lowest format.
Nonfunctional requirements	Relate to the nonfunctions (as opposed to functional requirements) that an IT system must satisfy from a qualitative perspective.
Nonstop	Something that never stops; refers to the availability of services.
Non-runtime properties	Characteristics of a portal when it is not running.
Object-oriented	An approach to programming that promotes reusability, extendibility, reliability, and portability. It is found in languages like Java.
On demand	When companies go beyond integration of processes, to sense and respond to fluctuating market conditions and provide products and services to customers.
Operations management	A group within IT responsible for a service-delivery environment meeting a pre-agreed service level.
Organization	A managed group of people, with allocated resources, that acts as a unit.
Outage	Refers to any time a service recipient does not receive service within the conditions set by a Service Level Agreement or preset expectations.

Outage minutes	A recommended metric for measuring availability. It provides a far more accurate and granular view than percentage uptime.
Parameter	A component has parameters that can be configured.
Partner	An independent enterprise or organization that shares accountability for a service.
Persistence	Refers to an object whose lifetime extends beyond that of the program which creates it. This is important when users want to revisit a portal and reuse their preset preferences.
Personalization	Enables information to be targeted to specific users based on business rules and user profile information.
Physical operational model	Describes the intended physical implementation of the logical operational model, or the "builder's view." Refers to the specific types of computers, networks, and software involved in the physical implementation.
Planned downtime	A period of time allocated to shutting down business services to allow for changes to the portal, like configurations or upgrades.
Policies	Management directives defined as a set of guidelines.
Portlet	An area of content on a portal page that addresses a predefined function, such as retrieving the latest news headlines, driving a search engine, searching a database, or displaying a calendar.
Portlet application	A collection of related portlets that can share resources with one another.
Pre-production	A non-live environment used for change management.
Problem management	The process of predicting, detecting, determining, resolving, and recovering from problems within the service-delivery environment, while maintaining the environment's integrity and the continuum of the business service.
Process	A structured flow of activities that integrate people and technology.
Production	Another term for the service-delivery environment or the live environment.

Productivity portlets	Portlets that enable the user to access productivity software such as Lotus Notes and Microsoft Office.
Prototyping	A method that helps define requirements, user interface changes, or technical concepts.
Quick-hit opportunities	Short-term improvement opportunities that require minimal effort (not requiring full implementation) and show a financial return and measurable results.
Resources	The personnel and skills an organization can use to enable the delivery of the required capabilities.
Risk	The exposure to loss, or the chance of injury or bad consequences.
Runtime properties	Characteristics of a running portal.
Self-adjusting	Software or hardware that adjusts itself to a normal situation.
Self-balancing	Software or hardware that balances itself and its resources to a normal state.
Self-healing	Software or hardware that identifies a fault, analyzes it, and recovers from it.
Sense and respond	Describes an organization that is able to respond better to customers and fast-changing conditions in the marketplace and the economy at large.
Service	The provision of specific results (deliverables) that satisfy the identified needs of clients
Service deliverer	The person responsible for providing services.
Service delivery environment	The overall combination of elements that delivers electronic business service(s). It implies the whole end-to-end environment (enterprise).
Service Level Agreement	A formal, written contract that is signed by all parties involved.
Service Level Objective	The criteria by which a service is measured, including service times, response times, and exclusions and penalties paid when objectives are not met.
Service provider	The organization responsible for actually delivering the service to clients. It defines and operates the value chain for the service.

Sideways scalability	The ability to scale the environment sideways, rather than upwards.
Signal-to-noise ratio	The concept of seeing meaningful information through a sea of "noise" or redundant information. A common problem in sensing business events.
Solution	Hardware, software, services, and processes that solve a business problem.
Static testing	The process of evaluating a program by walking through the code documentation, without executing the element or solution.
Supplier	A person or organization, external to the enterprise, that provides it with products or services.
Supply chain	The network that includes planning, designing, producing, and delivering products and services. The extended supply chain includes processes from suppliers' suppliers, all the way to customers' customers.
Supply-chain execution	Management of the activities of transportation, warehousing, and order-fulfillment
Supply-chain planning	A process that leverages all the partners in the supply chain to quickly and efficiently plan and move products to the end customer.
Tacit content	Potential knowledge not in an explicit form, such as thoughts still held in peoples' heads.
Test case	The process of verifying test conditions. It consists of input data and anticipated results for each test condition. A comparison of anticipated and actual test results will show if the result is correct or erroneous.
Test entry/exit criteria	Entry criteria establish the prerequisites to be met before testing starts. Exit criteria define the steps to be completed before the test level exits.
Test script	A document used to outline a sequence of actions that executes a test case. It includes detailed instructions for setting up and executing the test, and then evaluating the results.
Tiering an environment	A three-tier architecture of Web/application/data services that enhances the environment availability by enabling sideways scalability of selected components. It allows for

	single failure-point removal through replication or redundancy, and failover links.
To-be state	The next or envisioned state of the business or service-delivery environment in place.
Transaction	An agreement between a buyer and a seller to exchange an asset for payment.
Transcoding	The adaptation of content to meet the specific capabilities of a client device.
Two-phase commit	Ensures that either all the transaction-writes to a database occur or not, so the dtabase is in a consistent state.
UDDI	A collaborative XML-based project that aims to provide a global e-business registry to support the growth of B2B electronic commerce.
Upgrade	The process of installing a more recent version of software or operating system, or of increasing resources like processors, memory, disks, or cards.
Use-case scenario	Enables the role of each community to be clearly defined in the context of the business process and key business events, the content they access and provide in their roles, and the functionality they use.
User acceptance	The acceptance of a solution by users, effectively leading to acceptance by the business owner funding the project.
User Outage Minutes	The total number of minutes a business services is unavailable to an individual user.
Value chain	A series of linked business processes that create value in both products and services.
Web-based	An application created to use Web and Internet technologies.
Web-enabled	An application that has a Web interface so users can access it via a browser.
Web services	Encapsulated business functions, ranging from a simple request-reply to full business process interactions; self-contained, modular applications that can be described, published, located, and invoked over the Web. These services use open standards and a common infrastructure for description, discovery, and invocation (WSDL, UDDI, SOAP, and HTTP).

White-box testing	Testing that takes an inside view and looks at how something is done, rather than what is done. It includes testing paths, conditions, exceptions, and error-handling.

HISTORICAL TERMS USED IN THE BOOK

Bentley Prior(y)	The headquarters of the RAF Fighter Command, also known as Stanmore.
Bletchley Park	The headquarters of the British Government Code and Cipher School, and the Enigma code-breaking operation.
Bombe	A complex piece of engineering used for code-breaking. It was developed from a Polish concept and significantly enhanced by the mathematician Alan Turing.
Colossus	The first English electronic computer, developed at Bletchley Park to break the code of Enigma machines. Classified under the British Secret Act until 1974.
Cribs	Educated guesses from encrypted text that reduced the number of trials from billions to numbers that could be handled by the bombes. They relied on such things as the same messages encrypted with different keys, machine set-ups quirks, and repeated wheel-order and patch-panel settings.
Civilian Repair Organization	The organization responsible for the recovery of aircraft and its delivery to repair depots or manufacturing facilities.
Decrypts	Decrypted Enigma messages.
Dunkirk	A port in France from which a miraculous number of Allied troops were evacuated in May 1940.
Enigma	German military communication sent in coded form. The German high command believed the system to be unbreakable.
Map room	The operational heart of Storey's Gate, responsible for tracking events and modeling changing fronts on operational maps.
MI5/MI6	British intelligence organizations with internal and external mandates.
Ministries	Within the government, these included the wartime ministries of aircraft production, supplies, and food.

Storey's Gate	Cabinet war rooms.
Ultra	The British code-breaking capability for Enigma.
War Cabinet	A cabinet drawn from all political parties, assembled to run the war for its duration.
Whitehall	The heart of the British government and the location of the various ministries.

APPENDIX E

Credits and Sources

Photo Credit

The illustration in Figure 6.3 was used courtesy of the Imperial War Museum, London.

Bibliography

Briggs, Susan. *The Home Front: War Years in Britain 1939–45*. American Heritage, 1975.

Budianski, Stephen. *Battle of Wits*. Simon and Schuster, 2000.

Collier, Basil. *Leader of the Few: The Authorized Biography of Air Chief Marshal Dowding.*

Deighton, Len. *Blood, Tears and Folly.* HarperCollins, December 1993.

Deighton, Len. *Battle of Britain.* Jonathon Cape, 1980.

Deighton, Len. *Fighter: The True Story of the Battle of Britain*. Castle, May 2000.

Hodges, Andrew. *Alan Turing the Enigma*. Simon and Schuster, 1983.

Mason, Francis. *Battle over Britain.* McWhirter Twins, 1969.

Milward, Alan S. *War, Economy and Society 1939–1945.* Penguin Books Ltd, 1977.

Mosley, Leonard. *The Battle of Britain.* Time-Life Books, 1977.

Pawle, Gerald. *The War and Colonel Warden.* George G. Harrap & Co. Ltd., 1963.

Wintherbottom, FW. *The Ultra Secret.* Orion, 1974.

Web Sites for Background Information

http://www.aeroclocks.com/Sector_pages/sector_history.htm—Operations center clocks

http://www.availability.com/, http://www.tivoli.com/—Availability

http://www.battleofbritain.net/contents.html—Battle of Britain, 1940

http://www.bredemeyer.com/index.html, www-106.ibm.com/developerworks/patterns/—Software architecture

http://www.chu.cam.ac.uk/archives/—Churchill's Archive Centre

http://emep.worldonline.co.uk/docs/news16su.html—Bletchley Park code-breaking

http://www.fpp.co.uk/History/Churchill/WarRoom.html—Real history and Churchill

http://www.geocities.com/Broadway/Alley/5443/fcweek.htm—RAF Fighter Command Weekly July/November 1940

http://home.us.net/~encore/Enigma/enigma.html—The German Enigma Cipher Machine

http://www.ibm.com/services/e-business/ert-index.html, www.ibm.com/services/e-business/roi.html—Return on Web investment

http://www.iwm.org.uk—Imperial War Museum, London

http://www.jharper.demon.co.uk/btm1.htm—The British Tabulating Machine Company

http://www.managementscience.org/research/ab0107.asp—Use of project post mortems

http://ndad.ulcc.ac.uk/datasets/AH/statistics.htm#gen—Central Economic Intelligence Service (CEIS), National Digital Archive of Datasets (NDAD), archived digital data from UK government departments and agencies

http://www.optimizemagazine.com/—ROI

http://pan.net/history/enigma/enigma7.htm—The Y stations

http://www.pmi.org/—The Project Management Institute

http://www.pm2go.com/—The Standish Group ("Chaos, a recipe for projects success")

http://www.qaforums.com/, www.benchmarkqa.com/—Planning and testing

http://www.raf.mod.uk/history/timeline.html—RAF history

http://www.research.ibm.com/autonomic/index_nf.html—Autonomic computing

http://www.sdmagazine.com/—Software development

http://www.stable.demon.co.uk/bob/aa.html—The anti-aircraft command

http://www.techagreements.com/, www.metricnet.com/—Service levels

http://www.thebci.org/ , www.contingencyplanning.com/—Business continuity

http://www.winstonchurchill.org/eroomstour.htm—The Cabinet war rooms

Index

A

B

D

E

N

O

P

U

V

W

Y